Three

The Japanese Diet

Stability and Change in the Japanese House of Representative 1890-1990

DANIEL B. RAMSDELL
Central Washington University

Copyright © 1992 by
University Press of America®, Inc.
4720 Boston Way
Lanham, Maryland 20706

3 Henrietta Street
London WC2E 8LU England

Library of Congress Cataloging-in-Publication Data

Ramsdell, Daniel B.
The Japanese Diet : Stability and Change in the Japanese House
of Representatives, 1890-1990 / Daniel B. Ramsdell.
p.   cm.
Includes bibliographical references and index.
1. Japan, Kokkai.   Shuglin—History.
2. Japan—Politics and government—1868-   I. Title.
JQ1663.R36   1992   328.52'07209—dc20   91-36680 CIP

ISBN 0-8191-8494-2 (cloth : alk. paper)

Table of Contents

■

Preface

■

Since beginning work on this book a number of years ago I have wanted to call it "The Japanese Diet" in the hope that the title alone would propel it to the best-seller status in the United States. Now, however, I have learned that diet books are out and health/exercise books fill the top spots on the non-fiction best-seller lists, while serious works on Japan must engage in Japan bashing to win similar attraction. The English reading public, including Japan specialists, has been bombarded in recent years by a plethora of books by journalists, businessmen, scholars, and ex-government officials purporting to explain in a few hundred pages what makes Japan tick and, in the process, why "we" have a problem with Japan. Among other things this has caused attention to turn away from the continued output of scholarly studies on Japan. The hope of a best-seller thus demolished, I nevertheless stick to the preferred title as it is the appropriate term to describe the contents of the book.

The English word "diet" comes from the Latin *dies* (day) and is commonly used to describe some activity that has a daily regimen. Since its inception the Japanese national assembly has been officially known in English as "The Diet." Prior to 1946 the Japanese designation was Teikoku Gikai (Imperial Diet) and under the Constitution of 1947 it is Kokkai (National Diet).

In 1966 while perusing the tightly packed volumes of the proceedings of the Imperial Diet in the 1920s in the equally tightly packed reading room of the Kanagawa Prefectural Library I became fascinated by the appearance and reappearance of a few individuals rarely mentioned in standard studies of Japanese political history. Historians and political scientists long regarded the prewar Diet as inconsequential, a minor player in the scramble for political control. Hence, except for a few rarities, it was ignored as were most of the persons in it. Nevertheless, the men in the Imperial Diet had been recruited in one way or another to stand for election; to put themselves on the line and up for scrutiny by the press and the public. They had to be persons of some courage and substance.

I gradually began to acquire information about some of the faceless legislators for prewar times. Originally intending to confine the study to the Imperial Diet, I extended it to include the postwar period as it became apparent that the National Diet was indeed the product of its own past. The rules, customs and some of the individuals lived on in the more recent era.

The biographical data on each assemblyperson were entered in a computer database program which permitted the compilation of statistics which form the raw material for the study. These data are included in the many tables throughout the text and in the appendices. The task of compilation was time consuming, tedious at times and accompanied by the frustrations of a neophyte computer user. The immediate reward for this labor, aside from the opportunity to curse the computer,was in becoming acquainted with a number of truly exceptional men and women, many of them otherwise obscure, who served their nation and their constituents. To be sure, many of the 5,569 individuals remain unnoticed, components of the statistics. Many others, however, had incredibly varied careers, projecting themselves into virtually every walk of life, writing and performing copiously. They reflect membership in a society that was and is far from the stereotyped view of Japan as a conformist society composed of like minded interchangeable parts. Instead they represent a vibrant, energetic culture moving through the tumultuous times of the twentieth century. The other reward is the outcome: a wholly comprehensive set of statistics from which to draw conclusions and generalize about the political history of Japan, a major player on the world scene in modern times. Some of the generalizations resemble those reached by scholars in a more impressionistic way. Others do not, providing new evidence and interpretations about political recruitment in general and Japanese politics in particular.

Like everyone who has produced a scholarly book, I have received much assistance and support from a number of persons and institutions. While this is not conventional, I wish to list them now, in alphabetical order: Gary Bissiri, Karen Blair, Nancy Bracken, James Brennan, The Faculty Research Committee of Central Washington University, Carla Freeman, Earl Glauert, Beverly Heckart, Seichu Naito, Joe Ramsdell, Margie Ramsdell, Dave Storla, Warren Street, and Toshio Ueda. All have helped in various ways and I am grateful to them. Most of all I am indebted to my wife, Emiko Ramsdell, for all of the reasons that made this book possible.

It must be noted that, as this book goes to press, there have been two major changes in the leading left wing party of contemporary Japan. In late 1990 the Japan Socialist Party (JSP) officially changed its English language name to the Social Democratic Party of Japan (SDPJ). However, I have allowed the designation "JSP" to remain in both the text and the tables in the hope that purists will realize that for most of its existence it bore the earlier name. Then, at the end of July 1991, Doi Takako, the subject of a brief biography in Chapter Nine, resigned as head of the party, ostensibly to accept responsibility for the party's poor showing in the local elections in the spring of 1991. She was replaced by Tanabe Makoto.

Dedication

■

For Emiko

Chapter 1

Introduction

■

On November 29, 1890 the House of Representatives of the Japanese Imperial Diet was convened in Tokyo by the Emperor Meiji, thereby bringing into being the first elected national parliament in Asia. The three-hundred individuals seated in the hall had been elected by their fellow countrymen on July 1, 1890. Almost exactly one century later, on February 18, 1990, the thirty-ninth general election for the House of Representatives brought voters to the polls throughout Japan. In the one-hundred years of its existence 5,569 persons have participated in this deliberative body. In the pages that follow I have undertaken to analyze collectively all 5,569 members of this lower house of the Japanese parliament. I have confined the examination to the lower house because it was the sole elected body before the Second World War and it is the one with the greatest constitutional authority under the postwar constitution. In short, it is and has been by far the more important of the two houses of the Diet.

The study seeks to provide quantitative answers to a number of questions that have been raised about the Japanese political process in modern times. Among these is the extent to which the House of Representatives was, at any time or at all times, a "committee for managing the common affairs of the whole bourgeoisie." Did elected representative institutions naturally and inevitably attract individuals who sought to advance the interests of the "bourgeoisie" at the expense of the masses?

Also addressed is the composition of the elected political elite and the changes over time in this composition. Did the changes in Diet membership reflect other developments occurring within Japanese society? Related to this is the degree to which the development of Diet membership conformed to patterns found elsewhere in representative institutions. Does this development pattern indicate directions that other late-blooming "democracies" have followed or may follow in the future? How much did tendencies observable for the prewar (World War II) period continue under the new constitution after 1947?

An additional set of questions has to do with specific Japanese conditions. To what extent may compositional trends in the Japanese Diet membership be attributed to peculiarities in the history and culture of Japan? Related is the role of the Pacific War as a dividing line in Japanese political history. What general and particular distinctions can be discerned that separate the prewar from the postwar era? Are there other lines of periodic division and do they coincide with or contradict existing standard schemes of periodization for modern Japan? Japan has often been described as a paragon of stability and transitional "smoothness" in its modern history. Can this be measured quantitatively through the compilation of statistical biographical information on elected representatives?

Finally, on the macro-historical scale, there is the question of elected national assemblies as part of the "trappings" or "superstructure" of a modern capitalist state as it moves from semi-peripheral to core status in the modern world economy. Before the introduction of a parliament Japan would have to be regarded as peripheral in the world economy scheme developed by Fernand Braudel and Immanuel Wallerstein. Japan's adoption of a parliament, moreover, coincides quite closely with the commencement of Braudel's fourth secular trend. [1]

In addressing these questions I have developed a program which measures various characteristics of all members of the Diet. The characteristics are statistically enumerated in tables and charts which are interpreted in chapters on occupational background, education, professionalism, age, regional distinctions, party affiliation, political apprenticeship, and sex. The model is of my own creation, but bears resemblance to that employed by Colin Mellors, in his study of the membership of the House of Commons, *The British M.P.* [2]

The Prewar House and System

Before proceeding it is necessary to indicate the nature and functioning, both in law and in custom, of the House of Representatives. The lower of two houses created by the Constitution of 1889, this body was the only organ of representation at the national level. At first it had relatively little power and influence. The Emperor had the sole authority to convoke, open, close, prorogue and dissolve the House under the constitution. The annual session of the Diet was specifically limited to a period of three months. It quickly became the custom to convene the annual session formally in late December. After one or two days of organizational business the Diet was then adjourned for the New Year holidays, usually reconvening about January 21 of the following calendar year. Most regular sessions of the House of Representatives thus had only about sixty days in which business was conducted. Extraordinary or emergency sessions could also be called and frequently were, especially after an election in a year where the budget had not yet been approved. Such sessions were much shorter, usually only considering the budget or the specific emergency measure for which the session was called. [3]

In the early years of its existence the House of Representatives functioned as the chief constitutional organ through which opposition could be voiced to the *hanbatsu* dominated government. In the twentieth century its relative influence grew as a result of the expansion and bureaucratization of the political parties and the attrition of the genro. Its formal powers nevertheless remained severely limited. Its only advantage over the House of Peers was the provision that the budget had first to be submitted to the lower house. The legislative authority of the prewar Diet was largely confined to its capacity to pass or reject statutory acts and approve or disapprove Imperial ordinances issued while the Diet was not in session. It had the right to sanction constitutional amendments, but was not competent to introduce them. Although the Diet had the authority to pass it, the budget was submitted by the government. The constitution provided, moreover, that the Diet could neither reject nor reduce, without government concurrence, fixed expenditures based on powers assigned to the Emperor, those which were the result of existing statutes, or those that were related to the legal obligations of the government. In short, the principle was one of the superiority of law to the budget and the Diet's authority was supervisory in this realm. New taxes could not be applied without Diet consent, but the financial concern of the lower house was really limited to consideration of the budget estimates and not to the question of state revenue. Finally, the constitution stipulated that, should the Diet fail to approve a budget during its regular session, that of the preceding year should automatically go into effect.

As the influence of the House of Representatives grew, so also did its membership. Originally, the lower house consisted of 300 members whose eligibility was determined by a minimum age of thirty and the payment of 15 Yen annually in taxes. The membership of the house was raised to 381 in 1900, 464 in 1920 and to 466 in 1925. Accompanying these increases in membership were other revisions which enlarged the electorate from about 450,000 (males over twenty-five paying at least 15 Yen in taxes) to nearly 13,000,000 in 1925 when universal manhood suffrage was enacted. The nature of the electoral districts was also altered on each of the occasions when the franchise was extended. The original provisions in 1890 called for small, single member districts. In 1900 this was changed to create large districts, encompassing entire prefectures or designated municipalities, each of which elected from four to twelve members. In 1920 a bill was passed reverting to small sized districts with from one to three representatives. The Universal Manhood Suffrage Act of 1925 made the final prewar change to medium sized election districts of three to five Diet members. Table 1-1 indicates the consecutive changes in the number of members, size of the electorate and the number and size of electoral districts.

The fixed term for representatives under both the Meiji and 1947 constitutions was four years with a general election required at the expiration. Of the twenty-two elections held under the Meiji Constitution, only six came after a maximum hiatus. [4] Dissolution of the Diet was thus very common and was the prerogative of the government. After the final prewar revision of 1925 it was provided that elections should follow within thirty days of dissolution. The law also restricted election campaigns as to duration and expenses. Candidates, most of whom were endorsed by political parties, were obligated by the 1925 law to deposit a sum of 2,000 Yen in cash or public bonds as security and to forfeit that sum if they received less than ten percent of the votes in the constituency. Vacancies due to death or violation of the election law were filled by the next highest vote getter among the unsuccessful candidates, except that if the vacancy occurred after a member had taken a seat a new election was called. The expenses of an individual candidate in an election campaign were legally limited by a very complicated formula which usually came out to about 10,000 Yen in the 1920s. In practice, however, most campaigns far exceeded the legal figure. The estimated cost of a national campaign for a major party in 1928 was 10,000,000 Yen. In 1925 Tsurumi Yūsuke, himself a later successful candidate, called election costs the "curse of Japanese politics", continuing:

> In the first place, the necessity of great outlays has had a decisive influence on the character of candidates for Parliament. It has practically shut the door of the House to the middle class and also to the laboring people. Independent men who do not care to give pledges to their rich friends have found it impossible to get into political life. Some have somehow managed to raise expenses for one or two elections, but could not last long. There are cases of downright tragedy; the master of many a well-to-do family has gone into politics with sincere, patriotic motives and ruined not only his own career,but also the life of his whole family. To run for a seat in the House sends cold shudders through the hearts of the candidate's family and friends." [5]

TABLE 1-1
CHANGES IN THE ELECTION SYSTEM

ELECTION	DATE	ELIGIBLE VOTERS	AS % OF POP.	CAST VOTES	CONSTITUENCIES	SEATS	ELIGIBILITY	DISTRICTING SYSTEM
1	July 1, 1890	450,852	1.13	421,106	257	300	Males who have lived in the district for one year, paying 15 Yen in direct tax.	Small election districts: 214 single seat; 43 two seat. (130,000 pop. = one seat; 260,000 pop. two seats.
2	Feb. 15, 1892	434,594		398,457	257	300		
3	Mar. 1, 1894	440,113		391,870	257	300		
4	Sept. 1, 1894	460,483		392,036	257	300		
5	Mar. 15, 1898	452,637		396,177	257	300		
6	Aug. 10, 1898	502,292		397,906	257	300		
7	Aug. 10, 1902	982,868	2.18	859,276	105	376	Males who have lived in the district for 6 months, paying 10 Yen in direct tax.	Large election districts: Prefectures add districts with multiple seats; Cities as separate districts. 46 one seat districts to one 13 seat district. (120,000 pop. = one seat).
8	Mar. 1, 1903	958,322		818,682	105	376		
9	Mar. 1, 1904	762,445		639,821	106	379		
10	May 15, 1908	1,590,045		1,339,801	106	379		
11	May 15, 1912	1,506,045		1,338,528	107	381		
12	Mar. 25, 1915	1,546,411		1,417,136	107	381		
13	Apr. 20, 1917	1,422,126		1,300,154	197	381		
14	May 10, 1920	3,069,148	5.5	2,638,510	374	464	Males paying 3 Yen in direct tax.	Small districts: 295 one seat, 68 two seat; 3 three seat.
15	May 10, 1924	3,288,405		2,972,959	374	464		
16	Feb. 20, 1928	12,408,678	19.98	9,638,510	122	466	Males resident for one year in the district. Revised to 6 months in 1934.	Medium election districts: 53 three seat; 38 four seat; 31 five seat.
17	Feb. 20, 1930	12,812,895		10,446,188	122	466		
18	Feb. 20, 1932	13,103,679		9,723,116	122	466		
19	Feb. 20, 1936	14,304,546		11,132,677	122	466		
20	Apr. 30, 1937	14,402,497		10,203,686	122	466		
21	Apr. 30, 1942	14,594,287		12,142,447	122	466		

Continued on next page

TABLE 1-1 CONTINUED
CHANGES IN THE ELECTION SYSTEM

ELECTION	DATE	ELIGIBLE VOTERS	AS % OF POP.	CAST VOTES	CONSTI-TUENCIES	SEATS	ELIGIBILITY	DISTRICTING SYSTEM
22	Apr. 10, 1946	36,878,420	48.65	26,582,175	53	466	All persons 20 or older.	Large, prefecture-wide districts, plus others.
23	Apr. 25, 1947	40,907,493	52.38	27,361,607	117	466	All persons 20 or older.	Medium election districts: 3 to 5 seats per district.
24	Jan. 23, 1949	42,105,300		30,592,521	117	466		
25	Oct. 1, 1952	46,772,584		35,336,704	117	466		
26	Apr. 19, 1953	47,090,167		34,602,445	117	466		
27	Feb. 27, 1955	49,235,375		37,014,837	118	467	One seat-district added for Amami-Oshima.	
28	May 22, 1958	52,013,529		39,751,661	118	467		
29	Nov. 20, 1960	54,312,993		39,509,123	118	467		
30	Nov. 21, 1963	58,281,678		41,016,540	118	467		
31	Jan. 29, 1967	62,992,796		45,996,573	123	486	Five districts and 19 seats added.	
32	Dec. 27, 1969	69,260,424		46,989,573	123	486		
33	Dec. 10, 1972	73,769,636		52,425,078	124	491	One 5 seat district added for Okinawa.	
34	Dec. 5, 1976	77,926,588		56,612,755	130	511	Six districts and 20 seats added.	
35	Oct. 7, 1979	80,169,924		54,010,119	130	511		
36	June 22, 1980	80,925,034		59,028,834	130	511		
37	Dec. 18, 1983	84,483,256		56,779,690	130	511		
38	July 6, 1986	86,677,716	71.18	60,448,609	130	512	Redistricting creates one 6 seat and four 2 seat districts.	
39	Feb. 18, 1990	89,995,780		65,696,920	130	512		

Although the Diet sessions were normally of short duration, a singular lifestyle developed in Tokyo where the members spent their days when the Diet was in session. The rest of the year they were back in their districts, mostly rural areas in the early years. In a way, the annual migrations to and from the capital must have resembled in character if not in pomp the peregrinations of the daimyō in the *sankinkōtai* system of the Edo era.

Behavior in and out of the Diet hall was sometimes raucous. Ueki Emori (see Chapter Three), a major political party organizer, recounted how, in the very first Diet session in January 1891 he was attacked by *sōshi* (bullies) brandishing canes who appeared in organized formation in the gallery. Ueki's "karate" defense was no match and he required medical attention. This underscored an important qualification for Diet membership even in later years - intrepidity or the ability to defend oneself. This was a qualification rarely met despite the continuing peril faced on the floor and in nearby quarters. [6]

Ueki was, to be sure, an outspoken opponent of the h*anbatsu* dominated government which hired the bullies. He was a party member and responsible in some measure for the fact that the parties hit the ground running, immediately disputing with themselves and the government over the election of a vice-speaker in the first Diet session. Hayashida Kametarō, *shokikan* (Secretary) in the first assembly, wrote that "if a cooperative spirit had existed even a little in the opposition parties, it would have been possible to move rapidly toward the downfall of the *hanbatsu*. Their failure to do so perpetuated *hanbatsu* rule for longer than otherwise would have been the case." [7] The verity of this statement calls to mind the difficulty that the current permanent opposition has in cooperating against the government - LDP. Indeed, the nature of the struggle today between the *Yotō* (government or ministerial party) and the *Yatō* (opposition) resembles closely that of the parties versus the *hanbatsu* from 1890 until well into the twentieth century.

Another feature that hasn't changed much is the blameworthiness of some elected Diet members. Questionable activity has been a feature of parliamentarians throughout history and Japan has been no slacker in this regard. Corrupt politics was not learned from the West or anywhere else. It came naturally. In the last few years there have been the Tanaka Kakuei bribery case (still awaiting a final disposition), the Recruit scandal involving senior LDP politicians in 1988 and 1989, and the Pachinko - North Korea - JSP connection in 1989 and early 1990. [8] Nothing new here. One-hundred years ago the Constitution granted immunity to members while the Diet was in session and, in the very first session, the issue was raised because one elected member, Mori Tokinosuke, was incarcerated and missed the opening ceremony. He had been arrested for embezzlement. [9]

Another prominent member to spend time in prison was Uchida Nobuya (see Chapter Two). Uchida was an outspoken individual who did not take himself or others too seriously. He was something of an iconoclast. In one of several books he recalled election campaigning in the 1920s, by which time the political parties had become influential. One feature of election campaigns was to hold joint meetings at which several candidates made speeches to the assembled audience. Many politicians, including Uchida, developed reputations as effective speakers. Uchida recounted how a professional storyteller appropriated a story of a rickshaw man from his speech on reform of the House of Peers. [10] At such forums candidates also jockeyed for position in the order of presentation - some seeking to be first or next to last. According to Uchida noone wanted to be last because, by that time, the audience was likely to be in a foot-stomping mood. Shimada Toshio, once the last speaker, asked the crowd:"are your shoes important or is the nation important?" [11]

The Postwar House and System

Under the constitution adopted in 1947 the powers of the House of Representatives have been greatly augmented. It is now recognized as the highest organ of state power. The Prime Minister is chosen by the house and a majority of the cabinet ministers must also be members of the Diet. By custom, all Prime Ministers have been elected members of the lower house as have the vast majority of cabinet ministers. Usually only two or three members of the House of Councillors are included in the cabinet line-up and very rarely non-elected persons also serve. Although the new constitution also provided for a House of Councillors, with fixed six year terms, it gave clear precedence to the Representatives which may override dissenting action of the Councillors. No longer restricted to ninety days, the Diet is convened once a year and normally remains in session, unless dissolved for new elections, most of the time.

Since 1947 the system of medium sized election districts, originally instituted in 1925, has been in effect. There have been additions to the number of seats, as indicated in Table 1-1 and there have also been adjustments to the number of seats allowed in each district. Until 1986 each district was represented by from three to five individuals, except Amami-Ōshima which chose only one. A modification of the election law in that year created one district with six seats and reduced four districts to two representatives.

Stringent restrictions on campaign activity and funding, similar to those of the prewar era, continue to prevail. Just as prevalent is the circumvention of the legal restraints. Election campaigns are limited by law to a period of fifteen days, but many Diet members spend much of their time campaigning unofficially. There have been several liberalizing reforms in the laws governing election financing , most recently in 1975. As a result the government now picks up the tab for a number of items, including two free television appearances (five and one-half minutes each) and two free radio speeches (also five and one-half minutes each), plus a limited quantity of newspaper advertisements, costs of printing and distributing posters, and the expenses of a campaign car. The legal limits on campaign spending in 1986 ran from 13,624,000 Yen to 19,500,000 Yen. (Then about $80,000 to $110,000). However, actually costs running up to 75,000,000 Yen (about $440,000) are thought to be common. 12

Salaries of Diet members are fixed at no less than the highest paid civil servants. In 1980 this was 13,600,000 Yen (then about $60,444), plus annual allowances of 7,800,000 Yen for transportation, communication, etc. and 7,200,000 for legislative research expenses. Each also has two secretaries paid for by the government. Prior to the Pacific War being a legislator was not a full time job and most members had outside careers. This has changed dramatically, though there are still many who have additional sources of income. "Like members of Congress in the U.S., they are probably not deeply involved in those careers." 13

It is common knowledge that, since the end of the war, Japanese politics has been dominated by conservatives and that the LDP has organized every cabinet since it was formally organized in 1955. The LDP thus initiates almost all legislation which is, however, originated in the bureaucratic department with which it is concerned. Approval of legislation by the LDP's Policy Affairs Research Council is tantamount to its enactment into law. The Council is kept informed by the bureaucracy which gives very little information to the opposition parties. The latter, moreover, rarely introduce legislation in the Diet as it would be a waste of time. This state of affairs would seem to render the Diet almost impotent as a deliberative body, causing it to serve mainly as a rubber stamp to ratify decisions made elsewhere. The Diet does, however, examine and debate public issues of major national importance. Opposition parties attempt to embarass the government by provoking "slips of the tongue" in committee sessions which are often televised *in toto*. Moreover, Diet membership has clearly come to confer prestige, almost celebrity status and, of course, all prime ministers and almost all cabinet ministers - the national political leadership - are drawn from its ranks.

A major difference between Japanese and U.S. legislative behavior is the almost complete absence of lobbyists on the Japanese scene. It has been said that lobbyists do not exist because the parties themselves stand for interest groups. [14] Because of the multiple seat districting system that has prevailed since 1947, parties do not have to represent all voters in a geographical area. Instead they are tied to particular interest groups within the district in which they compete.[15] Although somewhat overgeneralized, it may be said that the LDP represents the interests of chambers of commerce, farmer organizations, medical societies, etc.; the JSP represents government workers' unions; the DSP some private sector labor organizations; and the Komeitō represents the interests of Sōka Gakkai. Only the JCP of the current political parties has no clear organizational constituency, except perhaps those alienated from the system.[16] "The principal problem for the Japanese parties during elections has not been to appeal to the greatest number of voters, but how to maximize the turnout of voters in their own special interest constituency." [17]

Along with the general population, the lifestyles of Diet members have undergone great changes since the prewar and early postwar years. Their salaries have grown at a commensurate pace. Some things remain unchanged, however, only transpiring at an elevated level. The continuing high cost of elections elicits criticisms and statements almost identical to those expressed by Tsurumi in 1925.

Since the war Diet members spend far more time in session and hence in the capital. They naturally reside there much of the year, returning to their districts periodically to raise money and make the rounds with support groups.

Accounts of the early postwar period provide a feeling of resemblance to the early years of the late nineteenth century. The lifestyle was simple and creature comforts were in short supply. Among those who have written about the early postwar is Tsuji Kan'ichi, a Diet member from Aichi Prefecture from 1946 to 1972. In 1950 Tsuji published an anecdotal description of life in the capital under the title of *Giin Shukusha*. The "Shukusha" was a kind of boarding house for Diet members in the early postwar years. It was located on a promontory about three *cho* from the streetcar stop at Akasaka Reservoir. One night's lodging for an eight mat room was one Yen, although gratituities would likely bring it up to about thirty Yen, still unbelievably inexpensive in the days of the postwar housing shortage. There was a fifty person capacity and lodging in the *shukusha* was apportioned according to party strength in the Diet. Within each party lots were drawn to determine the lucky lodgers. Tsuji stayed here for several years from 1947 onward, commenting that if politicians of rival parties "took a morning bath, party consciousness vanished like the mist." [18]

The *shukusha* was apparently off limits to some. Tsuji related an incident where a constituent brought a young woman to his quarters in the middle of the night. The young woman, a geisha, was the daughter of a geisha Tsuji had known in Nagoya. Though he insisted that "nothing happened", a few days later someone posted a notice about public morals in the lodgings, alluding to the midnight appearance of a woman of questionable reputation.[19] This kind of "sex scandal" hardly compares to that of today - Prime Minister Uno's brief tenure being cut short, in part, by sensationalized accusations of "womanizing" in 1989.

Tsuji also described a Diet member's occupation as representative of a "service industry." "It is continually people, people, people. Sometimes there are two or three teams of people, sometimes seven or eight and sometimes it is visitors on parade." [20]

Postwar parliament members have also found their lives threatened or exposed to bodily harm. Examples are too numerous to mention. The most spectacular occurred in 1960 with the massive street demonstrations and brawling in the Diet in May and June. Also occurring that year was the assassination of JSP leader Asanuma in October. Takase Den, among others, recited an incident somewhat earlier where he was surrounded by about 250 students in the Diet members reception hall. Despite cries of "bakayarō" ("you idiot!") which drowned out his attempts to respond to questions, the other Diet members present (most of them Socialists) remained silent, refusing to come to his assistance. [21]

Japanese politics and political behavior have, of course, been studied at great length. It hardly seems necessary to mention the many excellent general accounts. The great majority of these have been and continue to be the works of political scientists whose primary focus is on recent trends and current prospects. Among the generalized works particularly useful for this study are Ishikawa Masumi, *Nihon Seiji no Tōshizu* (1985) and *Sengo Seiji Kōzōshi* (1978), Masumi Junnosuke, *Nihon Seitō Shiron*, 7 vol. (1965-1980), and Wakata Kyoji, *Gendai Nihon Seiji to Fūdo* (1981) in Japanese and, in English, recent books by Hans Baerwald, *Party Politics in Japan* (1986) and Gerald Curtis, *The Japanese Way of Politics* (1988). Studies of political history have commonly been narratives of some length or concentrated upon a particular period or incident.[22] As for political elites, Takane Masaaki, *Political Elite in Japan* (1981) is a sociological approach, quantitative in nature, which examines certain political elites at intervals in modern times (1860, 1890, 1920, 1936 and 1969). Interested in modernization theory, Takane includes some Diet members among his political elites, but not all members. His emphasis is on elite political status rather than electability and he seeks to define "political elite" by quantitative methodology rather than attempting this same definition of elected assemblymen. Beyond this, election studies are relatively common, especially in English,[23] but recruitment studies, even of the recent past, much less in evidence.[24] To my knowledge there has been no single work in any language which attempts to analyze the composition of a parliamentary body over the whole course of its existence. Colin Mellors, mentioned above, has done a thorough recruitment study of the British House of

Commons covering a thirty year period, 1945-1974. Other works on the "mother of parliaments" are also available.[25] For the U.S. Congress recruitment studies include Donald R. Matthews, *U.S. Senators and Their World* (1960) and Susan Webb Hammond, "From Staff Aide to Election: The Recruitment of U.S. Representatives" (1987). In addition there are several comparative studies of national parliaments, though most are books with separate chapters on each of the countries whose assemblies are under review.

Previous recruitment studies providing statistical information on the members of the Japanese Diet for portions of the prewar period are all based on data collected by Masumi Junnosuke and included in Volume Five of his *Nihon Seitō Shiron*. Wakata, Pempel and Ishida have all used Masumi's figures.[26] A massive examination of postwar recruitment was published in 1980 under the editorship of Naka Kurō, *Kokkai Giin no Kōsei to Henka*, covering both houses from 1947 until 1979. Other scholars, working independently, have also collected statistics for selected periods, sometimes for a single Diet session. This list includes Ishikawa Masumi in *Sengo Seiji Kōzōshi* (1978), Scalapino and Masumi, *Parties and Politics in Contemporary Japan* (1962), Masumi again in *Postwar Politics in Japan, 1945-1955* (1985), Fukui, *Party in Power* (1969) and Curtis, *The Japanese Way of Politics* (1988). A comparison of my figures and those cited in these works is provided in Appendix B. Most of the postwar studies have emphasized political parties and distinctions between them in recruitment patterns. This is particularly true of the work by Wakata, Pempel, Naka, and Scalapino and Masumi. Some, including Fukui and Scalapino and Masumi, are also interested in factions within the parties, especially the LDP.

This study is relatively disinterested in parties and factions. The principal concerns are with all members regardless of party and with changes in the composition of the chamber over the course of time. Most of the studies referred to above subsume attributes such as education, occupational background, etc. to party affiliation in order make distinctions among them. Although Chapter Seven does take up party recruitment patterns, the primary emphasis remains temporal rather than spatial.

Fernand Braudel, the twentieth century macro-historian, has written that "the past always counts."[27] This is no less true in the political history of Japan than in the position of a town in sixteenth century Europe. A subsidiary intention here is to examine the extent to which incremental changes occurring over rather long stretches of time fit into Braudel's scheme of history - the secular trend. Japan's national assembly began to meet in 1890, just about the point in time in Braudel's reckoning of the beginning of a new secular trend. There is common agreement that, in the 1890s, Japan was edging away from her status as a "peripheral" area in the world economy dominated by the "core" states of Western Europe and

North America. As Japan advanced through the long course of this secular trend to the "semi-periphery" and then to the "core", the legislature and its membership constituted an important part of the "trappings" or superstructure of the state. This study may, thus, test the applicability of the Braudel/Wallerstein thesis as a major interpretation of world history, for there is no doubt that Japan has been a "major player" on the world scene in the twentieth century. She began to assume such a role, moreover, just as the national assembly came into being.[28]

A major related concern is the issue of continuity versus discontinuity in the development of modern Japan.[29] How much continuity or discontinuity has there been? How smooth have been the transitions and when did they occur? In politics, where have there been the greatest aberrations, quantum leaps, sudden changes? How "Japanese" has all of this been? Did the U.S. "democratize" Japan during the Occupation or was she already inherently "democratic"? Or has Japan never been "democratic"? [30] For that matter, what is parliamentary democracy?

In the chapters which follow I take up the attributes of the Diet membership in order: principal occupational background, education, political professionalism, age, region, party and apprenticeship with an additional special chapter on women in the postwar Diet. Each chapter, except those on age and region, concludes with a series of thumbnail biographies of individuals who exemplify some of the characteristics raised in that section. With a few exceptions I have selected less known individuals for this part. In each section I examine the total membership as well as compositional changes over time. When considering the entire membership, for analytical purposes, I use four cohort groups:

1. All members: 5,569 individuals elected between 1890 and 1990.
2. Prewar members: 3,537 individuals elected between 1890 and 1942.
3. All postwar members: 2,242 individuals elected between 1946 and 1990. This includes 210 persons also elected before the war and thus also listed in cohort group number two.
4. New postwar members: 2,032 individuals elected for the first time in 1946 or after.

The biographical information on these persons was derived from a variety of sources, the most important of which are: Japan. Kokkai. Shūgiin, *Gikai Seido 70-nen Shi*, Vol. IX, *Shūgiin Meikan* (1962) and Japan. Kokkai. Shūgiin, *Shūgiin Giin Ryakureki* (1940). The former of these contains brief biographies of all persons elected from the first election in 1890 through the twenty-ninth election in 1960. Also useful was Nihon Kokusei Chōsakai, ed., *Shūgiin Meiroku* (1977), especially for the postwar membership. Yearbooks such as *Yomiuri Nenkan* and *Asahi Nenkan* routinely include biographies of Diet members and, of course, there are annual editions of *Kokkai Benran*, published by Nihon Seikei

Shimbunsha. Newspapers also print abbreviated vitae at the time of elections. Most of the postwar lists of this sort have incomplete or inaccurate information, so it has been necessary to consult some full length biographies and, in some cases, local newspaper accounts for more background information.

Elite Status Formula

In the next two chapters I develop a typology for Diet members in which an "A" type has certain characteristics which I consider to be non-elite and in which a "B" type has elite characteristics. Later chapters develop this more fully and analyze groups of members by prefecture, sex, etc. according to an "elite status formula". The formula for analyzing cohort groups is as follows:

1. In assessing occupational backgrounds of a particular cohort group, agriculture and local government (as occupations) were considered to be non-elite. Education, central government service, journalism and law were considered to be elite occupations. In each of these six occupational categories the percentage differences between that of the cohort group and the national average was tabulated to get an elite status rating that was positive or negative. See example below.

2. For educational background, I added or subtracted the percentage differences between the national average and the cohort group for those attending (1) universities, (2) major universities, (3) Todai, and (4) Kyodai. I then added or subtracted the combined differences in these four areas and divided that total by three to arrive at a positive or negative educational elite rating. See example below.

3. Local assembly membership was considered non-elite. If the percentage in the cohort group with local assembly experience was higher than the national average the difference was recorded in the non-elite column. If the local assembly membership percentage was lower than the national average, the difference was recorded in the positive column. In this way, a plus or minus elite status rating was obtained for this apprenticeship category. See example below.

4. The identical procedure was used for company directorships, except that such apprenticeship represents a weaker degree of non-elite background. Thus, I halved the differences between the percentage in this cohort group and the national average. See example below.

5. High frequency of election was taken to represent elite status. Hence, the average number of times elected for the sub-group was compared to the national average. If the cohort group figure was higher the difference was measured in positive elite status points. If the figure was lower, it stood on the negative side. See example below.

The points achieved in each of the above categories were then added to arrive at the elite status rating for the cohort group under consideration. The following is an illustrative example:

This example uses the cohort group of all prewar members from Fukuoka Prefecture. 138 individuals.

Category	National percentage	Fukuoka percentage	Elite Status rating	
Occupations				
Agriculture	17.7	10.1	+7.6	
Education	7.1	2.9	-4.2	
Central government	10.9	17.3	+6.4	
Local government	8.4	6.5	+1.9	
Journalism	8.2	8.7	+0.5	
Law	11.1	7.2	-3.9	
				+8.3
Education				
University	40.4	38.4	-2.0	
Major university	35.5	34.8	-0.7	
Todai	10.7	11.6	+0.9	
Kyodai	1.6	2.9	+1.3	
			-0.5	
			divided by 3 = -0.2	
Local Assembly members	61.9	50.7	+11.2	
Company directorships	49.1	47.1	+2.0	
			divided by 2 = +1.0	
Average number of times elected	2.66	2.41		-2.5
				+9.7
Overall prewar Fukuoka members elite status rating			+17.9	

It will be seen that what I have chosen to regard as "elite" occupations are those requiring, for the most part, a university education and a "modern" rather than "traditional" role in society.   In short they are "bourgeois" occupations and the elite status might well be considered to represent a non-rentier class; an urban or "bourgeois" elite. Although the earliest Diets were not particularly bourgeois and hence not very elite, the division used here to distinguish elite from non-elite status is justified, because the occupations so delineated and the universities attended came to have great prestige in Japanese society at large. Local assembly membership and company directorship affiliations, designated non-elite, also reflect a more local or regional outlook as will be explained later.[31] This is the reason for including them here. Other factors, including several occupations like medicine which seem, at first glance, to be "elite" have been excluded. The percentage figures for such occupations are very small, however, and the prestige of some, including medicine, is subject to question.

In Meiji times high social status was assumed by many to be derived from other factors than those designated here as "elite" or "modern." Local landlords, heavily represented as agriculturalists in the early Diets, would likely be considered elites, but I justify their designation as non-elite by the fact that the occupation itself was already regarded as non-modern. Moreover, the agricultural sector was neglected in early modern Japan in terms of resources devoted to its modernization. This tendency began even before the Constitution created the Diet and continued thereafter. The progressive enhancement of bourgeois characteristics in the Diet membership paralleled the growth of the industrial sector in Japan. The result was that those landlords who might earlier be considered elite on the local scene were now clearly regarded by the nation as a whole as representative of traditional rather than modern values. There is, in addition, sufficient disagreement on class structure in modern Japan to question the desirability of rating individuals on that basis. Hence, it is suitable to have an "elite" rating based on "modern" qualities - education, occupation, and apprenticeship.

NOTES

1 See Fernand Braudel, *The Perspective of the World* (Vol. 3 of *Civilization and Capitalism 15th-18th Century*, English translation, 1984), Chapter One, particularly pp. 78-80.

2 Colin Mellors, *The British MP: A Socio-Economic Study of the House of Commons* (1978).

3 The shortest emergency session lasted two days. There were three of this duration during the Pacific War. The average length of an extraordinary session was slightly more than ten days.

4 The 21st general election, April 30, 1942, was held five years after the previous one because of the emergency conditions occasioned by the war.

5 Tsurumi Yusuke, "The Liberal Movement in Japan", in *The Reawakening of the Orient and Other Addresses*, ed. by Sir Valentin Chirol, Yusuke Tsurumi, Sir James Arthur Salter. (1925), pp. 76-77.

6 Ueki Emori, *Ueki Emori Nikki* (1955), pp. 371-374.

7 Hayashida Kametarō, *Nihon Seitō Shi* (1927), V. 1, p. 304.

8 The Recruit affair was particularly scandalous. It surfaced late in 1988 when it was revealed that Ezoe Hiromasa, Chairman of Recruit Incorporated, had provided unlisted stock in Recruit Cosmos (a real estate development company) to high government officials in advance of their listing on the stock exchange. Most high ranking LDP members were implicated, including Prime Minister Takeshita and former Prime Minister Nakasone. Takeshita, among others, was forced to resign.

9 Hayashida, *Nihon Seitō Shi*, p. 304.

10 Uchida Nobuya, *Fūsetsu Gojūnen* (1951), p. 80.

11 Uchida, *Fūsetsu Gojūnen*, pp. 81-82.

12 See Gerald Curtis, *The Japanese Way of Politics* (1988), pp. 165-188 for details on recent campaign financing laws and the ways around them.

13 Izumi Shoichi, "Diet Members", in *The Japanese Diet and the U.S. Congress,* ed. by Francis R. Valeo and Charles E. Morrison (1983), pp. 62-63, 75.

14 For this and the material in the preceding paragraph, see Kan Ori, "The Diet in the Japanese Political System", in *The Japanese Diet and the U.S. Congress*, p. 17.

15 For an interesting article on interest group politics in Japan, see Ishida Takeshi, "The Development of Interest Groups and the Pattern of Political Modernization in Japan", in Robert E. Ward, ed., *Political Development in Modern Japan* (1968), pp. 293-336. Ishida describes the process of forming a "typical" Japanese interest group and notes the historical development of such business and labor organizations. He does not tie the interest groups to the political process itself, but is mainly concerned with how Japanese interest groups conform to or depart from patterns of "modernization" developed by Westerners from their own expereince. Alfred B. Clubok in "Political Party Membership and Subleadership in Rural Japan", in Bernard Silberman and Harry Harootunian, ed., *Modern Japanese Leadership* (1966), pp. 385-409 also provides useful information on "local notable politics" and how the LDP relies on this mode of electoral behavior. William E. Steslicke, *Doctors in Politics: The Political Life of the Japan Medical Association* (1973) considers pressure groups with particular emphasis on the rise of the JMA in the 1960s.

16 See Hashimoto Mitsuru, "Dantai Shozoku", Chapter Eleven of Naka Kurō, ed., *Kokkai Giin no Kōsei to Henka* (1980), pp. 219-258.

17 J. J. Foster, "Ghost-hunting: Local Party Organization in Japan", *Asian Survey*, 22:9 (Sept. 1982), p. 855.

18 Tsuji Kan'ichi, *Giin Shukusha* (1950), p. 5.

19 Tsuji, *Giin Shukusha,,* pp. 3-7.

20 Tsuji, *Giin Shukusha*, p. 2.

21 Takase Den, *Ichi Daigishi no Negoto* (1957), pp. 20-22.

22 To mention but a few: Shinobu Seizaburō, *Nihon Seijishi,,* 4 vol. (1976-1982); Banno Junji, *Meiji Kenpō Taisei no Kakuritsu* (1971); Yamanaka

Einosuke, *Nihon Kindai Kokka no Keisei to Kanryōsei* (1971); Ota Masao, *Taishō Demokurashi Kenkyū* (1975); Toyama Shigeki, et. al., *Shōwa Shi* (1955 and later editions); Haruta Kunio, *Nihon Kokkai Jishi* (1987).

[23] Election studies include Yuzu Masao, ed., *Kokusei Senkyō to Seitō Seiji* (1977); Takabatake Michitoshi, *Gendai Nihon no Seitō to Senkyō* (1980) and, in English, R.H.P. Mason, *Japan's First General Election, 1890* (1969); Edward J. Drea, *The 1942 Japanese General Election: Political Mobilization in Wartime Japan* (1979); Robert A. Scalapino, "Elections and Political Modernization in Prewar Japan", in Robert E. Ward, ed., *Political Development in Modern Japan* (1968), pp. 249-291; Scott Flanagan and Bradley Richardson, *Japanese Electoral Behavior: Social Cleavages, Social Networks and Partnership* (1977); Vernon Bogdanour and David Butler, ed., *Democracy and Elections: Electoral Systems and Their Political Consequences* (1983); Steven R. Reed, "The People Spoke: the Influence of Elections on Japanese Politics, 1949-1955", *Journal of Japanese Studies* (Summer 1988), pp. 309-339.

[24] Among recruitment studies, mention may be made of Aoyama Takenori, *Gikai Kōsei no Mondai to Kentō* (1977) in addition to those cited hereafter in this chapter. In English, there are H. Taylor, *Qualifications of Politicians* (1967); Young C. Kim, "Political Recruitment: the Case of Japanese Prefectural Assemblymen", in *American Political Science Review* (December 1967), pp. 1036-1052; Jung-suk Youn, "Candidates and Party Images: Recruitment to the Japanese House of Representatives", in John C. Campbell, ed., *Parties, Candidates and Voters in Japan: Six Quantitative Studies* (1981), pp. 101-115; Ezra N. Suleiman, ed., *Parliaments and Parliamentarians in Democratic Politics* (1986).

[25] See W.L. Guttsman, *The British Political Elite* (1963); P.W. Buck, *Amateurs and Professionals in British Politics 1918-1959* (1963); A. Ranney, *Pathways to Parliament* (1965); M.D. Rush, *The Selection of Parliamentary Candidates* (1969).

[26] Wakata Kyōji, *Gendai Nihon no Seiji to Fūdo* (1981); T.J. Pempel, *Policy and Politics in Japan: Creative Conservatism* (1982); Ishida, "The Development of Interest Groups", pp. 306-309.

[27] Braudel, *The Perspective of the World*, p. 50.

[28] Braudel, *The Perspective of the World*, Chapter One, pp. 21-88, cited above in note 1. See also Immanuel Wallerstein, *The Modern World System,* Vol. 1, *Capitalist Agriculture and the Origins of the European World-Economy in the Sixteenth Century* (1974), Vol. 2, *Mercantilism and the Consolidation of the European World-Economy 1600-1750* (1980).

[29] See Ishikawa Masumi, *Sengo Seiji Kōzōshi* (1978), pp. 1-12.

[30] On this last question, see, for example, Gavan McCormack and Yoshio Sugimoto, *Democracy in Contemporary Japan* (1986), particularly the Introduction, pp. 9-17.

[31] See Hans Baerwald, *Party Politics in Japan* (1986), p. 20.

Chapter 2

OCCUPATIONS

■

An analysis of the occupational backgrounds of Diet members may properly begin with a glance at Table 2-1 which breaks down all 5,569 members according to their primary occupational activity prior to their initial election. This table denotes the four cohort group categories explained in the Introduction: all members, prewar members, all postwar members, and new postwar members. With few exceptions the patterns for all postwar and for new postwar members are very similar. Thus, in the comparative graph 2-1, the postwar figures include all postwar members.

Many members, especially in the early years, pursued more than one career before seeking elective office. Many others continued old careers while in office or after leaving the Diet. Still others changed occupations or principal areas of interest. It has been difficult at times, therefore, to pick a single primary occupation. Nevertheless, after weighing all of the information available, a decision had to be made on each individual. It is important to underestand, however, that while a single primary occupation has been entered in each case, a great many members had multiple careers and multifarious interests.

Before proceding to analyze the data, some of the occupational categories require additional explanation. Those listed under agriculture, which are particularly numerous in the early years, invariably were landowners whose principal source of income and prestige came from the possession of land used for agricultural purposes. Few of these men engaged much in the arduous labor associated with farming. Many, moreover, had additional pursuits, a fact that is revealed by noting that nearly half (45.8%) of all members with agricultural backgrounds also served business as presidents or directors of companies.

A few other occupational categories also require explanation. Obviously, many of those classified under the heading of Labor/Socialist movement served for a while as blue collar workers before they moved into union work. Most of

TABLE 2-1

IMPERIAL AND NATIONAL DIET

Primary Occupation

	ALL MEMBERS NO.	%	ALL PREWAR NO.	%	NEW POSTWAR NO.	%	POSTWAR NO.	%
Agriculture	735	13.2	625	17.7	123	5.5	110	5.4
Business/Banking	1368	24.6	992	28.1	429	19.1	376	18.5
Education	402	7.2	252	7.1	158	7.0	150	7.4
Higher Education	93	1.7	51	1.4	51	2.3	42	2.1
Govt. (Central)	414	7.4	230	6.5	204	9.1	184	9.1
Govt. (Home Min.)	234	4.2	157	4.4	86	3.8	77	3.8
Total C. Govt.	648	11.6	387	10.9	290	12.9	261	12.9
Local Govt.	356	6.4	296	8.4	64	2.9	60	3.0
Journalism	424	7.8	289	8.2	162	7.2	135	6.6
Law	544	9.8	391	11.1	190	8.5	153	7.5
Labor/Soc.	120	2.2	16	0.5	114	5.1	104	5.1
Medicine	149	2.7	94	2.7	59	2.6	55	2.7
Military	55	1.0	51	1.4	6	0.3	4	0.2
Politics	404	7.3	52	1.5	362	16.2	352	17.3
Religion	20	0.4	11	0.3	10	0.4	9	0.4
Women's Orgs.	7	0.1	0	-	7	0.3	7	0.3
Writing	22	0.4	8	0.2	15	0.7	14	0.7
Blue Collar	50	0.9	2	0.1	49	2.2	48	2.4
White Collar	149	2.7	12	0.3	137	6.1	137	6.7
Soka Gakkai	10	0.2	0	-	10	0.4	10	0.5
Other/None	13	0.2	8	0.2	6	0.3	5	0.2
	5569		3537		2242		2032	

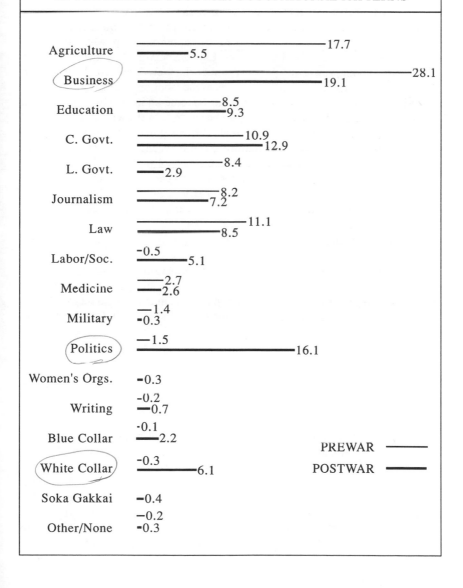

GRAPH 2-1
IMPERIAL AND NATIONAL DIET COMPARISON
OF PREWAR AND POSTWAR OCCUPATIONAL PATTERNS

Agriculture — 17.7 / 5.5

Business — 28.1 / 19.1

Education — 8.5 / 9.3

C. Govt. — 10.9 / 12.9

L. Govt. — 8.4 / 2.9

Journalism — 8.2 / 7.2

Law — 11.1 / 8.5

Labor/Soc. — -0.5 / 5.1

Medicine — 2.7 / 2.6

Military — 1.4 / -0.3

Politics — 1.5 / 16.1

Women's Orgs. — -0.3

Writing — -0.2 / -0.7

Blue Collar — -0.1 / 2.2

White Collar — -0.3 / 6.1

Soka Gakkai — -0.4

Other/None — -0.2 / -0.3

PREWAR ——
POSTWAR ▬▬

these persons sat in the Diet after the war and came either from the government railway workers union (Kokurō) or the teachers union (Nikkyosō). They are listed under Labor/Socialist movement instead of blue collar or education, however, because of their early and strong commitment to union work and their identification with it rather than the trade or profession. Clearly, many listed under education or blue collar categories also belonged to unions. Such affiliation is taken into account in a category associated with apprenticeship, which is considered in Chapter Seven. Also listed under Labor/Socialist movement are some individuals in both prewar and postwar times who were intellectuals, trained in law, but who devoted their primary energies to the labor or socialist causes.

Under the heading of politics, which has become an increasingly prominent category, some hard decisions also had to be made. On the whole, those placed in the politics column were persons who also engaged in other productive activities for which they received remuneration. Even in recent times, few came out of universities to embark immediately on careers as "politicians". Most, however, devoted themselves primarily to politics or political causes from an early point in their adult lives. In postwar times the majority of those for whom politics is listed as the primary occupation served apprenticeships as secretaries or assistants to Diet members before succeeding to their patron's seat or launching out on their own. This has been a conspicuous feature of political recruitment in recent Japan.[1]

The category "white collar worker" includes either professionals in fields like engineering or accounting (whose numbers were too small to list as a separate category) or to persons with management positions in the private sector. It also includes a few who had positions like hospital administrator, YMCA director, etc.

Agriculture

Agriculture is one of the occupations which displays markedly different patterns for the prewar and postwar periods. It is also one where a relatively consistent downward trend is visible over the entire century. (See Table 2-3). The grand total of those with a primary occupation in agriculture is 13.2% which is the second highest figure for any category. Most of these members came in the prewar period (17.7% of all prewar members), especially in the period up to about 1920. Election laws and districting were always designed (they still are) to favor rural constituencies and, after 1920, as the election law was broadened to include all adult males (1925) and then women (1946), the fall off of agriculturalists was rapid. The most precipitous drop in the agricultural membership was between 1946 and 1947 when postwar land reforms probably had some effect. In recent elections the number of successful candidates from agriculture has fallen to insignificant proportions. The heyday, by contrast, was in the late 19th century when agriculture took first place in the September 1894 election and in the balloting of March 1898. Over twenty-five percent listed agriculture in this latter election, but it may be argued that this was a low figure given the heavy concentration of population on the land and the equally heavy tax burden borne thereon. In a sense, therefore, it is possible to contend that agriculture was underrepresented from the very beginning.

A look at the pattern for new members (See Table 2-3) reveals that scant effort has been made at any time since the end of the war to recruit members from the agricultural sector.

It is not surprising to find that, as a group, members from agriculture were among the least well educated for a numerous category. The overwhelming majority had served in local assemblies before advancing to the national level. Agricultural interests have consistently been more prominently represented in local and prefectural assemblies. The law creating prefectural assemblies in 1878 enfranchised middle and upper class landlords so that "the agrarian middle class received its political emancipation before the corresponding class in urban centers. It is not surprising that these provincial landlords, with their new privileges, were destined to become an important factor in Japanese politics."[2] The fact that over eighty-five percent of the agriculture delegates had local assembly experience differentiates them from nearly every other cohort group by a wide margin. Agriculture delegates also had a high percentage with company directorships, but a very poor ratio of reelectability. (See Table A-1, Appendix A)

The aggregate profile of the agriculture Diet member is of an individual with relatively little education (not likely to be a college graduate), interested in local affairs (revealed in local assembly membership), frequently involved in local business concerns, but not likely to serve long at the center of power in Tokyo.

Party affiliation of agriculture members was overwhelmingly conservative, both before and after the war, but since far more served in the prewar Diet this tendency shows up much more clearly for the prewar era. This means that most prewar agriculture members belonged either to the Seiyūkai or the Minseitō and their antecedents (80 percent). In the postwar period nearly sixty percent were LDP members and another ten percent independents. This is not to say, however, that conservative parties drew most of their membership from the agricultural sector.

On the whole the agriculture members stand for the prewar economy and its values. They represent local elites, not prepared for national leadership by formal training, but whose prominence enabled them to be put forward as candidates and secure election by their constituents. As the franchise extended and power and prestige moved to the cities, representatives from the agricultural sector diminished. The influence of the rural electorate in perpetuating the rule of the conservative LDP has, however, continued and is widely recognized.

TABLE 2-2
IMPERIAL AND NATIONAL DIET
Primary Occupation By Election and Year
(Figures are percentages)

Election	1	2	3	4	5	6	7	8	9	10	11	12	13
Agriculture	11.5	12.1	15.7	19.1	25.7	20.7	17.0	18.2	20.8	15.6	14.8	15.6	14.7
Business/Banking	19.9	20.4	22.0	18.8	23.4	26.3	25.5	27.3	27.0	28.2	29.7	28.6	25.4
Education	13.4	10.8	11.3	10.6	8.3	9.1	8.8	8.2	6.2	6.6	4.6	6.9	5.8
Higher Education	1.2	0.3	0.3	0.3	1.0	0.9	0.8	0.3	0.2	0.7	1.9	1.2	2.7
Govt. (Central)	10.3	7.1	7.0	6.7	5.3	4.3	6.1	6.3	5.2	6.6	7.3	6.7	6.3
Govt. (Home Min.)	5.6	10.5	5.3	5.5	3.7	2.4	2.4	1.3	3.2	2.6	3.6	4.7	3.9
Total C. Govt.	15.9	17.6	12.3	12.2	9.0	6.7	8.5	7.6	8.4	9.2	10.9	11.4	10.2
Local Govt.	17.1	20.4	18.7	21.6	13.3	14.9	9.0	9.5	7.4	6.6	3.4	2.7	3.1
Journalism	4.7	4.3	5.3	4.3	5.0	6.7	8.8	8.2	8.7	11.1	13.8	15.1	17.6
Law	8.4	7.1	7.7	7.0	7.7	7.9	13.8	12.9	14.6	15.4	16.5	14.4	14.5
Labor/Soc.	-	-	-	-	-	-	-	-	-	-	-	-	-
Medicine	1.6	1.2	1.7	0.3	1.3	1.5	2.7	2.4	1.0	2.4	2.2	1.2	4.3
Military	0.3	0.9	0.3	0.6	0.7	0.9	0.5	0.3	0.5	0.9	1.0	0.5	-
Politics	3.7	3.7	4.7	4.3	4.0	3.4	3.7	3.7	4.0	2.4	1.5	2.0	1.9
Religion	1.6	0.6	-	0.3	0.3	0.9	0.5	0.8	0.5	0.5	0.5	0.2	0.2
Women's Orgs.	-	-	-	-	-	-	-	-	-	-	-	-	-
Writing	0.3	-	-	-	-	-	-	0.3	0.2	-	-	-	-
Blue Collar	-	-	-	-	-	-	-	-	-	-	-	-	-
White Collar	-	-	-	-	-	-	-	-	-	0.2	0.2	-	-
Soka Gakkai	-	-	-	-	-	-	-	-	-	-	-	-	-
Other/None	0.3	0.3	-	0.6	0.3	0.3	0.5	0.5	0.5	-	-	-	0.2
Year	1890	1892	1894	1894	1898	1898	1902	1903	1904	1908	1912	1915	1917

Continued on next page

TABLE 2-2 CONTINUED
IMPERIAL AND NATIONAL DIET
Primary Occupation By Election and Year

Election	14	15	16	17	18	19	20	21	22	23	24	25	26
Agriculture	16.1	12.9	10.5	9.2	10.1	12.0	11.5	12.9	11.1	5.7	4.9	4.5	4.1
Business/Banking	27.6	25.4	26.8	25.5	24.4	21.4	20.2	24.8	26.2	25.7	29.9	22.7	19.5
Education	5.8	4.3	3.6	4.7	3.2	3.5	3.2	4.0	13.9	10.3	4.7	6.9	7.1
Higher Education	1.6	1.6	3.2	2.4	3.2	3.1	2.4	3.0	2.8	2.7	2.8	1.7	1.5
Govt. (Central)	6.7	8.8	9.9	9.0	10.5	7.5	8.3	8.7	6.2	7.8	12.0	12.2	14.1
Govt. (Home Min.)	3.8	5.8	6.0	5.1	6.9	6.4	7.3	6.6	2.3	3.2	4.1	9.0	7.7
Total C. Govt.	10.5	14.6	15.9	14.1	17.4	13.9	15.6	15.3	8.5	11.0	16.1	21.2	21.8
Local Govt.	3.0	3.3	1.7	1.9	2.5	2.3	2.0	3.0	3.0	3.2	4.3	2.6	3.4
Journalism	13.7	17.2	16.9	17.3	15.8	16.8	16.6	12.1	9.2	12.0	11.1	11.1	12.2
Law	13.9	13.1	14.8	16.5	16.2	16.6	16.2	14.0	9.6	10.8	10.0	12.8	11.6
Labor/Soc.	-	-	0.2	0.2	-	1.2	3.2	1.3	6.2	7.8	5.1	6.0	6.9
Medicine	2.8	3.9	2.8	3.4	2.1	2.1	3.0	2.1	3.2	1.5	0.9	1.7	1.7
Military	1.0	1.0	1.1	0.9	1.7	1.7	1.2	4.0	-	-	-	0.2	0.4
Politics	3.0	2.1	2.1	3.0	1.9	2.1	2.2	2.1	3.6	2.7	2.1	2.8	3.4
Religion	0.2	-	0.2	0.2	-	0.2	0.2	0.2	1.1	0.4	-	0.2	0.4
Women's Orgs.	-	-	-	-	-	-	-	-	-	0.2	0.2	-	-
Writing	0.2	0.2	0.4	0.4	0.6	0.6	0.6	0.4	0.4	0.2	1.1	0.4	0.6
Blue Collar	-	-	-	0.2	-	0.2	0.2	0.2	0.6	1.5	1.5	0.9	0.9
White Collar	0.4	0.4	0.2	0.4	0.8	0.6	0.6	0.6	-	3.2	4.9	3.9	4.3
Soka Gakkai	-	-	-	-	-	-	-	-	-	-	-	-	-
Other/None	0.4	0.2	0.2	-	-	0.4	0.8	0.2	0.6	0.2	0.4	0.4	0.2
Year	1920	1924	1928	1930	1932	1936	1937	1942	1946	1947	1949	1952	1953

Continued on next page

TABLE 2-2 CONTINUED
IMPERIAL AND NATIONAL DIET
Primary Occupation By Election and Year

Election	27	28	29	30	31	32	33	34	35	36	37	38	39
Agriculture	4.6	3.8	3.4	3.4	2.9	4.3	3.9	3.3	3.1	3.1	3.5	2.1	1.2
Business/Banking	19.4	20.0	19.3	19.1	17.3	20.6	17.9	16.3	14.1	15.1	11.1	13.5	12.3
Education	7.0	7.2	7.3	6.9	6.0	5.1	5.9	5.5	5.1	4.5	4.9	4.1	3.9
Higher Education	2.3	1.1	0.9	0.6	0.6	0.2	1.2	2.0	2.3	2.2	2.9	2.7	2.5
Govt. (Central)	14.1	14.9	14.3	16.3	14.0	12.8	11.6	8.6	6.8	6.7	6.3	7.0	8.4
Govt. (Home Min.)	7.4	5.6	5.6	5.4	4.5	3.7	2.0	1.8	1.0	1.2	0.8	1.0	-
Total C. Govt.	21.5	21.5	19.9	21.7	18.5	16.5	23.6	10.4	7.8	7.9	7.1	8.0	8.4
Local Govt.	3.2	3.0	2.8	2.8	3.3	3.1	2.4	1.6	1.6	1.4	1.6	1.8	2.9
Journalism	9.3	10.6	11.3	9.0	8.6	7.3	5.7	5.5	4.7	4.9	4.5	4.7	5.5
Law	11.4	8.9	8.8	6.0	5.8	5.7	6.1	4.9	5.5	5.5	5.9	5.9	6.8
Labor/Soc.	7.4	6.4	6.9	5.4	6.6	4.7	5.7	6.3	5.9	5.1	5.9	3.9	5.5
Medicine	2.7	2.5	3.2	2.4	2.7	2.6	2.6	2.5	2.5	2.0	2.7	2.1	2.0
Military	1.1	0.8	0.6	0.4	0.2	0.2	0.2	0.2	0.2	0.2	0.2	0.2	0.2
Politics	3.2	4.0	5.1	9.6	14.4	16.1	21.2	28.4	34.1	34.2	37.4	37.9	35.5
Religion	0.4	0.4	0.6	0.9	-	-	-	-	-	-	-	-	0.2
Women's Orgs.	-	0.2	0.4	-	-	0.2	-	-	0.2	0.2	0.2	0.2	0.2
Writing	0.4	0.2	0.4	0.4	0.6	0.6	1.0	1.0	0.8	0.8	0.4	0.4	0.6
Blue Collar	1.5	2.5	3.0	3.9	3.3	1.8	2.9	2.5	1.6	2.5	1.7	1.4	1.6
White Collar	4.6	6.8	6.0	7.7	8.0	9.5	8.4	9.0	9.2	9.4	8.8	10.2	9.6
Soka Gakkai	-	-	-	-	1.4	1.4	1.2	1.4	1.4	1.0	1.0	1.0	1.2
Other/None	-	-	-	-	-	-	-	-	-	0.2	0.2	-	-
Year	1955	1958	1960	1963	1967	1969	1972	1976	1979	1980	1983	1986	1990

TABLE 2-3

IMPERIAL AND NATIONAL DIET

Primary Occupation of New Members By Election and Year (Figures are percentages)

Election	1	2	3-4	5-6	7	8	9	10	11	12	13	14	15
Agriculture	11.5	15.1	21.1	28.3	15.8	15.1	28.3	17.5	19.4	21.6	16.6	18.8	13.5
Business/Banking	19.9	20.5	25.7	30.7	28.9	35.5	31.7	32.5	31.1	31.4	31.3	32.9	27.4
Education	13.4	9.6	9.4	7.0	8.9	9.7	2.5	8.3	3.6	9.8	6.0	5.4	4.0
Higher Education	1.2	0.6	-	-	0.4	-	0.8	1.0	1.0	2.6	3.3	1.1	0.8
Govt. (Central)	10.3	5.4	3.0	2.7	5.0	4.3	2.5	6.3	8.7	6.5	4.6	5.1	9.1
Govt. (Home Min.)	5.6	11.4	1.9	2.3	1.6	1.1	4.2	1.5	3.6	7.2	4.0	4.7	6.7
Total C. Govt.	15.9	16.8	4.9	5.0	6.6	5.4	6.7	7.8	12.3	13.7	8.6	9.8	15.8
Local Govt.	17.1	21.7	22.6	12.8	8.9	9.7	8.3	6.8	2.0	2.0	2.6	3.2	3.6
Journalism	4.7	3.6	3.4	3.9	6.2	6.5	6.7	8.7	10.7	6.5	13.2	7.9	15.1
Law	8.4	6.0	7.5	7.4	12.4	14.0	10.8	12.1	15.3	10.5	9.9	12.3	9.1
Labor/Soc.	-	-	-	-	-	-	-	-	-	-	-	-	-
Medicine	1.6	1.2	1.1	1.6	3.5	2.2	1.7	3.4	3.1	0.7	7.9	2.9	5.6
Military	0.3	1.8	1.1	0.4	0.8	-	0.8	1.5	1.0	0.7	-	1.4	1.6
Politics	3.7	2.4	2.6	1.9	0.4	-	1.7	-	-	0.7	-	2.9	0.8
Religion	1.6	0.6	-	-	0.4	1.1	-	-	-	-	-	-	-
Women's Orgs.	-	-	-	-	-	-	-	-	-	-	-	-	-
Writing	0.3	-	-	-	-	1.1	-	-	-	-	-	0.4	0.4
Blue Collar	-	-	-	-	-	-	-	-	-	-	-	-	-
White Collar	-	-	-	-	-	-	-	0.5	0.5	-	-	0.7	0.8
Soka Gakkai	-	-	-	-	-	-	-	-	-	-	-	-	-
Other/None	0.3	-	0.4	-	0.4	-	-	-	-	-	0.7	0.4	-
Total number	300	166	265	258	228	93	120	206	196	153	151	277	252
Year	1890	1892	1894	1898	1902	1903	1904	1908	1912	1915	1917	1920	1924

Continued on next page

TABLE 2-3 CONTINUED
IMPERIAL AND NATIONAL DIET
Primary Occupation of New Members By Election and Year

Election	16	17	18	19	20	21	22	23	24	25	26	27	28
Agriculture	16.8	12.6	14.8	11.8	17.2	18.3	11.9	7.6	3.1	3.7	4.2	7.0	4.4
Business/Banking	29.4	27.6	25.8	21.3	23.7	29.2	28.2	27.1	30.8	13.8	6.3	8.8	23.5
Education	4.0	4.7	0.8	5.5	4.3	6.4	15.8	6.7	2.6	9.2	14.6	3.5	10.3
Higher Education	4.0	2.4	3.1	2.4	1.1	2.5	2.3	1.8	1.5	1.8	-	-	-
Govt. (Central)	8.7	9.4	10.1	7.1	4.3	7.9	6.0	9.8	16.9	15.6	22.9	14.0	11.8
Govt. (Home Min.)	4.6	1.6	7.8	7.1	4.3	4.5	2.6	4.9	5.6	22.9	8.3	12.3	2.9
Total C. Govt.	13.3	11.0	17.9	14.2	8.6	12.4	8.6	14.7	22.5	38.5	31.2	26.3	14.7
Local Govt.	1.7	1.6	3.1	4.7	4.3	4.0	2.6	2.7	5.1	1.8	6.3	7.0	-
Journalism	9.2	13.4	13.3	10.2	12.9	6.9	9.1	11.1	9.2	6.4	10.4	5.3	4.4
Law	13.9	17.3	14.1	17.3	10.8	8.9	6.7	8.4	8.2	7.3	6.3	5.3	5.9
Labor/Soc.	0.6	-	-	4.7	9.7	-	6.0	5.3	3.1	2.8	4.2	5.3	2.9
Medicine	2.9	3.9	1.6	1.6	3.2	1.0	3.4	2.7	1.0	3.7	2.1	7.0	2.9
Military	2.3	0.8	3.1	1.6	-	7.4	-	-	-	0.9	2.1	1.8	-
Politics	-	2.4	0.8	0.8	2.2	1.5	2.8	1.8	1.0	-	8.3	3.5	7.4
Religion	2.3	0.8	-	-	-	0.5	1.3	0.4	-	-	-	-	1.5
Women's Orgs.	-	-	-	-	-	-	-	0.4	0.5	-	-	-	1.5
Writing	0.6	0.8	-	0.8	-	0.5	0.3	0.4	1.5	0.9	2.1	-	-
Blue Collar	-	-	-	0.8	-	0.5	0.7	1.8	3.1	2.8	-	5.3	10.3
White Collar	0.6	0.8	1.6	0.8	1.1	-	-	7.1	6.7	5.5	2.1	14.0	10.3
Soka Gakkai	-	-	-	-	-	-	-	-	-	-	-	-	-
Other/None	-	-	-	1.6	1.1	-	0.7	-	-	0.9	-	-	-
Total number	173	127	128	127	93	202	386	225	195	109	48	57	68
Year	1928	1930	1932	1936	1937	1942	1946	1947	1949	1952	1953	1955	1958

Continued on next page

TABLE 2-3 CONTINUED

IMPERIAL AND NATIONAL DIET

Primary Occupation of New Members By Election and Year

Election	29	30	31	32	33	34	35	36	37	38	39
Agriculture	5.1	4.2	1.0	7.1	4.2	2.4	1.3	2.8	1.2	1.6	2.3
Business/Banking	13.6	16.7	10.8	23.2	7.4	7.2	9.2	5.6	3.6	17.2	10.5
Education	6.8	4.2	2.9	3.0	6.3	6.4	7.9	-	3.6	3.1	3.8
Higher Education	-	2.8	2.0	1.0	4.2	3.2	2.6	2.8	3.6	3.1	3.2
Govt. (Central)	8.5	9.7	7.8	3.0	3.2	4.0	1.3	5.6	8.3	10.9	12.0
Govt. (Home Min.)	-	-	-	-	2.1	1.6	-	-	1.6	1.6	-
Total C. Govt.	8.5	9.7	7.8	3.0	5.3	5.6	1.3	5.6	8.3	12.5	12.0
Local Govt.	1.7	1.4	2.0	4.0	1.1	-	2.6	-	2.4	3.1	7.5
Journalism	6.8	5.6	4.9	5.1	2.1	0.8	3.9	5.6	4.8	1.6	6.8
Law	8.5	4.2	4.9	5.1	11.6	7.2	3.9	8.3	8.3	9.4	12.8
Labor/Soc.	11.9	2.8	4.9	7.1	7.4	5.6	1.3	2.8	8.3	3.1	5.3
Medicine	3.4	-	3.9	3.0	2.1	2.4	1.3	2.8	4.8	1.6	1.5
Military	-	-	1.0	-	-	-	-	-	-	-	-
Politics	16.9	33.3	32.4	26.3	42.1	47.2	52.6	41.7	41.7	20.3	21.8
Religion	-	1.4	-	-	-	-	1.3	-	-	-	0.8
Women's Orgs.	3.4	-	-	1.0	-	0.8	-	-	-	-	0.8
Writing	1.7	-	1.0	1.0	2.1	-	-	-	-	-	-
Blue Collar	6.8	5.6	3.9	1.0	-	2.4	-	11.1	1.2	1.6	1.5
White Collar	5.1	8.3	9.8	8.1	4.2	9.6	10.5	8.3	7.1	21.9	8.3
Soka Gakkai	-	-	6.9	1.0	-	-	-	-	-	-	1.5
Other/None	-	-	-	-	-	-	-	2.8	1.2	-	-
Total Number	59	72	102	99	95	125	76	36	84	64	133
Year	1960	1963	1967	1969	1972	1976	1979	1980	1983	1986	1990

Business

The most numerous single occupational classification for Diet members is business and banking with approximately one-fourth of the grand total. The percentages are somewhat higher for prewar delegates (28.1) compared to 19.1 for those elected after 1946. Tables 2-2 and 2-3 reveal a consistently high level of business delegates overall and for new members throughout the prewar era. There was a drop in the wartime election of 1942 followed by a resurgence to a high level of 29.9% in 1949. After that, business membership tailed off, particularly among recruits. This is mainly because of the emergence of more "pure politicians" whose primary occupation is classified as politics, but whose connections to and relations with the business world are well known.[3] In the two most recent elections the percentage of newly successful business affiliated candidates shot back up over the ten percent mark.

Like their colleagues from agriculture, business members of the Diet were relatively undereducated with only 34.3% attending universities, compared to 49.6% for all members. Few graduates of the major national universities entered the national assembly following business careers. Businessmen also had high percentages in local assembly membership, especially in the postwar era where the percentage is 46.7 compared to 32.8 for all members. Needless to say, almost all businessmen turned Dietmen had company affiliations. They also had a rather low professionalism rate: average number of times elected was 2.75 against the overall average of 3.12. Most of the low reelectability was in the prewar period. Very few female members came from the world of business.

The overall pattern for business persons who served in the Diet is one that reflects the pre-modern traits also seen for agriculture. The composite profile of the businessman Diet member shows that he was probably not a university graduate, but had some previous experience in local elected government and, of course, corporate concerns. He was not likely to be reelected more than twice. Since the preponderance of business members was in the prewar era when reelection was less common and the influence of the Diet was less pronounced, the lower professionalism rate of businessmen Diet members is to be expected. On the whole, disparities between the business category and the total membership are greater in the postwar than in the prewar period, generally reflecting the prewar model. The conscious recruitment before the war of *narikin* (parvenu) attests not only to the corporate orientation of the political parties, but also the importance of wealth in election campaigns. [4]

It is not necessary to undertake a statistical analysis to show that the businessmen elected to the Diet were affiliated with conservative parties. Since all prewar parties were conservative (in world terms), this is relatively meaningless until

1946 and after. However, for the prewar period as a whole the business affiliates parallel the overall average quite precisely: 75.7% of businessmen compared to 75.8% of all prewar Diet members belonged to the Seiyūkai, Minseitō, or their antecedents. In the postwar it is not surprising that 88.3% of the businessmen politicians were in the ranks of the LDP.

Education

I have decided to divide education as an occupation into two sub-categories, one labelled higher education and the other simply education. The latter refers to teaching careers at all levels below that of the university. This division of the field was necessary because of the significant differences in training and outlook between university professors on the one hand and public school teachers on the other, a distinction that is not confined to Japan. It can readily be seen (Table 2-1) that neither of these fields constituted a major occupational category, but education does occupy sixth place for all members, prewar and postwar. It stands in fourth place for new postwar members. If combined, the two fields represent fifth place for all members of the House of Representatives.

With but 1.7% overall and 2.3% for the postwar period, higher education would appear to be an insignificant occupational category. However, a brief look at those coming to the Diet from university professorships highlights some rather well known features of Japanese society. Since, moreover, professors have high status in this society, their presence and prominence sheds further light on the elite element in society.

Those from higher education were much more likely than the overall average to have attended a university, especially a major university, much less likely to have served in a local assembly or as a company director, and somewhat more likely to be associated with parties of the left. Among prewar cohorts from higher education this profile is much the same, except that the reelection potential is substantially above average: 3.38 compared to 2.66. Conversely, in the post-war period members with backgrounds in higher education were much less likely than average to be reelected whereas their tendency toward the left is even more pronounced. Though few in number, professorial Diet members represent the extreme of the "B" type - national rather than local or regional in character and outlook. The "B" type is better educated, less common in local assemblies and board rooms, more liberal and reelectable; in short, an elite type. "B" types are also more urban and "modern."

Diet members whose previous careers were as teachers (Education) demonstrate a pattern that differs significantly from that of the professors. In every grouping the teachers were less well educated than the average. To be sure, this is partly because normal schools were not classified as universities in prewar times and hence fall under the heading of "Other Schools." Forty percent of those in the education category attended such institutions. For the postwar period (and it must be remembered that many postwar representatives attended school before the war), the "other schools" figure rises to fifty-five percent. Teachers were also less likely to have served as company directors and, since the war, in local assemblies. Women, however, are much more in evidence here. Education is the largest single occupational grouping for women Diet members. Educators were also much more likely to have labor union backgrounds in, of course, the rather militant Japan Teachers Union.[5] This, in turn, means that a greater than average percentage of educator representatives were JSP members, although more than half of the teachers in the Diet belonged to the LDP in the postwar years. Teachers have a lower than average professionalism rate.

Government

Much has been written elsewhere about the bureaucratization of the Japanese Diet.[6] Members of the civil service who served in elected government have, indeed, been numerous throughout most of the history of parliamentary institutions in Japan. Bureaucrats in the national legislature have the third largest number and percentage over the entire period (648 individuals = 11.6%), lagging slightly behind law in the prewar period and also standing behind business and politics in the postwar.

In compiling the data for this study I decided to separate out those who had served in the Home Ministry because (1) it was the most numerous by far of the government departments providing successful candidates, (2) the Home Ministry administered elections until 1946 giving its affiliates a strong advantage, and (3) it was identified with some of the most conservative elements in prewar government. The Occupation abolished this ministry in 1946 and purged many of the Home Ministry politicians, including those sitting in the House of Representatives. Nevertheless, there have continued to be representatives from the Home Ministry in the National Diet throughout the postwar era up to the present. Significantly, the largest percentage of Central Government bureaucrats (and second largest of Home Ministry members) was attained in the elections of 1952 and 1953, immediately after the end of the Occupation when many purgees were reinstated. Over thirty-eight percent of the new members elected in 1952 were former bureaucrats with twenty-three percent of them products of the Home Ministry. Since the late 1960s the numbers with such occupational backgrounds have fallen off substantially. (See Tables 2-1, 2-2, and 2-3). Some of the postwar era bureaucrats did not have long civil service careers, but were purged or entered politics when their ministries were abolished or reduced in size and function.

Discrepancies in the educational and other background factors between Home Ministry and other bureaucrats are most noticeable in prewar times when the Home Ministry affiliates were more inclined toward the non-elite type. Overall, however, the variations are relatively slight and the central government bureaucrats turned politician will be analyzed as a single group.

Government officials as Diet members have been much better educated than the overall average with large percentages of university graduates (93% in the postwar). Of all the central government officials elected to the House of Representatives 45.3% attended Todai. This is more than three times the rate for all members. Among postwar members sixty-three percent were Todai products, again more than three times the overall average. Admission to the central government bureaucracy was, and remains, tantamount to the attainment of super elite status in Japan. It is hardly surprising, therefore, to find so many coming from the super elite university. Generalizations about Todai domination of the Japanese government[7] really stem from its preponderance in the permanent bureaucracy rather than from its role in elective office.

In other respects, the central government graduates fulfill the "B" or elite type rather well. They had fewer than average company directors, especially in prewar times, and much smaller percentages who served in local elected bodies. They were more successful at winning reelection than usual, especially after the war, and were almost all affiliated with conservative parties (eighty-nine percent to the LDP in the postwar). The average age of new Diet members from the bureaucracy was higher than the norm. This, again, is to be expected, since parties did not recruit from the bureaucracy at its lower, junior levels until very recently.[8] Except for the overwhelmingly conservative caste, these are all elite "B" traits. As will be seen later, however, (Chapter Six) party affiliation is not crucial in determining elite status.

Local Government

As an occupational category local government also figured prominently in the early years of the House of Representatives, but it had tailed off to insignificance even before the Pacific War. This was the most numerous occupational background on two occasions - the election of 1892 (tied with business) and the election of September 1894. By 1912 the percentage coming to the Diet from careers in local government had fallen to less than five percent and it never again exceeded that figure. It was natural that government service at the local level should serve as a major source of recruitment in a day when many of the professional occupations were as yet undeveloped and before the modern civil service system had come into effect. Later, when modern universities began to turn out graduates for national rather than local leadership, few such graduates went into local government careers. Instead, they entered the central government bureaucracy and the professions such as journalism and law from which some later sought election to the national parliament.

As a group, local government cohorts stand squarely in the non-elite "A" category - undereducated with many serving as local assembly members (73.6%, 82.4% before the war), but few serving as company directors. Their professionalism, measured in reelectability, was lower than the national average, particularly before the war. On the whole they were less likely to join left wing parties and were more heavily represented in government sponsored parties and among independents in the early years of the system.

Journalism

The profession of journalism was the background for 434 National Diet members. This is 7.8% of the total with the figure slightly higher for the prewar membership (8.2% compared to 7.2% for the postwar). The highest totals for journalists were in the period from the mid-1910s until the outbreak of the Pacific War. Much of this was the era of the so-called Taishō Democracy in which the House of Representatives was dominated by the political parties. In the elections of 1917, 1924, 1928 and 1930 journalists were the second most common profession. These were all elections in which the Kenseikai (later Minseitō) fared well. Journalists were often attracted to the party originally founded by the followers of Ōkuma Shigenobu. After the war, the army of ex-journalists dwindled somewhat with only about half as many members as in prewar elections. Still, the postwar contingent has been fairly consistent - ranking between 8.6% and 12.2% of the total lower house until 1967, and hovering around five percent in the 70s and 80s..

Journalist members of the Diet definitely fall into the "B" classification, substantially larger percentages coming from universities but fewer than average numbers having served in local assemblies. Somewhat fewer had company directorships and they have a much higher than average retention rate. All of these patterns hold for prewar and postwar journalists turned Diet members. As an occupation associated with the private sector, fewer journalists than average attended national universities, including Todai. It is interesting to note the very high percentage of Waseda graduates among the journalist members of the Diet. Of all journalists 26.7% were products of this one institution (29.1% for postwar members).

As noted, journalists in prewar tended to be recruited by the Kenseikai (Minseitō). In the postwar period, however, the party affiliation of journalists has followed the national pattern very closely. In age, journalists were younger than the norm when first elected. It is quite clear that, at least from the 1910s on, a journalistic career has been looked on with favor as a source of recruitment for Diet candidates.. This study has not made an attempt to ascertain the news organizations from which these Diet members were drawn, but it can be said with assurance that a majority worked for the national press where they became familiar with the operation of the central government. When Diet membership became a full time job with year round commitments, journalists began to follow the representatives from morning until night. This became so severe that Takase Den complained that "a Diet politician has no days when he is free of journalists."[9] Some writers seem to have become proteges or, at least, so familiar with Diet operations, that they were recruited by the parties to run for office. Very recently, there have been successful candidates from broadcast journalism, especially television. Many journalists had relatively brief careers in that profession before joining the ranks of the Diet. Some returned to it afterward.

Law

In most modern parliamentary systems it is assumed that many members will be from the legal profession.[10] Indeed, it is common for the English language press to refer to representatives as "law-makers" and to take for granted their background in law. In the case of Japan, however, where the pool of attorneys from which candidates may be recruited is not so large as in Anglo-Saxon countries, the number and percentage of lawyers is much smaller than might be expected.[11] Nevertheless, the legal profession has been a major source of Diet members. The overall total of 544 (9.8%) puts it in fourth place. It was third for the prewar era and fourth or fifth for the postwar years. It is somewhat surprising to note the decline in lawyers in the postwar period, especially from the 1960s onward. This is due, no doubt, to the great rise of "pure politicians", many of whom graduated from the law departments of universities but never stood for the bar. The number went back up in the 1990 election when seventeen new members (12.8%) were attorneys.

The rise and fall of lawyers in the Diet closely parallels the pattern of the journalists. Lawyers were most conspicuous from the early 20th century up to the Pacific War. Even in the postwar era lawyers and journalists - two "modern" professions depending heavily on literary skills - rose and fell in tandem.

The general profile of the lawyer/Diet member suggests category "B", but not quite so markedly as with journalists or educators.. Attorneys are, of course, better educated than the average and slightly better educated than journalists. This holds for both prewar and postwar eras. Among the universities producing lawyers who served in the Diet we see a different arrangement than with journalists and educators. Whereas Todai graduates are common among lawyers (22.8%) but rather rare for journalists, the universities which began as law schools - Meiji, Chūō, and Nihon - all have contributed a sizeable number of lawyers for the Diet. In contrast, fewer than normal have come from Waseda and Keiō, the humanities universities *par excellence* in modern Japan.

Elsewhere, the legal profession in the Diet follows the "B" type by having fewer than normal company directors, but departs by coming close to the norm with local assembly members. Assemblymen lawyers were more likely to be reelected before the war, but less likely since. In prewar times lawyers were more common than average among the ranks of the Minseitō and its antecedents. After the war, while more attorneys served the LDP than any other party, they are in fact well below the average for the LDP and somewhat above the average in the ranks of the JSP and JCP. The average age for newly elected attorneys is below the overall norm.. On the whole, thus, while learning toward the "B" type, the legal profession in the Diet is close to straddling the fence.

Politics

As explained earlier, the occupational category Politics has been applied to those whose main careers were in elective politics. These are primarily persons who held official, remunerated posts in political parties before they were elected to the Diet. They were men (and a few women) who have trained themselves or were trained by others for careers in politics. Undoubtedly, most of these individuals did have other interests, but they have been identified by themselves and the public as devoted primarily to the profession of politics. Very few of these "pure politicians" served in the Diet before the war, but a great many have been elected since, particularly in the decades of the 1970s and 1980s. The reasons for this have been deduced and explained elsewhere.[12] Interestingly, however, very few of these politicians seem to have direct business connections through directorships, at least prior to Diet service. "Pure politicians" have, however, become the most numerous occupational category since the election of 1972. Their numbers, moreover, steadily mounted in every election since that time until 1990, when they dropped off slightly. The number of new members also fell in 1986 and 1990 from previous figures.

In assessing the characteristics of this category we may dismiss the prewar members as there were but fifty-three of them. For the postwar period "pure politicians" statistically adhere close to the norm in education, but deviate significantly in company directorships as already noted. Slightly more than the average percentage had previously served in local assemblies. In party preferences, "politicians" were more likely to be recruited by the opposition parties than by the ruling LDP. They were particularly more prominent among the minor centrist parties - DSP and Komeito - where they commonly served as party officials. Since these parties put forward only a few candidates in carefully selected districts and most are successful, it stands to reason that they would pick their own leaders to run for national office. This accounts for the higher percentage of "pure politicians" among the ranks of the tightly organized minor parties which do not have a national constituency. Significantly, although 27.6% of the "politicians" elected to the Diet since 1946 belonged to the JSP, very few had affiliations with labor unions, another major source of JSP recruitment.

Other Occupations

All of the other occupational categories are relatively insignificant in percentage terms, but they nevertheless deserve some comment. Medicine accounted for 149 persons overall for 2.7% of the total lower house membership. This percentage has held up in almost identical fashion for both prewar and postwar time periods. Medical personnel in the Diet fall closer to the "A" (non-elite) than the "B" (elite) type and they parallel rather closely the overall figures for party preference.

In the prewar period there were very few retired military personnel who served in the Diet: merely 1.4% of the prewar total. This is substantially less than is found in the British House of Commons where a military career was seen as useful preparation for legislative activity.[13] Not so in Japan. The largest number of ex-military persons was elected in the wartime election of 1942, but even then the percentage was only four. After the war, retired military ceased to stand for election or sit in the Diet, in part because all military officers were purged[14] and, of course, because the conventional military services were eliminated under the new constitution.

Of the other enumerated categories such units as religion, writing and women's organizations are significant only for their insignificance. The categories of blue collar and white collar workers are also small in number, though both have grown since the end of the war. In particular, the category of white collar worker has begun to assume importance, reaching a figure in excess of ten percent in 1986.

As a category, blue collar worker is rather insignificant at the national level. Obviously, those in this category are non-elites and entirely identified with left wing parties and union membership. A separate category called labor/socialist movement has also been devised for those persons whose careers were closely bound up with the prewar socialist movement or who, after the war, entered elective politics from the leadership of the labor unions. This has been explained in the introduction. Persons so identified represented 2.2% of all Diet members and 5.1% of the postwar aggregate. Their numbers have been rather consistent, between 3.9% and 7.8% following each election since 1946. They have been among the most secure of candidates with a reelection rate in excess of the national average. They too fall into the "A" group in terms of education and local assembly membership. Representing left of center parties, it has become commonplace to note that union leadership has been a springboard to a secure Diet seat in the JSP.[15]

Finally, a word may be said about the white collar occupational grouping. Persons in this category have been on the rise in the last several decades as engineers and company employees below the board room level have been recruited. Since the overwhelming majority have served in the postwar Diet, the statistics for the few in the prewar era may be safely ignored. On the whole, white collar types fall into the "B" or elite group - better educated than average, fewer company directors and local assembly members and more "professional" in their reelectability. A slightly greater than average percentage of white collar Diet members belonged to the opposition parties.

Capsule Biographies

An example of a Diet member from the field of agriculture is Arai Shōgo. Arai was born in Tochigi Prefecture in a wealthy farming family (gōnō) in 1856. He had a formal private education that included tutoring in Chinese classics and English. His wife was the daughter of Etō Shimpei, famous junior member of the Meiji government who led the Saga Rebellion in 1874. Arai never knew Etō, but may have picked up some of his anti-establishment qualities.

Arai began his political involvement, like so many other early political figures, in the newspaper business. He founded and began to publish the *Tochigi Shimbun* in 1881 and the following year he was a charter member of the Tochigi Jiyūtō, which was one of the most active local chapters before the promulgation of the constitution. Arai was a primary leader in 1885 of a group which planned an expedition to Korea to promote Kim Ok-kyun and his reformist party. Late in that year Arai and others were arrested by Japanese authorities after leaving Osaka with a large supply of munitions destined for Korea. This affair is known as the Osaka Incident for which Arai was convicted and imprisoned. He was not exceptional in Japan's parliamentary history as an ex-convict who won election to the national assembly. Arai was released from prison in 1887 in a general amnesty. Thereafter he was more nationalistic, but he retained membership in the Jiyūtō, winning election to the first Imperial Diet under that banner in 1890. He was reelected continuously through the sixth general election in 1898 and again in 1904. He died in 1906 while serving in the Diet.

Arai also stands as an example of a popular rights agitator who became a respected Diet member. His career in the house was not greatly distinguished, but he simultaneously occupied a government position as head of the Northern Division of the Colonization Bureau after 1896.

A business affiliate with a long Diet career, serving both before and after the war, was Uchida Nobuya. Elected seven straight times from 1924 to 1942, Uchida reflects the embourgeoisement of the parties in the interwar period.

He was, above all, an entrepreneur, a capitalist on a large scale. Graduating in 1905 from Tokyo Higher Commercial School (later Hitotsubashi University), Uchida went to work for Mitsui Bussan. But, at the time of the outbreak of the First World War, he perceived the coming need for shipping. He thus resigned from Mitsui Bussan and opened his own shipping company - Kōbe Uchida Kisen - with one ship. The firm expanded greatly and Uchida became wealthy, organizing and presiding over one shipping company after another. His was a classic success story.

It was as a wealthy war profiteer that Uchida was well known and he was recruited after the war by Hara. He was already recognized as a "soft touch", on everyone's list for big contributions to worthy causes. In the Diet in the 20s and 30s Uchida was something of an opportunist. He was originally elected as a Seiyūkai representative from Ibaraki. He maintained this allegiance while rising to high party posts by the early 1930s. He was often associated with maverick conservative Tokonami Takejirō, though he did not bolt the party with Tokonami in 1927. However, in 1934, he accepted a portfolio (Minister of Railways) in the Okada Cabinet against the wishes of the party. He was consequently drummed out of the Seiyūkai.

In 1936 he was implicated in the famous Railway scandal, but was found innocent. While still holding his Diet seat he was named governor of Miyagi Prefecture in 1940. During the war he supported the Tōjō government, joined and was a leader of the IRAA. He also served briefly as Minister of Agriculture and Commerce in the reorganized Tōjō Cabinet from February to July 1944. After that he was appointed a member of the House of Peers, an honor that lasted little more than a year.

When the war ended Uchida was one of those active in forming a new political party, the Shimpotō. He was purged, however, and debarred from office. While waiting out the Occupation he wrote a caustic, gossipy biography that flailed at many politicians, past and present.[16] The Occupation over, he recaptured his electoral base, returning to the Diet in 1952 and 1953. He died at age 90 in 1971.

Uchida was perhaps more typical of Diet members than some of the misfits described elsewhere in this study. He was certainly representative of successful businessmen who turned to politics. To be sure, not all opportunists came from the business world, but he clearly reflects the kind of background that the conservative political parties sought in the 1920s.

Included next is Fukuchi Gen'ichirō, not because of his longevity as a Diet member or even his role in electoral politics, but because he is representative of the all-purpose individual often found in the Diet before the system matured. He could legitimately be classified in occupation as a journalist, literary figure or educator. For statistical purposes he has been placed in the latter category.

Fukuchi was born in Hizen, the son of a physician, in 1841. He studied Dutch at Nagasaki and, in 1858, went to Edo to study English. He then became an interpreter in the service of the Bakufu in which capacity he travelled to Europe in 1861 and again in 1865. While in Europe he acquired a deep interest in oratory and newspapers. He also studied Shakespeare. When he returned to Japan he opened a private school and, in 1870, launched the *Koko Shimbun* which supported the Bakufu. The publication was quickly suspended by the new government and Fukuchi then joined the new Meiji government, accompanying the Iwakura Mission as an interpreter from 1870 to 1874. Immediately after returning from this voyage he became editor of *Tokyo Nichi Nichi Shimbun*. This newspaper, the first Tokyo daily, became a kind of official organ of the Meiji oligarchy. As its editor, Fukuchi wrote critically of the popular rights movement, but his was the first paper to reveal to the public the sale of property by the Hokkaido Colonization Commission in 1881. He also organized a public protest meeting in connection with this scandal.

In 1882, on prompting by the administration, Fukuchi was one of the founders of the Teiseitō, a government party designed to counter the organizations of Itagaki and Ōkuma. Fukuchi and *Tokyo Nichi Nichi* consistently supported the principle of unrestricted imperial sovereignty in the constitution that was under preparation through the 1880s. He also served in the Tokyo-fu assembly and was its speaker in the 1890s. In 1888 he left *Tokyo Nichi Nichi* and reasserted his interest in the stage. He founded Kabuki-za to revitalize Kabuki and wrote several books about it.

Elected to the Imperial Diet as an independent in 1906, he died before his initial term was up, but he was an "impact person" in political, journalistic, educational and artistic circles from the 1880s until the time of his death in 1908.

An example of a university level educator in the Diet is Uehara Etsujirō who had a long and distinguished life in both categories. Uehara was elected eight times before the war and five times after in a parliamentary career than spanned four decades.

Uehara was born in Nagano in 1877 and went abroad for his higher education at the University of Washington (1907) and the University of London where he received a Doctor of Science degree in 1910. While in the U.S. he took up journalism as a reporter for *Nichibei Shoho*. He then returned to Japan where he assumed professorships at Meiji and Rikkyō Universities. He was also principal for a time of a girls' higher school in Zushi, Kanagawa Prefecture.

He entered politics at the suggestion of Inukai Tsuyoshi in 1917. Thereafter, he was a consistent follower of Inukai and a strong voice in the call for universal suffrage in the 1920s. In the Katō Takaaki Cabinet, when universal manhood suffrage was enacted in 1925, he was Parliamentary Councillor of Communications. He also worked for reform of the House of Peers, though this effort was less successful.

When Inukai joined the Seiyūkai to become its president, Uehara went with him and quickly assumed high party rank. From 1932 to 1936 he was Vice-Speaker of the House of Representatives. In the late 1930s he was associated with the Kuhara faction of the Seiyūkai, but in 1940 he joined Hatoyama Ichirō, Katayama Tetsu and others in organizing the Dōkōkai, which stood in opposition to the IRAA. Needless to say, Uehara was denied government "recommendation" in the 1942 election. He consequently went down to defeat, a result that probably saved his political career.

Out of government, Uehara was not purged by the Occupation and was, hence, active in organizing the Jiyūtō at the end of the war. He was elected for that party in 1946 and repeated in 1947, 1949 and 1952. After losing in 1955, his final electoral victory came in 1958 as a member of the LDP. He continued an active political life in the postwar decade with advisory positions in the several conservative parties. He was Minister of State and then Home Minister in the First Yoshida Cabinet (1946-47). Of course, the Home Ministry was then abolished. In 1955 he attended the initial Afro-Asian Conference in Bandung, Indonesia and also took a seat as government representative at the 11th meeting of the U.N. General Assembly in 1956.

As might be expected of someone with a scholarly background, Uehara produced several books, including a six volume history of political rights in Japan (*Nihon Minken Hattatsu Shi*), published between 1958 and 1971, the last several volumes posthumously. His recollections, also published after his death, as *Hachijūro no Omoide*, reveal an enthusiastic idealist, representative of mainstream political goals in 20th century Japan.

Kobashi Ichita is a near perfect example of what used to be called the "bureaucratization of Japanese politics" through the movement of former government officials into the upper echelon of the political parties and hence the Diet. The best known of this type are prime ministers such as Katō Takaaki, Hamaguchi Osachi and Wakatsuki Reijirō. The high point of the phenomenon was in the 1920s when "Taishō Democracy" was in full swing. The Home Ministry was the bureaucratic department which provided the largest number of such parliamentarians.

Kobashi fits the description well. He was born in Kumamoto in 1870, graduated from the Law Faculty of Todai in 1898 and went to work in the Home Ministry. Therein he was one of several younger officials who became followers of Hara Kei. Kobashi joined the Seiyūkai when Hara became prime minister in 1918.[17] He first stood for election in 1920 and he was reelected in 1924 and 1928. By the latter year he had joined Tokonami Takejirō first in the Seiyūhontō and then the Minseitō. He was briefly Education Minister (July to November 1929) in the Minseitō Cabinet headed by Hamaguchi. He had to resign due to the Echigo Railroad Scandal. In 1937 he became mayor of Tokyo.

He was, in many ways, typical of Japanese politicians in the party era. A bureaucrat with elite educational credentials, he rose through the ranks of the Home Ministry to join the dominant political party at the top, not in the lower echelons. He followed his patron from party to party, became involved in a bribery scandal, but remained active in political affairs. He died in 1939.

Many interesting Diet members had journalistic backgrounds. Yamaji Jōichi is an appropriate representative of this occupation. He was a Waseda graduate and associated in the Diet with the Kenseikai/Minseitō line descended from Ōkuma's Kaishintō. Yamaji was also representative of a characteristic not so common in Japan as in Britain - a politician with connections to the overseas empire.

Yamaji, from Hiroshima, graduated from Waseda in Political Economy in 1906 and began a journalistic career with a local newspaper in Tottori Prefecture. Before long he was in Korea as an editor for *Daikan Nippō*, a Japanese language daily. In Korea he became part of the apparatus of imperialism, working part time first for the Government of Korea and then, after 1910, for the Government-General. He also edited a magazine in Seoul, *Shin Hantō*, which extolled the virtues of Japanese rule.

In 1912, when he was thirty (the minimum age) he entered politics, winning the first of ten consecutive campaigns in Hiroshima. Technically, Yamaji ran as an independent in his first election, but he soon joined the Dōshikai which became the Kenseikai and then the Minseitō. Within the party he was influenced by Adachi Kenzō, another former adventurer in Korea. The Adachi faction was the more expansionist group in the party. When Adachi bolted to form a separate party in 1932 - Kokumin Dōmei - Yamaji went along to become its first Secretary-General. However, he did not go as far as Nakano Seigō and other strident nationalists and Yamaji hence returned to the Minseitō in 1935. He was elected under that banner in 1936 and 1937. He died in 1941.

Many journalists in the Diet were Wasedans. Most, moreover, were associated in one way or another with Ōkuma's party. The number of such who emerged in the era of "Taishō Democracy" was particularly high. Yamaji's career exemplifies this pattern well.

Shimada Toshio is representative of the attorney turned politician: the type so common in the United States. This variety of elected politician has been less common in Britain, but Shimada resembled British Tory representatives in his elite background in education and government.

Born in Shimane Prefecture in 1877, Shimada came to Tokyo and graduated from Todai in Political Economy in 1900. He then went to work for the Tokyo municipal government, rising to department head of Education. After a trip to England in the late 1900s, he returned to take up the practice of law. Recruited to politics, he ran successfully for the Diet from Shimane in 1912 as a Seiyūkai candidate. He lost in 1915, but rebounded in 1917 and 1920. He was also defeated in the 1924 election, but then won six consecutive times from 1928 to 1942.

He remained loyal to the Seiyūkai mainstream throughout, serving as Chief of the Legislative Bureau in the Inukai Cabinet (1932). Later in the 1930s he at first defended the authority of the Diet against the encroachments from the military, but eventually sided with the pro-military faction led by Nakajima Chikuhei. He was Minister of Agriculture in the Hirota (1936-37) and Yonai (1940) cabinets.

During the war Shimada supported the IRAA, was an advisor (komon) and assumed a cabinet post (Agriculture and Commerce) in the Koiso Cabinet (1944-45). Like many other party politicians he was adaptable during and immediately after the war. In 1945 he became Speaker of the House of Representatives and when the last Diet elected under the old system was dissolved in late 1945 he predicted that a newly elected body would have a similar composition.[16] He was correct, of course, except for the purges. Shimada himself was purged, unable to stand for reelection in 1946 and he died in 1947.

During the party era of the 1920s and 1930s Shimada became a "Tokyo insider" - a good example of the party politician in the days of "bourgeois democracy." He practiced law throughout his parliamentary career and also lectured at Waseda and Chūō universities.

Yamaguchi Kikuichiro represents the occupational category of professional politician. He is very typical of the postwar phenomenon in the conservative ranks of an incumbent politician who was always successful in election campaigns. He was not so prominent, however, to become a household word. Although most long term LDP members, including Yamaguchi, secured cabinet rank, it must be remembered that few became prime minister and were the subject of major biographical treatment.

Yamaguchi was a consummate politician, although he did do a few other things. Born in Wakayama in 1897, Yamaguchi enrolled at Waseda in Commerce but did not graduate. In 1930 he was elected to the Wakayama prefectural assembly, becoming speaker for two terms beginning in 1937. In 1942 he was persuaded to run for the Diet as a government recommended candidate from Wakayama. He was successful for the first of eleven consecutive terms that stretched until 1969 when he retired. He was one of the few "recommended" wartime victors who were not purged.

During the twenty-seven year interval of his service in the Diet, Yamaguchi's party affiliation moved from the IRAA to the Jiyūtō in 1945 to the LDP when it was founded ten years later. He held many committee posts, cabinet positions under Yoshida and Kishi, and high rank in the LDP. He was named Speaker of the House of Representatives in 1965. He travelled widely, including a visit to China in the 1950s. His book, *Hoshutō kara Mita Shin Chūgoku* (1955) was influential on the pro-Peking wing of his party in the late 1950s and 1960s.

Yamaguchi is representative of the unspectacular, rather "gray" figures who have come to make up the Japanese government since World War II. They are not as colorful or as varied in their backgrounds as many of the earlier figures. They are not particularly controversial[19], do not arouse strong emotions, and generally represent the interests of the growing middle class. Yamaguchi is a good example of the "committee of the bourgeoisie" in postwar Japan.

NOTES

1 Each member has two secretaries provided at government expense. Most also hire someone for their district office and some also hire additional secretaries at their own expense. See Izumi, "Diet Members", p. 74.

2 Tsurumi, "The Liberal Movement", p. 73.

3 See, for example, Joji Watanuki, *Politics in Postwar Japanese Society* (1977), pp. 11-12; Jun'ichi Kyogoku, *The Political Dynamics of Japan* (1987), pp. 114-116; Ronald J. Hrebenar, "The Money Base of Japanese Politics", in Ronald J. Hrebenar, ed., *The Japanese Party System* (1986), Chapter Three, pp. 55-79; Nathaniel Thayer, *How the Conservatives Rule Japan* (1969); Haruhiko Fukui, *Party in Power: the Japanese Liberal Democratic Party and Policy Making* (1969), pp. 162-165.

4 For an interesting and frank account of a wealthy *narikin* who was enticed into politics in the teens and twenties, see Uchida Nobuya, *Fūsetsu Gojūnen*, especially pp. 71-90.

5 The teachers union is described in detail in Benjamin C. Duke, *Japan's Militant Teachers: a History of the Left-Wing Teachers' Movement* (1972), although this book is now out of date in terms of the union's political activities.

6 See Izumi, "Diet Members", pp. 70-71; Thayer, *How the Conservatives Rule*, pp. 226-228. See also Reed, "The People Spoke", pp. 309-339. Reed argues that the electorate preferred bureaucratic candidates. "The massive entry of bureaucrats into the conservative parties was more a matter of electoral response to bureaucratic candidates than of elite recruitment." (p. 324). For prewar times, see Robert A. Scalapino and Junnosuke Masumi, *Parties and Politics in Contemporary Japan* (1962).

7 These generalizations are more often made in broad accounts of Japan and/or by individuals not very familiar with the Japanese reality. The view that Todai has commanding dominance in many fields is, however, widespread in "popular" culture, both in Japan and elsewhere. See, for example, Warren Tsuneishi, *Japanese Political Style* (1966), pp. 97-98. Tsuneishi also writes about the preponderance of Todai graduates in the upper echelons of the bureaucracy, both prewar and postwar (pp. 79-81). Misstatements about

Todai influence in politics are found in Charles G. Cleaver, *Japanese and Americans: Cultural Parallels and Paradoxes* (1976), p. 106 and newspaper and magazine accounts, especially in the United States. For example, in *The Washington Post Weekly*, April 18-24, 1988, Fred Hiatt has a bylined article, entitled "In Japanese Politics Its All in the Family". Hiatt quotes an informant as saying that "more than half of all Diet members are alumni" of Todai. My figures show that 21.3% of the 1988 members of the House of Representatives and 20.6% of the House of Councillors had Todai affiliation. Also see Herman Kahn's influential 1970 book, *The Emerging Japanese Superstate; Challenge and Response*, pp. 64-66. Kahn may be responsible more than any other single individual writing in English for popularizing the notion of the Todai "club" as dominant in government and business.

8   Since the 1970s the LDP has been recruiting from junior and lower levels. See Curtis, *The Japanese Way of Politics*, pp. 91-92.

9   Takase, *Ichi Daigishi no Negoto*, p. 33.

10 Mellors, citing other sources, says that the proportion of lawyers in the British House of Commons between 1945 and 1974 was 15.6%. "Comparable figures for other legislatures include: United States, 55%, Brazil 50%, France 32%, Italy 27%, Germany 19%." (Mellors, *The British M.P.*, p. 59). An earlier work detailing the prominence of lawyers in American politics is Heinz Eulau and John D. Sprague, *Lawyers in Politics* (1964).

11 There are several reasons for the paucity of attorneys in Japanese elected assemblies. The most obvious is the fact that there are far fewer lawyers in Japan than in the United States because there is much less litigation. Izumi contends that detailed legal knowledge is not necessary for Diet membership and that lawyers are not, by their role in society, in good positions to gather votes. (Izumi, "Diet Members", p. 70). Wakata Kyoji makes essentially the same contention in *Japanese Diet Members: Social background, General Values and Role Perception* (1977), p. 86. However, the issue is more complicated. Although *bengoshi* (practicing attorneys), *kenji* (public procurators), and law professors are not numerous, it has been noted that the number of persons doing legal work in Japan ranks third among major nations on a per capita basis, trailing only the U.S. and Britian. See Stephen Clayton, "More Lawyers Than Meet the Eye", *PHP* (Nov. 1984), p. 8. See also John O. Haley, "The Myth of the Reluctant Litigant", *Journal of Japanese Studies* (Summer 1978), pp. 359-390 and J. Mark Ramseyer, "Reluctant Litigant

Revisited: Rationality and Disputes in Japan", *Journal of Japanese Studies* (Winter 1988), pp. 111-123. For additional works, see note 8 in Chapter Three.

[12] See, for example, Izumi, "Diet Members", pp. 71-72 and Bradley Richardson and Scott Flanagan, *Politics in Japan* (1984), p. 273.

[13] Mellors notes that in the period of his study (1945-74) 11.9% of all MPs had served in one branch or another of the British armed forces. Almost all were conservatives: about twenty-five percent of the Conservative MPs had military experience. (Mellors, *The British MP*, p. 99).

[14] 122,235 career military personnel were purged. This represented 53,854 army officers, 27,691 navy officers and 39,394 members of the military police. See Hans Baerwald, *The Purge of Japanese Leaders Under the Occupation* (1957), p. 81.

[15] Izumi, "Diet Members", p. 71. Also J.A.A. Stockwin, "The Japan Socialist Party: a Politics of Permanent Opposition", in Ronald J. Hrebenar, ed., *The Japanese Party System* (1986), pp. 6-7 and Richardson and Flanagan, *Politics in Japan*, p. 81. This is to name but a few readily available in English. All of these works are based on Japanese sources.

[16] Uchida Nobuya, *Fūsetsu Gojūnen.*

[17] Peter Duus, *Party Rivalry and Political Change in Taisho Japan* (1968), p. 32.

[18] Uchida Kenzo, "Japan's Postwar Conservative Parties", in Robert Ward and Sakamoto Yoshikazu, ed., *Democratizing Japan: The Allied Occupation* (1987), p. 321.

[19] Obviously, prime ministers arouse more controversy, especially Tanaka Kakuei.

Chapter 3

Education

■

The general educational preparation of Diet members is outlined in Tables 3-1 and 3-2. The major divisions of educational accomplishment from elementary to university require no further explanation. It is, however, important to point out that the criterion used here is highest level of education *attended*, not necessarily completed. Actually, a rather large number of Japanese, including politicians of prominence, attended universities but dropped out before graduation. This was particularly common before the war, but has also been observed in recent decades. Ten universities have been singled out and considered "major" for analytical purposes. These ten were so designated because (1) they are the most prestigious universities in Japan, (2) they were all in operation before the Pacific War and can thus be included for both prewar and postwar times periods, and (3) no other university contributed a significant percentage of members over the entire period covered by this study. It must also be acknowledged that the same may be said of Hōsei, Tōhoku and Hokudai, all of which were included as "major" though none produced more than one percent of the total Diet membership.

Those indicating high school as the highest level of education were practically non-existent before the war. This is because the prewar *kōtōgakkō* were university preparatory institutions and hence rarely the terminal stage in anyone's education. Even after the war the percentage listing high school is statistically insignificant. One rather interesting item is that a full one-third of those in the "high school" category for the postwar period were women. This will be discussed in the section on the female members of the Diet in Chapter Nine.

TABLE 3-1

IMPERIAL AND NATIONAL DIET

Education

Election	1	2	3	4	5	6	7	8	9	10	11	12	13
University	15.6	16.7	15.7	12.5	18.3	22.0	32.2	30.5	30.9	38.2	46.2	50.6	54.3
Major University	12.9	13.3	13.3	10.3	13.6	17.4	26.3	25.1	26.0	31.0	40.8	44.0	47.9
TODAI	4.0	2.8	3.7	3.0	3.0	3.4	7.4	6.3	4.5	5.9	8.5	10.9	14.3
KYODAI	-	-	-	-	-	-	-	-	-	0.2	0.7	1.0	1.2
WASEDA	0.6	0.6	1.3	1.5	2.0	3.7	3.2	3.2	4.2	3.3	6.1	7.4	7.5
KEIO	6.2	6.8	7.0	4.3	6.3	7.6	6.6	8.2	7.4	7.6	9.7	8.9	8.9
MEIJI	0.9	1.9	0.7	0.6	0.3	1.2	3.5	2.9	4.0	4.3	4.8	5.2	4.6
CHUO	0.6	0.9	0.3	0.9	2.0	1.5	4.8	3.9	5.0	7.3	9.0	7.7	8.0
NIHON	-	-	-	-	-	-	-	-	0.7	1.2	1.0	2.0	2.2
HOSEI	0.6	0.3	0.3	-	-	-	0.5	0.3	0.2	1.2	0.5	0.7	0.7
TOHOKU	-	-	-	-	-	-	-	-	-	-	-	-	-
HOKUDAI	-	-	-	-	-	-	0.3	0.3	-	-	0.5	0.2	0.5
High(er) School	-	-	-	-	-	-	-	-	-	0.2	-	-	-
Middle School	-	0.3	0.3	0.9	0.7	0.6	1.1	1.6	1.7	1.7	2.9	2.7	2.9
Elementary	-	-	-	0.3	1.0	1.5	2.1	2.1	0.5	0.7	0.5	-	-
Private education	46.7	49.5	49.0	49.8	47.7	48.8	42.8	39.2	40.8	32.2	22.0	19.9	17.1
Other Schools	6.5	7.1	8.0	7.3	8.7	8.5	7.4	8.9	6.9	8.8	10.7	9.9	10.4
None listed	31.1	26.3	26.3	29.2	23.7	18.3	14.4	17.6	18.8	18.2	17.7	16.4	15.2
Year	1890	1892	1894	1894	1898	1898	1902	1903	1904	1908	1912	1915	1917

Continued on next page

TABLE 3-1 CONTINUED
IMPERIAL AND NATIONAL DIET
Education

Election	14	15	16	17	18	19	20	21	22	23	24	25	26
University	53.6	61.8	63.6	69.2	68.6	66.9	66.2	67.2	54.2	64.1	67.3	73.2	72.8
Major University	47.0	55.6	58.2	64.6	61.7	60.8	60.5	58.7	45.0	53.8	57.3	62.5	61.3
TODAI	13.5	17.2	19.7	20.3	21.5	21.2	20.9	21.3	12.2	13.5	17.7	25.7	24.6
KYODAI	1.8	2.7	2.4	3.0	4.2	4.4	4.7	4.4	3.8	4.0	5.6	5.8	5.8
WASEDA	7.3	11.7	13.3	15.8	13.3	15.0	15.0	13.7	11.1	12.2	10.0	9.9	10.7
KEIO	7.1	7.0	3.9	4.5	3.6	2.3	1.6	3.0	2.3	3.0	2.1	2.6	1.5
MEIJI	3.6	5.1	5.4	7.1	6.3	5.0	5.3	3.5	4.9	5.7	5.1	3.4	3.9
CHUO	7.5	6.0	5.6	5.6	5.3	6.0	5.1	4.7	3.6	4.6	5.3	5.4	4.7
NIHON	3.6	3.7	5.6	6.2	6.5	5.0	5.5	3.8	4.3	7.2	8.3	7.3	7.7
HOSEI	2.4	1.8	1.9	1.7	0.8	1.5	1.4	0.8	1.7	2.3	2.1	0.9	0.9
TOHOKU	-	-	-	-	-	-	0.8	1.1	0.9	1.3	1.1	1.1	1.3
HOKUDAI	0.2	0.4	0.4	0.4	0.2	0.4	0.2	0.4	0.2	-	-	0.4	0.2
High(er) School	0.4	0.6	0.4	0.4	0.4	0.2	-	0.2	2.8	1.3	1.7	0.9	1.1
Middle School	3.6	3.5	3.4	3.4	4.2	4.4	3.2	5.3	4.3	5.9	6.2	3.0	4.3
Elementary	0.2	-	0.2	0.2	-	-	0.2	0.2	0.4	0.6	0.6	0.9	0.9
Private Education	10.9	6.8	5.4	3.0	2.3	1.9	1.2	0.2	-	-	0.2	-	-
Other Schools	11.1	11.9	14.1	11.8	11.8	12.5	14.2	16.5	22.8	13.9	12.4	15.2	14.6
None Listed	20.2	15.4	12.8	12.0	12.6	14.1	15.0	10.4	15.4	13.9	11.5	6.9	6.4
Year	**1920**	**1924**	**1928**	**1930**	**1932**	**1936**	**1937**	**1942**	**1946**	**1947**	**1949**	**1952**	**1953**

Continued on next page

TABLE 3-1 CONTINUED
IMPERIAL AND NATIONAL DIET
Education

Election	27	28	29	30	31	32	33	34	35	36	37	38	39
University	71.5	71.1	71.5	72.2	70.6	71.7	70.9	73.0	72.8	74.4	75.0	78.3	78.1
Major University	60.3	60.8	58.4	59.5	60.1	58.6	58.3	58.9	56.6	60.5	58.4	61.1	58.8
TODAI	24.9	23.8	26.1	26.8	24.7	25.1	23.2	22.7	19.0	21.3	19.8	21.3	19.1
KYODAI	6.5	6.6	6.2	5.8	6.8	5.9	4.5	4.3	4.1	3.7	2.9	3.1	2.9
WASEDA	10.8	8.7	9.6	10.5	10.3	9.2	10.8	11.9	12.9	11.9	11.9	12.3	12.5
KEIO	1.9	2.8	2.6	3.0	3.5	4.1	4.3	5.5	6.5	7.6	7.2	8.2	7.8
MEIJI	3.0	3.2	2.8	3.2	2.9	2.9	3.1	2.3	2.5	2.9	2.9	2.3	2.9
CHUO	4.6	5.1	5.1	3.4	3.3	3.9	5.5	6.3	6.1	6.8	8.4	7.4	6.8
NIHON	7.0	7.0	5.8	4.5	4.7	4.1	3.3	2.7	2.3	2.9	2.7	3.7	3.3
HOSEI	0.6	0.4	0.6	0.6	0.8	1.0	1.2	1.0	0.6	1.0	0.6	0.8	1.2
TOHOKU	0.8	1.7	1.7	1.5	2.3	1.8	2.0	1.6	2.0	1.6	1.4	1.4	1.4
HOKUDAI	0.2	0.4	0.2	0.2	0.8	0.6	0.4	0.6	0.6	0.8	0.6	0.6	0.8
High(er) School	0.4	0.8	0.6	0.6	1.0	1.6	2.0	1.8	2.5	2.5	4.1	4.7	8.2
Middle School	3.6	2.8	3.2	1.9	3.1	3.7	3.5	2.7	3.5	2.9	2.5	2.0	1.9
Elementary	0.8	1.5	2.1	2.1	3.1	3.7	3.1	3.1	2.7	2.3	2.0	0.6	0.4
Private Education	-	-	-	-	-	-	-	-	-	-	-	-	-
Other Schools	16.7	18.3	16.9	18.2	18.5	17.5	18.7	18.2	17.8	17.6	16.4	14.5	11.3
None Listed	7.0	5.5	5.6	4.9	3.7	1.8	1.8	1.2	0.6	0.2	-	-	-
Year	1955	1958	1960	1963	1967	1969	1972	1976	1979	1980	1983	1986	1990

TABLE 3-2
IMPERIAL AND NATIONAL DIET
Education (Highest Level Attained)

	All members		Prewar		All Postwar		New Postwar	
	No.	%	No.	%	No.	%	No.	%
University	2763	49.6	1430	40.4	1492	66.5	1333	65.6
Major University	2328	41.8	1254	35.5	1235	55.1	1074	52.9
TODAI	773	13.9	380	10.7	444	19.8	393	19.3
KYODAI	140	2.5	56	1.6	108	4.8	84	4.1
WASEDA	433	7.8	243	6.9	221	9.9	190	9.4
KEIO	251	4.5	168	4.8	89	4.0	83	4.1
MEIJI	210	3.8	143	4.0	82	3.7	67	3.3
CHUO	250	4.5	139	3.9	121	5.4	111	5.5
NIHON	167	3.0	79	2.2	102	4.5	88	4.3
HOSEI	57	1.0	34	1.0	27	1.2	23	1.1
TOHOKU	31	0.6	5	0.1	31	1.4	26	1.3
HOKUDAI	16	0.3	7	0.2	10	0.4	9	0.4
High(er) School	79	1.4	6	0.2	74	3.3	73	3.6
Middle School	181	3.3	101	2.9	85	3.8	80	3.9
Elementary	52	0.9	23	0.7	30	1.3	29	1.4
Private Education	843	15.1	842	23.8	2	0.1	1	0.0
Other Schools	792	14.2	430	12.2	387	17.3	362	17.8
None Listed	859	15.4	705	19.9	172	7.6	154	7.5
	5569		3537		2242		2032	

Almost one-fourth of the prewar Diet members were educated privately. The nature of this private education included specialization in a wide variety of subjects including English, other foreign languages, mathematics, and commerce, but it was mainly made up of the study of Chinese Literature or Classics or Japanese Literature and Classics, including Kokugaku. This kind of pre-modern education was mostly acquired before the Meiji Restoration and was an important educational source of politicians (and others) in the early years of the system. It dropped precipitously as time passed, the modern educational system came into effect, and the qualifications were relaxed for both candidates and electors. As a category used in this study private education disappeared entirely after the war, except for one person elected in 1949.

The category of "other schools" is designed to incorporate all "modern" institutions which do not fall under the heading of the graduated school system running from elementary to the university. For the prewar period, this means specialized schools such as normal schools, technical schools, training institutions and Seinen Gakkō. The percentage coming from such educational backgrounds rose as those receiving private education fell. By 1937 the figure had reached 23.7%. After the war, the level from "other schools" has fluctuated rather widely from a low of 12.4% (1949) to a high of 22.8% (1946). The overall postwar figure is 17.8%.

A surprisingly large number of Diet members did not publicly indicate the nature of their education. Thus, the number of "none listed" is relatively high. The figure was highest of all for the first election in 1890. The percentage fell off gradually thereafter, but it tended to go back up each time the election law was modified to permit more voters. There continued to be more than ten percent in this column until the end of the Occupation. It fell to 6.9% in 1952 and then slowly disappeared altogether. Nevertheless, we end up with 15.4% "none listed" for the entire Diet membership (this is the second highest for any category); 19.9% for the prewar years (third highest); and 7.6% for the postwar era. In the early years those not indicating a formal education doubtedlessly had either acquired private education or perhaps had stopped at an early point in the modern system. It likely means an elementary or middle school level of training or some kind of private tutoring.

It is immediately apparent from Table 3-1 and Graph 3-1 that the ascending curve for those attending universities drops back after the war to the level of elections 13 and 14 (1917, 1920), then accelerates more rapidly than before to reach and exceed the prewar peak (1930) within three elections by 1952, the first post-Occupation election. University attendance among Diet members reached a plateau at that point which lasted until the 1980s when it began to rise again. (See Graph 3-2) There was also a prewar plateau from 1930 to 1942. This gives some credence to the notion that the pattern set in prewar times was resumed after the end of the Occupation, with the latter representing therefore an unusual aberration in the otherwise smooth evolution of parliamentary government.

Another observation is that the gap between the overall university and the major university categories has widened substantially in the postwar period. Before the war the widest percentage margin was 8.5 in 1942; the overall difference for all members elected before the war was 4.9%. After the war the gap between all university and major university assemblymen rose to an all-time high of 19.3% in the election of 1990. The overall postwar margin was 12.7%. The rising disparity has been very steady, almost constantly growing election by election. This reflects, indeed it proves, the emergence and gradual expansion of the Japanese higher educational system which now includes more than 450 universities in all regions of the country.

It is appropriate now to examine in somewhat greater detail and analyze the statistical data on Japanese men (and a few women) coming from major univerities to the national assembly at Nagata-chō in Tokyo. Here may be tested the cliches about the overwhelming dominance of Tokyo University (Todai) in the corridors of power in the Japanese government.[1] The importance of Todai as Japan's premier institution of higher learning is, to be sure, substantiated by Diet membership figures. It should not be overblown, however. A total of 773 (13.9%) of all persons ever elected to the House of Representatives attended this one university. The percentage was 10.7 before the war, but 19.8 for all who served in the postwar period. Table 3-1 and Graph 3-1 further reveal the preeminence of Todai and note how its graduates (or matriculants) began to rise in numerical significance, especially toward the end of the Meiji era, topping ten percent for the first time in the election of 1915. The Todai contingent rose steadily and rather quickly after that to reach a plateau at just over twenty percent in the 1930s and 1940s. With the end of the war and the purge of most sitting members, the Todai group plummeted to 12.2% in 1946. As seen in several other realms in this study, the pattern of growth jumped back to the prewar level after the Occupation came to an end. The leap for Todai affiliates was from 17.7% to 25.7% between the 1949 and 1952 elections. A "Tibetan" plateau in which Todai cohorts were never lower than 22.7% nor higher than 26.8% was maintained until the election of 1976. The figure dropped under twenty percent in 1979 and has hovered around that point ever since. Most of the time the Todai percentages were about double those of the next most productive university Waseda, but they do not equal the prominence of the Oxbridge connection in the British House of Commons.[2]

GRAPH 3-1
UNIVERSITY ATTENDANCE

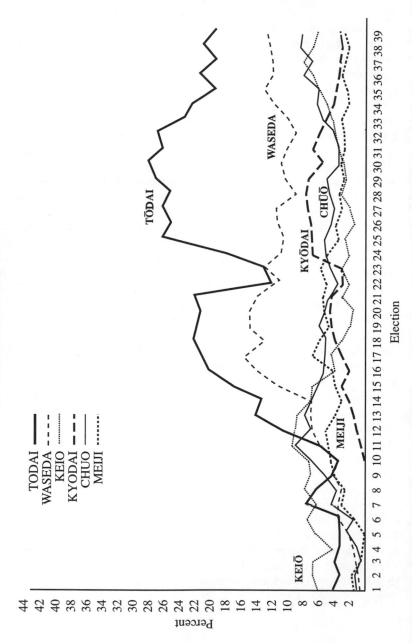

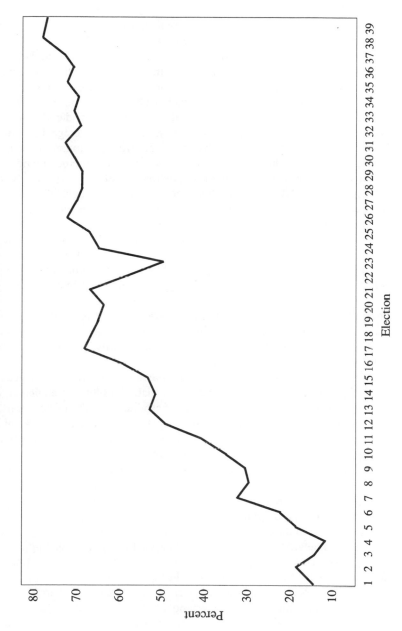

GRAPH 3-2
UNIVERSITY ATTENDANCE

The conspicuous role of Todai, not only in providing successful candidates for national elective office, but in other areas of *national* leadership, is most clearly evident when we correlate university attendance with occupation. Here we see that Todai represents the most extreme example (at least in the education category) of what I have been calling the "B" or "elite" type. Everyone knows that Todai stands for elite status. The occupational background of Todai affiliates in the House of Representatives suggests what have been considered high prestige occupations in modern Japan. There were far fewer than average Todai matriculants who engaged in farming or business, the two most common occupations overall and also for the prewar period. These are non-elite occupations. But, Todai students are very prominent in government service at the national level (38.2% overall; 34.4% prewar, 42.0% postwar) and also law. The disparity in law between Todai alumni and all representatives is, however, much greater before the war (plus 11.0%) than after (plus 2.6%). Todai cohorts were not notably above or below the national average in other occupational categories.

The elite quality of the Todai connection is further revealed by the lower than average figures for company directors and local assembly membership and the somewhat higher than average level of professionalism. In particular, Todai grads were 32.6% less likely than average to have been members of local elected bodies before advancing to the national level. Todai educated Diet members were also more likely to be found in conservative political parties, but not to a preponderant degree. There have been Todai recruits in all of the major and minor political parties in the postwar era.

Admission to Todai is presumed to imply a high level of intelligence and capability as well as national leadership potential. Thus it has been that organizations (political parties) preparing slates of candidates, just like corporations of national significance, have consistently sought to recruit from the ranks of Todai alumni. It is also well known that Todai has been particularly prominent in filling top government posts, including cabinet ministers.[3]

The other highly prestigious national (Imperial) university - Kyodai - has been nowhere near as conspicuous in the Diet. The overall totals for Kyodai alumni are 140 (2.5%) of the total, with 1.6% for the prewar and 4.9% for the postwar era. To be sure, Kyodai did not open its doors until 1897 and none of its graduates hence entered the Diet until the election of 1908. The percentage of Kyodai alumni eased upward over the prewar period, continuing an ascending curve after the war to reach a peak of 6.8% in the election of 1967. Their numbers have dropped since that time to less than half the highest level.

Statistically, Kyodai grads also display elite characteristics. Farmers and businessmen are uncommon, with government bureaucrats and lawyers numerous. They were much less likely than average to have served in local assemblies,

somewhat less likely to come from executive board rooms (prewar) and conspicuous in their electoral success. The average number of times elected for Kyodai
Dietmen was 4.07, the highest for any university returning as many as one percent of the total membership. On the average, however, Kyodai men (there were
no women) were less conservative than those from Todai. They were more frequent in the Minseitō in the prewar period and less common in the LDP for the
postwar. Kyodai graduates were also more numerous than average in both the
DSP and the JCP.

From its inception Kyodai had a more academic reputation with a sense of
academic freedom. As reflected in its Diet membership, Kyodai seems less political than Todai, perhaps more independent and, as it turns out, less conventional,
conformist and conservative than its counterpart in the Kantō.

For the most part, graduates of the famous private universities in Japan follow
a different pattern than that observed for the two great national institutions. The
products of the private schools do not precisely fall into the non-elite "A" category: they rather tend to fall close to the overall averages in many areas with a
few noteworthy exceptions. Each of the private universities, however, displays
some special characteristics.

Waseda and Keiō are normally regarded as the two most renowned and prestigious private universities in Japan. This is due, in part, to their venerable antiq-
uity and to the stature of their founders. Keiō University grew out of Keiō
Gijuku, founded by Fukuzawa Yukichi in 1858. I have listed as Keio educated
(and hence university educated) anyone who attended this institution either before
or after it became Keiō University in 1890. Waseda was founded by Ōkuma
Shigenobu in 1882. As the institution associated with a prominent official, it is
not surprising that Waseda has always been an important source of recruitment
for Diet members. Fukuzawa, on the other hand, disdained government service
and his school has long been identified with the private sector, particularly big
business. Only about half as many Keiō products as compared to Wasedans have
entered the House of Representatives.

Waseda holds second place among universities providing National Diet members with 433 individuals, good for 7.8% of the grand total. The percentage is 9.9
for all those elected since the end of the Pacific War. Since the election of 1924
Waseda graduates have maintained a consistent level which has been over ten
percent for all elections save four since that time. The high point of 15.8% was
reached in the 1930 election. In prewar times Waseda matriculants were invariably numerous following elections in which the Dōshikai-Kenseikai-Minseitō
(the party of Ōkuma and followers) fared well. One such year was 1930 as were
1936 and 1937 when the Waseda total was also high. Since the war the Waseda
percentage has fluctuated only slightly, moving between a low of 8.7% (1958)

and a high of 12.9% (1979). Overall, recruitment of Waseda alumni as new members of the Diet was most conspicuous in the 1920s and 1930s, the era of prewar party government.

In comparison with other Diet members Waseda graduates statistically stand out in only a few categories. As noted in the previous chapter, they were particularly common in the field of journalism where, at 26.7%, they were nineteen percentage points above the average. The figure (and discrepancy from the norm) is greater for the prewar era than after, but lofty in the postwar as well. In other occupations Waseda graduates were rather less common than the norm in government service and law. The other major distinction, for prewar times, is that Waseda men were overwhelmingly more likely to be members of the Minseitō. The reasons for this have already been noted. Obviously, therefore, they were much less likely to be recruited by the Seiyūkai, although some did switch to that party in the many mergers and breakups of the 1920s. Waseda affiliated Diet members come very close to the norm in the apprenticeship categories: local assembly members, company directors, labor union affiliations. Since the war they have been only slightly more common in the LDP than in the opposition parties. Waseda graduates were eminently reelectable, both before and after the war.

As the oldest school of its kind, in existence for more than thirty years before the first Diet convened, Keiō had more of its graduates in the early sessions than any other institution. After the mid-1920s, however, as Waseda graduates increased, those from Keiō declined to relative insignificance. After the war, the Keiō contingent remained very small (usually under four percent) until the elections of the 1980s when it has climbed back up, reaching 7.8% in 1990.

As noted, Keiō students were not normally politically oriented. As Diet members their occupational backgrounds suggest an "A" pattern with more than normal members in agriculture and business. They were also much more common in journalism (though not to the degree of Waseda), but less prevalent in government and law.[4] The "A" pattern for Keiō affiliates is also seen in their frequency as company directors. They were not so common in local assemblies. In overall statistical profile, Keiō-ites in the Diet are most notable for their business orientation. Here they stand out above all other universities, further strengthening the contention that Keiō is the businessman's institution *par excellence* in modern Japan.[5]

Of the other private universities, only three - Meiji, Chūō and Nihon - produced enough Diet members to merit attention. Each provided between 3.0% (Nihon) and 4.5% (Chūō) of all members, with Chūō and Nihon somewhat more prominent after the war and Meiji slightly more so in the prewar era. All three of these institutions began as law schools.[6] Hence, the profile of their graduates in the Diet is distinguished most clearly by the high percentage of attorneys. In other categories, Meiji leans moderately toward the "A" or non-elite side with a few more company directors and local assembly members than average, a more conservative party line-up, and a lower than average level of professionalism. Chūō seems more elite, but only very slightly, whereas Nihon University graduates are a bit more inclined toward the "B" or elite profile - fewer than average businessmen and farmers, fewer company directors and local assembly members, but a better than average likelihood of a long Diet career, except in the postwar period.

A comparison of all university educated members with the total membership reveals significant discrepancies in only a few categories. Agriculture and business occupations are substantially lower in prewar times, but not much below the norm after the war. There is a smaller percentage of university graduates who served in local assemblies before moving on to the "big time" and, of course, the numbers in central government service and law are higher than average, especially for the prewar era. University persons were also quite a bit more likely to be reelected than the norm, particularly in prewar times. It is interesting that the party line-up for university affiliates in the postwar era deviates only marginally from the national average. Of course, about sixty-five percent of all postwar members attended universities.

There is little point in breaking down the other educational classifications, such as elementary, middle school or high(er) school, because the number and percentages for each are so very small. The somewhat higher percentages for all of these categories after the war reflects (1) that participation in the "modern" educational system had become complete and (2) the eligibility of women, many of whom ceased their formal education with high school graduation. (See Chapter Nine)

One other sub-category in the educational sphere deserves passing mention. This is the department or faculty of a university to which a future Diet member was admitted and with which, therefore, he was affiliated and from which he graduated (if he graduated). In both prewar and postwar times, students in Japan were admitted, following competitive examinations, to a "faculty" of a particular university.[7] The number and name of the "faculty" (*bu*) vary from institution to institution. Almost all multi-purpose universities, however, have a faculty of law and of politics and economics. Some schools, such as Chūō University, subsume political science under the law faculty, while others like Waseda, Meiji and Nihon have a separate "faculty" of political science and economics. Of Diet members coming from universities in the postwar period the largest number have been students from law faculties. They were one-third of the total in 1983 and have been consistently above twenty-five percent since the end of the Occupation in 1952. The next highest totals have come from faculties of politics and economics, or a combination thereof. About fifty percent of all Diet members elected in the last three elections studied in law or politics and economics faculties of Japanese universities.

It must be noted that admission to and graduation from a law faculty does not imply even a "major" in law, much less admission to the bar. From the inception of the Imperial university system in the nineteenth century, the law faculty has simply been regarded as the one most suitable as preparation for a government career.[8]

In the prewar period it is more difficult to come up with the kind of breakdown shown in Table 3-3 because a sizeable number of persons studied law or politics/economics privately without attending a university. Therefore, in the figures for prewar times I have included all those who either attended a law faculty or studied law privately. After about 1910 the vast majority of such persons were university graduates. The same principle was used for politics/economics.

Graph A-8 (Appendix A, p. 219) also reveals the pattern for the prewar period. Those who had studied law privately or enrolled in the law faculty of a university reached the twenty percent mark in the first election of the twentieth century (1902). The figure remained at or above twenty percent, reaching a high point of thirty-five percent in 1932. Students of politics/economics display a similar curve, though at a lower level. Diet members so educated did not top ten percent until 1924, but they remained above that level consistently thereafter including the postwar period. The peak of politics/economics educated members was 21.2% in the wartime election of 1942. Law and politics/economics combined account for fifty percent or more of all Diet members for the years from 1936 to 1946. After the war, the combined figure has been over forty percent regularly since 1952.

Conversely, though it is hardly surprising, the number and percentage of Diet members who studied Chinese and/or Japanese classics and literature was very high at first, then began to drop and finally dwindled with a rush after 1912.[9] That such a decline would occur in those educated privately is to be expected, but that so many had received formal training of this type is testimony to the prevalence of such education among local elites. The high figure of classically educated Diet members also suggests that it was not only (or even primarily) those educated in "modern" subjects such as law, mathematics or English who participated in the new "bourgeois" system of elections created by the constitution.

Ichishima Kenkichi[10] was an early Todai student who was deeply involved in national politics in his youth, served for a short time in the Diet, and then turned to a career in university administration. Here is offered a brief sketch of his career as representative of Todai graduates in the early years of the Diet system.

TABLE 3-3
IMPERIAL AND NATIONAL DIET
EDUCATION
University Faculty Attended or Major Subject of Private Education
(Figures are Percentages of those Elected Each Year)

Election	Year	Law	Politics/ Economics	Chin./Japan. Classics, etc.
1	1890	6.3	3.3	34.2
2	1892	7.7	2.5	43.5
3	1894-1	10.0	2.3	40.3
4	1894-2	9.1	4.3	42.1
5	1898-1	11.0	2.7	40.3
6	1898-2	10.4	3.1	42.1
7	1902	21.9	5.4	36.1
8	1903	22.8	5.0	31.3
9	1904	19.9	4.2	32.8
10	1908	24.5	5.2	17.1
11	1912	26.0	9.6	14.0
12	1915	24.2	9.2	17.0
13	1917	27.3	7.9	14.3
14	1920	30.1	8.2	8.4
15	1924	31.0	12.6	5.9
16	1928	33.2	14.4	4.7
17	1930	33.7	17.8	2.2
18	1932	35.4	17.1	1.7
19	1936	34.7	18.8	1.7
20	1937	32.3	18.9	0.9
21	1942	28.0	21.2	0.2

Continued on next page

| | | | **TABLE 3-3 CONTINUED**
IMPERIAL AND NATIONAL DIET
EDUCATION
University Faculty Attended or Major Subject of Private Education
(Figures are Percentages of those Elected Each Year) | | |

Election	Year	Law	Politics/ Economics	Chin./Japan. Classics, etc.
22	1946	21.5	14.2	
23	1947	23.6	14.4	
24	1949	26.0	15.3	
25	1952	13.8	19.5	
26	1953	31.0	19.4	
27	1955	30.1	17.9	
28	1958	28.1	19.8	
29	1960	31.4	18.3	
30	1963	28.5	17.7	
31	1967	28.0	17.2	
32	1969	31.5	18.1	
33	1972	26.2	16.9	
34	1976	25.4	12.5	
35	1979	28.9	16.9	
36	1980	31.4	17.1	
37	1983	33.1	18.2	
38	1986	32.0	16.0	
39	1990	29.5	26.4	

From Niigata, Ichishima was a student at Todai in 1881 and 1882 when he came under the influence of Ono Azusa. He joined Ono's study group, the Otokai, which was active in promoting Ōkuma Shigenobu and in the founding of the Kaishintō. Ichishima also studied British political theory with Ernest Fenollosa, a political moderate. Ichishima, however, dropped out of Todai just before completing his course and then turned to journalism in his native Niigata. In 1883 he was imprisoned for violation of the Press Law while serving as editor of *Niigata Shimbun*.

Ichishima won election to the House of Representatives three times under the Kaishintō banner: in September 1894 , March 1898 and August 1898. Only in his thirties, he nevertheless withdrew from the part-time work of national electoral politics to full-time employment at Waseda University. He had previously worked with Takada Sanae and others from 1882 in support of Ōkuma's efforts to found a private university. When his last Diet term expired in 1902 he became head librarian at Waseda where he also served as a trustee for over forty years.

He was also active in book publishing, particularly in efforts to locate rare books and bring them to publication. In his later years he became interested in *zuihitsu* (literary miscellany), contributing significantly to the promotion of this important literary genre.

It is clear that Ichishima's career outside of the Diet was more important than the role he played within. This too, however, is typical, particularly in the earlier years of the parliamentary process in Japan.

Tsurumi Yūsuke, chosen here as a representative Todai product for the later prewar period, is a name familiar to English reading students of modern Japan. He had impeccable connections to go along with an elite background and an almost unbelievably active career. He was initially the protege of Nitobe Inazō, the early twentieth century's most important popularizer of Japan to the outside world. He was the son-in-law of Gotō Shimpei and the father of two famous scholars of the postwar: Tsurumi Shunsuke and Tsurumi Kazuko.

Born in 1885, Tsurumi graduated from Todai in 1910 and immediately went to work for the central government in the Railway Ministry. He also worked for the Colonization Ministry before leaving government service in 1924. He continued thereafter to travel extensively in Europe, Asia, North America and Australia. In the 1920s, even before his election to the Diet, he was a strenuous advocate of people-to-people diplomacy. Because of his ability to speak and write in English, he was in great demand in the U.S. and Britain, contributing articles and giving speeches. He saw it as his duty to explain Japan's international position and defend it, if necessary. But he also contributed to the stereotyping of Japan by playing to foreign sentiments. In a 1925 volume, Tsurumi wrote on "The Liberal Movement in Japan" of which he said that he would "explain how democratic, not to say radical ideas made rapid progress in Japan partly under the influence of President Wilson's lofty idealism, and later as a result of the overthrow of autocratic systems in Europe. This [Japanese] middle class, backed by the rising labor movement, was making a steady advance upon the conservative party, in spite of the limited suffrage and the strategic position of the bureaucracy, when like a bolt from the blue sky came the Immigration Bill of 1924, bringing in its train grave consequences for the future of Japan."[11] Tsurumi also went on record in 1925 advocating voting rights for women.

In 1928 Tsurumi ran for the Diet from Okayama, winning as a minor party candidate - the Meiseikai. Since the two major parties were almost evenly split from 1928 to 1930, Tsurumi gained attention because he held the deciding vote in certain deliberations. He was rejected at the polls in 1930 and 1932, but bounced back in 1936, 1937 and 1942, the last time with government endorsement. When the war ended in 1945 Tsurumi immediately took up the task of organizing a new political party - the Shimpotō. He was this party's first Secretary General in November 1945. In that capacity he communicated with the Occupation authorities, but the purge axe fell on him in early 1946. He was later depurged and elected as a conservative to the House of Councillors for one term, 1953-1959. He served as Welfare Minister in the first Hatoyama Cabinet (1954-55).

Throughout his life Tsurumi was a whirlwind of activity. He wrote more than a dozen books, including best-selling novels such as *Haha* (1930). He was the organizer of the Japan chapter of the Institute of Pacific Relations and Japan's representative to most of its meetings in the 1920s and 1930s. Originally, a "Taishō liberal", Tsurumi drifted rightward, a not uncommon phenomenon in the troubled 1930s. He died in 1973.

There were many products of Waseda University in the House of Representatives. As noted, they were usually associated with the political party founded by Ōkuma and they were often journalists in their early careers. Tagawa Daikichirō fits these qualities and adds a few others. Tagawa was born in Nagasaki in 1869 and, after graduating from Waseda (then known as Tokyo Semmon Gakkō) in 1890, he became a reporter for *Hōchi Shimbun* and *Miyako Shimbun*. During the wars with China (1894-95) and Russia (1904-05) he was an interpreter with the army in the field. In 1908 he joined the Tokyo city government, the same year that he won his first election to the Imperial Diet. He ran as a minor party candidate from Nagasaki.

In his first three election victories (1908, 1912, 1915) he was on the independent left, a precarious position. He lost in 1917. In 1920 he returned to the win column with the Kenseikai, but he soon moved leftward to become a combative "liberal" in the mold of Ozaki Yukio. In fact, he followed Ozaki thereafter, joining the Kakushin Club in 1921. In 1924 he switched to a Tokyo district, lost in the general election but gained a seat as a replacement for another candidate in 1927. He was not reelected in 1928, but did succeed in 1930, 1936 and 1937, each time with Ozaki. During the war until 1942 he refused to support the IRAA. Naturally, he was blacklisted by the government in the 1942 election and, despite support from Ozaki, he went down to defeat.[12]

In 1947 Tagawa returned to the Diet, winning on the JSP ticket, again from Tokyo. Unfortunately, however, he died five months later in October 1947. Tagawa displayed the independence and individualism sometimes associated with Wasedans. He was an active Christian, a sign in itself of non-conformity. His 1938 book, *Kokka to Shūkyō* (The State and Religion) was a serious attempt in the age of ultranationalism to reconcile Christianity with the prevailing concept of *kokutai*.[13] He lectured at several universities in the 20s and 30s, was a trustee of Meiji Gakuin and, after the war, active in peace organizations. He also authored many books on a wide variety of subjects - city government, political parties, theology, finance and the British monarchy and parliament.

Some of those informally educated had illustrious careers, not always in politics. Suehiro Shigeyasu was a writer first and politician second, but he exemplified the spirit of many early Meiji figures - versatility, commitment and talent.

Suehiro was born in Ehime in 1849, the son of a samurai. He studied Chinese literature and classics at the old Han school, worked briefly in local government, before going off to Tokyo in his early twenties. He was briefly employed in the Finance Ministry of the new Meiji government, but soon turned to journalism and politics. While working as an editor for *Chōya Shimbun* in 1875 he was arrested for violating the Press Law. Undeterred, he joined others in forming the Jiyūtō in 1881 and was an active voice in the politics of the popular rights movement from that time forward.

Suehiro is best known for his political novels which were published in the 1880s under the pen name of Suehiro Tetchō. *Setchūbai* (Plum Blossoms in the Snow) in 1886 became immensely popular, particularly among the youth congregating in the capital. It was set in the 21st century where Japan had become a world leader in every category due mainly to the enlightenment of the Emperor and the wisdom of elected representatives. Suehiro here anticipated the constitution by two years. While George Sansom and Donald Keene[14] have gently ridiculed Suehiro's futurism, Japan's present condition as a world leader in many categories (to the chagrin of practically every other nation) makes him seem more prophetic than naive.

In any event, Suehiro not only wrote political novels, but he practiced politics. He was elected in the first Diet campaign in 1890 with Kaishintō sponsorship and then again in the fourth election of September 1894, this time as an independent from Ehime. Donald Keene describes him as an idealist who was regarded by others in the Diet as something of a nuisance.[15] He expired before his Diet term did in 1896, still short of his fiftieth birthday.

Although he was elected to the Imperial Diet only once, included here is a brief biography of Ueki Emori as a representative with a premodern private education. He could also have been included as an "amateur", a politician by occupation, or as a journalist. He was all of these, mostly simultaneously, in his short life.

He was born in Tosa-Han in 1857, the eldest son of a samurai. He studied at the Han school and, then, in 1873, he went to Tokyo where he enrolled at a private school, Kainan. Here he was exposed to the ideas of the Meirokusha and Fukuzawa Yukichi.

At the tender age of twenty he joined the Risshisha, founded earlier by fellow Tosan Itagaki Taisuke. Ueki quickly became one of Itagaki's leading theorists, helping to revive the Aikokusha. He was the most vigorous mover in bringing together the various popular rights movements from all over the country into a single political party. This goal was finally realized in 1881 when the Jiyūtō came into being.

In the 1880s Ueki was a member of the Kōchi Prefectural assembly and engaged in editorial writing for newspapers such as *Kōchi Shimbun* and *Jiyū Shimbun*, the organ of the Jiyūtō. He was also active in organizing the "sake-sellers assembly", a movement in 1882 to bring down the high tax on sake. He is most famous, however, for his "draft" constitution, which was one of several prepared by liberals in 1880 and 1881. In his version Ueki advocated a unicameral Diet elected by universal suffrage, unconditional civil rights, and sovereignty with the people. He also recommended a federal system rather like that of Switzerland. Frequently thereafter, he called for a constituent assembly to prepare the constitution.

Needless to say, these ideas were far too radical for the established leaders who ignored the demands from the left to produce a conservative constitution that gave very little power to the representatives of the people.[16] The oligarchy could not and did not still the voice of Ueki, however. He was elected to the first Diet and in the two years of life remaining to him he continued to speak and write of the "natural rights of man", the spirit of resistance, world peace, and the emancipation of women. He was one of a very rare breed in calling for women's rights in the nineteenth century.

Ueki stands historically as a passionate advocate of ideals which continue to stir the minds of youth one-hundred years later. Perhaps for this reason, he has received a good deal of attention from modern writers, including Ienaga Saburō and, among foreigners, Joseph Pittau and Roger Bowen.[17] His own works are all political polemics which show a keen appreciation of Western political theory as well as the Japanese cultural tradition. He was a genuine reformer, probably well ahead of his time. He died in 1892 before the second Diet election, at the age of 35. Rumors that he was poisoned persist to this day.

Andō Masazumi is used here as one who attended "other schools." He is also representative of many prewar Diet members in the variety of experience he brought to politics. And he stands as an interesting example of an Occupation purgee as he was a consistent opponent of militarism.

Andō was born in 1876, the son of the head of Shinryūji Temple at Asakusa, Tokyo. He attended several universities, finally Tokyo Foreign Language School. After finishing his schooling in 1899 he began adult life in the priesthood, but soon turned to journalism, first as a reporter and then as managing editor and director of *Tokyo Asahi Shimbun*. He also sought and won election to the Asakusa-ku assembly, serving briefly as its speaker.

He took up national electoral politics in 1920, winning as an independent from Tokyo in that year. He subsequently joined the Seiyūkai and was reelected seven consecutive times until 1942. He succeeded in the wartime election despite non-endorsement by the Tōjō government. During his initial tenure in the national assembly he rose to prominence in the Seiyūkai, serving as Parliamentary Councilor for Education in the Tanaka Giichi Cabinet (1927-29) and as Parliamentary Vice-Minister for Education in the short-lived Inukai Cabinet (1932). He developed a reputation for hostility to the military and was one of only a handful of Diet members who openly criticized government regulations curtailing freedom of speech during the Pacific War.

Immediately after the war Andō played an important role in the founding of the Jiyūtō where he was an avid supporter of Hatoyama Ichirō. Nevertheless, he was purged because of his prominence and despite his opposition to militarism. When the Occupation ended he reentered politics and was successful as a Jiyūtō candidate in 1952, 1953 and 1955. He was Minister of Education in the first Hatoyama Cabinet (Dec. 1954 to March 1955) when his announcement of a plan to revise social science education drew criticism from educational circles.

Andō died on October 14, 1955. He authored a number of books, most notably on Buddhism and the relationship between politics and religion.

NOTES

1   See note 5 in Chapter Two. Popular accounts too numerous to mention also repeat this endlessly. In addition to the works cited in Chapter Two, see William Ouchi, *Theory Z: How American Business Can Meet the Japanese Challenge* (1981), pp. 21-22 for misleading commentary about Todai and other Japanese universities. Ouchi's 1981 book was a best-seller in the U.S. See also Rodney Clark, *The Japanese Company* (1979), p. 36 and M.Y. Yoshino, *Japan's Managerial System* (1968), p. 90 for Todai garduates as business executives.

2   Mellors, *The British M.P.* (p. 40) provides figures indicating that 32.7% of all British MPs between 1945 and 1974 were graduates of either Oxford or Cambridge. For the Conservative Party of Great Britain, more than fifty percent of the successful candidates in each election during this period were "Oxbridge" affiliates. (p. 48). For Labour, the figures were substantially lower: between 14.5% and 20.8% of Labour MPs were so connected.

3   Baerwald, *Party Politics*, pp. 20, 30, 163. See also Richardson and Flanagan, *Politics in Japan*, pp. 277-279 and Hans Baerwald, *Japan's Parliament: an Introduction* (1974), p. 65. Akira Kubota, *Higher Civil Servants in Postwar Japan* (1969), pp. 70-72 discusses the prominence of Todai grads in the bureaucracy.

4   Although an advocate of constitutional government and a parliament, Fukuzawa himself was critical of the bickering of the political parties and adopted the position of a "diagnostician". He consistently eschewed taking a position in government, a view that may have been promoted at Keiō in its early years. See Carmen Blacker, *The Japanese Enlightenment* (1964),, p. 121.

5   The original idea for Keiō was to turn out "civilized students." This meant Western studies, especially about Britain, were stressed in accordance with Fukuzawa's contempt for Asian civilization. Keiō eventually became an eminent private university in many fields, but never had a strong tradition of advancing its students into government service. In addition to Blacker, see John Hall, "Japanese History", in *Twelve Doors to Japan* (1965), p. 407.

6   Chūō University was originally founded in 1885 as Igirisu Hōritsu Gakkō (English Law School). Its name was changed to Tokyo Hōgakuin Daigaku in

1903 and to Chūō Daigaku in 1905. Nihon University was known as Nihon Hōritsu Gakkō at its founding in 1889. Meiji University was Meiji Hōritsu Gakkō when founded in 1881, became a university in 1903.

7 This applies to multi-purpose universities, but not, of course, to specialized institutions like medical colleges.

8 At present the curriculum of a law faculty normally consists of one and one-half to two years of general education followed by two or two and one-half years of more specialized legal study. "Legal education in the universities resembles that of American undergraduate political science departments rather than American law schools and must be limited to the fundamentals necessary for students considering positions in government and industry." (Hakaru Abe, "Education of the Legal Profession in Japan", in A.T. von Mehren, ed., *Law in Japan*, pp. 159-160). Admission to the bar requires passing the national law exam followed by two years of additional training at the Legal Training and Research Institute (Shihō Kenkyūjo). This training concludes with another bar exam. The system turns out less than 500 practicing attorneys a year. (See Abe, "Education of the Legal Profession", pp. 155-156. Also *Encyclopedia of Japan*, Vol. 4, p. 381 and Takaaki Hattori, "The Legal Profession in Japan: Its Historical Development and Present State", in von Mehren, *Law in Japan*, pp. 111-152). However, as noted in Chapter Two (note 11), there are many more persons doing legal work than the figure for practicing attorneys seems to suggest.

9 The following subjects of study have been included in the classifications of Chinese or Japanese classics and literature: Kangaku, Kanseki, Kokugaku, Shūshigaku, Kōgaku, Wagaku, and Yōmeigaku.

10 He was also known, primarily in Tokyo, as Ichijima.

11 Tsurumi Yusuke, "The Liberal Movement in Japan", p. 67.

12 Ozaki was accused, not for the first time, of lese majeste for remarks he made in a speech supporting Tagawa's candidacy.

13 Tagawa Daikichiro, *Kokka to Shūkyō* (1938).

14 George Sansom, *The Western World and Japan* (1950), pp. 415-416; Donald Keene, *Dawn to the West: Japanese Literature in the Modern Era: Fiction* (1988), pp. 89-92.

15 Keene, *Dawn to the West*, p. 92.

16 Ueki's "draft", however, was realized in the 1947 constitution.

17 Ienaga Saburo, *Ueki Emori Kenkyu* (1960); Joseph Pittau, *Political Thought in Early Meiji Japan 1868-1889* (1967), esp. pp. 65-66, 101-114; Roger Bowen, *Rebellion and Democracy in Meiji Japan: A Study of Commoners in the Popular Rights Movement* (1980), pp. 192-212 et. seq.

Chapter 4

The Diet as a Profession
■

What constitutes a professional politician in an electoral system? Others[1] have attempted to answer this question in the British and American systems. In all cases professionalism is determined by length of service or electability. Mellors and Buck consider years of service as the determinant of professionalism whereas Matthews prefers to use the number of times an individuals was elected as the standard. This study follows the example of Matthews because, with thirty-nine elections over one-hundred years, it suits the Japanese situation better. Mellors groups all British MPs into two categories of "amateurs" or "professionals" and he arbitrarily decides that all MPs with ten or more years of service are professionals while all others are considered "amateurs."[2] I will not be this rigid at fixing a line dividing professionals and amateurs. The earlier chapters have taken up the matter of professionalism in association with educational and occupational backgrounds. This chapter will consider the overall picture of permanence (or non-permanence) in order to see what kinds of patterns emerge and how much continuity and change there has been. Professionalism, so defined in electoral politics, is, of course, important because leadership is invariably exercised by those with much experience, namely the professionals.

Tables 4-1 and 4-2 provide a generalized view of permanence and electability over the course of time. Table 4-1 shows that the average length of service of Diet members, based on number of times elected, steadily increased, as it surely had to, in the early years of the system. I believe that it is reasonable to conclude that the average number of times elected meant next to nothing until about 1903, by which time the average was 2.8 and the size of the House of Representatives had increased from the original 300 to 376. The numbers in the table exceed the statutory membership limits frequently in the early years because it was the law to seat the person who received the next highest number of votes if, for any reason, the seat became vacant. Thus, although 300 persons were actually elected in

		TABLE 4-1		
		IMPERIAL AND NATIONAL DIET		
		Professionalism		
Election	**Year**	**Avg. No. of times elected***	**No. of members**	**New seats**
1	1890	1.0	321	
2	1892	1.48	322	
3	1894-1	1.83	300	
4	1894-2	2.13	329	
5	1898-1	2.03	300	
6	1898-2	2.56	328	
7	1902	2.24	376	76
8	1903	2.80	380	
9	1904	3.04	404	
10	1908	2.68	422	3
11	1912	2.58	413	
12	1915	2.72	403	
13	1917	2.95	414	2
14	1920	2.56	504	83
15	1924	2.51	513	
16	1928	2.70	467	2
17	1930	2.99	468	
18	1932	3.23	475	
19	1936	3.41	481	
20	1937	3.80	494	
21	1942	3.15	473	

Continued on next page

		TABLE 4-1 CONTINUED IMPERIAL AND NATIONAL DIET Professionalism		
Election	Year	Avg. No, of times elected*	No. of members	New seats
22	1946	1.59	469	
23	1947	1.97	474	
24	1949	2.13	468	1
25	1952	3.03	467	
26	1953	3.49	467	
27	1955	3.88	474	
28	1958	4.23	471	
29	1960	4.60	467	
30	1963	4.92	467	
31	1967	4.71	486	19
32	1969	4.71	491	5
33	1972	4.67	491	
34	1976	4.18	511	20
35	1979	4.41	511	
36	1980	5.11	511	
37	1983	5.02	511	
38	1986	5.27	512	1
39	1990	4.48	512	

*This figure is the average number of times all members had been elected prior to and including the numbered election.

1890, 321 sat in the Diet before the next election in 1892. This practice was discontinued altogether under postwar election laws.

After 1903 the figure for average number of times elected fluctuated slightly on either side of this line (with a high of 3.04 and a low of 2.51) through the early part of the twentieth century until 1932. One of the reasons why the figure did not rise much is because of the addition of new seats, particularly the seventy-six added in 1902 and the eighty-three in 1920. Prewar Japan may be said to have acquired a "professional" House of Representatives in the election of 1932 when the average experience of the total membership exceeded three successful election campaigns. It remained above three until the end of the war with the high point of professionalism reached in the election of 1937.

After the war the massive Occupation purges deprived most veteran members of their eligibility with the result that the process of building a professional assembly had to start all over again. Of the members elected in 1946, 385 (82%) were newcomers. The success rate, measured by average number of times elected, remained low throughout the Occupation, but once restraints were removed and the surviving prewar politicians were depurged, many returned to the electoral wars. Over half of the 210 individuals who served in both prewar and postwar Diets were not elected after the war until the Occupation was over. Most of these returned in 1952, pushing the experience figure back over 3.0. It then rose steadily throughout the 1950s and 1960s. It dipped in the late 1960s and 1970s, mainly because new seats were added, but it went up again to exceed five in the three elections of the 1980s. It fell back to about 4.5 when 133 new members came aboard in 1990. Thus, we have a repetition of the prewar pattern and a rather thorough "professional" assembly has become well established.

The above table indicates that 41.6% of all 5569 members of the Japanese National Diet (House of Representatives) served but one term or less. They were rank amateurs. For the prewar period when the Diet had little power, the number of one-timers was close to half the total. For the postwar period the figure is lower, but still nearly one-third of all persons elected since 1946 have but one such experience. For all members, prewar and postwar, the average number of times elected was 3.12. It was 2.66 for the prewar era and 4.19 for the postwar (3.92 for new postwar members).

If amateur assemblyman status may be assigned to those who served less than three terms, a reasonable estimate it seems to me, then fifty-nine percent of the entire membership falls into that category. This breaks down to 66.4% (about two-thirds) for prewar representatives and fourty-four percent for postwar members (47.9% for new postwar). Such high percentages for amateurs may suggest to some political immaturity,[3] but one must take into consideration the unusual circumstances which twice arose in the course of Japan's parliamentary history.

TABLE 4-2
IMPERIAL AND NATIONAL DIET
PROFESSIONALISM
Number of Times Elected

No. of times	All members		Prewar members		All Postwar		New Postwar	
	No.	%	No.	%	No.	%	No.	%
1	2319	41.6	1658	46.9	664	29.6	661	32.5
2	1001	18.0	688	19.5	331	14.7	313	15.4
3	558	10.0	370	10.5	205	9.1	188	9.3
4	390	7.0	238	6.7	174	7.8	152	7.5
5	310	5.6	153	4.3	173	7.7	157	7.7
6	267	4.8	121	3.4	169	7.5	146	7.2
7	200	3.6	96	2.7	127	5.7	104	5.1
8	157	2.9	66	1.9	116	5.2	91	4.5
9	109	2.0	40	1.1	86	3.8	69	3.4
10	101	1.8	45	1.3	70	3.1	56	2.8
11	48	0.9	15	0.4	40	1.8	33	1.6
12	36	0.6	12	0.3	32	1.4	24	1.2
13	25	0.4	12	0.3	18	0.8	13	0.6
14	20	0.4	10	0.3	14	0.6	10	0.5
15	10	0.2	5	0.1	8	0.4	5	0.2
16	9	0.2	2	0.1	7	0.3	7	0.3
17	3	0.1	1	-	3	0.1	2	0.1
18	2	-	1	-	1	-	1	-
19	1	-	1	-	1	-		
25	1	-	1	-	1	-		
NA	2	-	2	0.1	2	0.1		
	5569		3537		2242		2032	

First of all, the initial Diet could have no experienced members and, secondly, the Occupation purge created an almost identical situation where, in most cases, previous service was *prima facie* evidence of ineligibility. Before the war newcomers made up over twenty-five percent of all electees on all but three occasions (14% in 1903, 23% in 1912, and 19% in 1937). Since the war, rookies totalled less than twenty-five percent on every occasion since 1952 until the exceptional election of 1990. Other than that percentages of newcomers have exceeded twenty percent only when new seats were added.

The figures in Tables 4-2 and 4-3 substantiate the notion that the prewar Imperial Diet was mostly made up of amateurs with little experience. This body had very little power at first, though it gradually acquired more and it did provide the basic training ground in which was tested the style of operation for the more powerful postwar institution. The lower house is now constitutionally supreme and, since the end of the Occupation, has steadily become more and more professional. This does not necessarily mean that it has become more effective or responsive to the wishes of the electorate. Nor does it, I think, imply any greater evidence of "democracy." The growth of professionalism does, however, indicate stability, since lower turnover bespeaks greater continuity.

Other factors affecting career longevity in the Diet include availability of funds, crowd pleasing oratorical ability and audacity. Tsuji Kan'ichi once wrote, "a politician must be audacious. He sometimes must have the ability to play the crowd."[4] Tsuji went on to wonder about his own possession of this quality, but the notion of politician as actor, frequently found elsewhere in electoral systems, was also apparent in Japan in the days before television.

The need for financial support has already been commented on in a general way. It early elections it was less necessary than it later became. "When voting was introduced it was a great novelty and few people knew anything about Western electoral methods. In the first campaign of 1890, for example, expenses were almost nothing. For example, the noted scholar Nishi was returned from the city of Okayama with the entire outlay of one yen ... This was the amount he spent for his transportation in a rickshaw from his village to Okayama." [5]

If, however, knowing "Western electoral methods" meant extravagant outlays, Japanese candidates proved quick studies. Tsurumi called the extraordinary cost of elections "the curse of Japanese politics." It affected professionalism, not only by screening out some candidates with meager funds, but causing before the war "the fear or I should say dread of dissolution on the part of M.P.'s. Being in a hard-earned position, costing so much, they tremble at the thought of dissolution."[6] This statement was uttered in 1925, but was a factor later as well.[7]

Hoshi Hajime, who served both before and after the war, once wrote a primer for Diet campaigners, published as *Senkyō Daigaku* in 1924.[8] This book pre-

TABLE 4-3
IMPERIAL AND NATIONAL DIET
PROFESSIONALISM
Average Number of Times Elected for New Members

Election	Year	No. new members	Avg. no of times elected
1	1890	321	3.46
2	1892	166	2.46
3/4	1894	265	2.28
5/6	1898	258	2.36
7	1902	228	2.92
8	1903	93	2.02
9	1904	120	2,08
10	1908	206	2.53
11	1912	196	2.75
12	1915	153	2.39
13	1917	151	2.38
14	1920	277	2.55
15	1924	252	2.94
16	1928	173	3.31
17	1930	127	2.87
18	1932	128	2.83
19	1936	127	3.36
20	1937	93	2.86
21	1942	202	1.78

Continued on next page

TABLE 4-3 CONTINUED
IMPERIAL AND NATIONAL DIET
PROFESSIONALISM
Average Number of Times Elected for New Members

Election	Year	No. new members	Avg. no of times elected
22	1946	386	3.53
23	1947	225	3.77
24	1949	195	3.96
25	1952	109	5.34
26	1953	48	4.27
27	1955	57	5.04
28	1958	68	5.19
29	1960	59	5.56
30	1963	72	5.49
31	1967	102	5.38
32	1969	99	4.99
33	1972	95	4.21

This table indicates the average number of times elected for representatives whose first successful run was in the year indicated. It is not necessary to go beyond 1972 because the average becomes meaningless when the highest possible figure (for number of times elected) is six.

The elections of 1894 (3 and 4) and 1898 (5 and 6) have been combined in this table.

scribed a kind of campaign by the numbers in which twelve chapters told of campaign financing and such things as how to make a speech after losing an election. Hoshi provided marginal subtitles to each section consiting of numerical points to follow from one to whatever. No shrinking violet, Hoshi also recorded his own campaign speeches as models for others to follow.

One other element deserves attention when considering professionals versus amateurs. Certain "classes" of Diet members (those elected for the first time in a given year) had longer or shorter average life spans. Table 4-3 indicates that the original "Class of 1890" had an average Diet life span of 3.46 elections, the highest for the entire prewar period. Other successful prewar groups were the "Class of 1928", the first elected under universal manhood suffrage, and the "Class of 1936", when the "liberal" political parties scored well just before the February 26 Incident. The least successful "class" was that of 1942, the wartime election which featured "recommended" candidates promoted by the Tōjō government under the banner of the Dai Nihon Taiseikai.[9] In this election the government compiled a list of 466 such "recommended" candidates which included 235 incumbents and eighteen former members. Of those recommended 381 (81.8%) were elected, but about one-third of the votes and eighteen percent of the seats went to opposition candidates who officially ran as independents. This included several vigorous critics of the Tōjō government such as Ozaki Yukio, Saitō Takao and Nakano Seigō. Most of the 381 "recommended" candidates were purged by the Occupation and hence ineligible to stand for election in 1946, 1947 or 1949. Of all the persons elected in 1942, only 126 (27%) were ever elected again after the war. Of these 126, thirty-seven were elected during the Occupation, but eighty-nine (seventy-one percent of the 126 and nineteen percent of the 466 total Diet membership) came back after the Occupation ended. These factors back up the contention that the Occupation promoted discontinuity.[10] They also strengthen the argument that prewar political trends were resumed when the Occupation came to an end.

In the postwar period the "Class of 1952", the first after the Occupation, and the "Class of 1960", a small group of fifty-nine, both had great success. Although most members of the "Class of '52" have passed from the scene, in 1990 thirteen members of the "Class of '60" were still active in the Diet. By the mid-1980s sixteen members of this group had achieved cabinet status. Of course, almost all LDP members who are elected five or more times are likely to win at least one cabinet appointment.[11] Table 4-4 also suggests that the wartime and Occupation periods together represented a kind of aberration and that the trend toward professionalism was resumed with the election of 1952 when the figures approximate those of 1936 and 1937. The elections of 1942, 1946, 1947 and 1949 are all "irregular" in relation to the elections which preceded and followed the 1940s, resembling instead the "immature" amateur quality of the earliest years of the Diet. After the Occupation was terminated and purgees returned, the trend toward a more professional Diet becomes visible once again with only slight variations when new seats were added.

Party distinctions in terms of professionalism are difficult to compute with much meaning for the prewar years because of the many shifts and changes in party allegiance. Since, moreover, a large majority (2676 out of 3537 = 75.7%) of all prewar members were ultimately associated with one or the other (sometimes both but at different times) of the two bourgeois parties descended from the Jiyūtō and the Kaishintō, party figures on average length of service would not differ much from the numbers cited for the entire prewar membership.

For postwar times, however, it is possible to make some observations about professionalism based on party affiliation. LDP members (including those who belonged to conservative parties before the 1955 merger) had an average Diet life expectancy of 4.44 times elected (4.12 for new postwar members). The figures for the JSP are close to these: 4.03 (3.91). The JCP, which has elected ninety-six persons altogether, has a much lower average at 2.96. This is due, in part, to the purging of the JCP Diet membership in 1950 and 1951, causing an unnatural drop.[12] JCP electoral successes also fluctuated greatly on several occasions, lowering the averages further. The DSP had averages of 3.72 (3.76), again not greatly different from those of the LDP and JSP as well as the postwar composites of 4.22 and 3.94. The Kōmeitō, which did not enter the national fray until 1967 and has so far elected 103 individuals, has only a slightly lower rate, due entirely to the fact that none of its representatives can have been elected more than nine times.

A regional and prefectural breakdown on the basis of electability reveals no startling discrepancies. A table to this effect is found in Appendix A. Of the regions Hokkaido had the highest overall rate of professionalism. This is to be explained in part by the fact that Hokkaido did not participate in the first six elections when the turnover rate was very high. The more populous regions, such as Kantō and Kinki, generally seem to have more professionals. As a region Kantō had the highest overall average after Hokkaido as well as the high prewar figure. Kinki has been the area with the greatest continuity in the postwar era. It should be stressed, however, that except for Okinawa[13], the difference between the highest and lowest regional averages is only about .5 number of times elected. For the prewar era the discrepancy between Kantō (highest) and Chūbu (lowest) is about .6. For the postwar period the differences are even slimmer. Moreover, none of the regions maintained its prewar rank in the postwar, suggesting that there is no single region where there has been established a stronger sense of stability in Diet seats. When we look at individual prefectures in an effort to see

TABLE 4-4
IMPERIAL AND NATIONAL DIET
PROFESSIONALISM
Number of Times elected by Election

Election	Year	Times Elected (% of those elected each year)				
		1	2-3	4-6	7-10	More than 10
1	1890	100				
2	1892	52	48			
3	1894-1	46	54			
4	1894-2	39	45	16		
5	1898-1	54	26	20		
6	1898-2	31	45	24		
7	1902	61	20	15	6	
8	1903	24	50	20	7	
9	1904	30	44	15	11	
10	1908	49	23	21	8	
11	1912	47	29	14	7	2
12	1915	39	39	14	5	2
13	1917	36	37	15	9	3
14	1920	55	24	13	7	2
15	1924	49	28	16	6	1
16	1928	37	40	17	3	3
17	1930	27	46	20	4	3
18	1932	27	36	28	6	3
19	1936	26	32	33	10	0 (less than 1%)
20	1937	19	36	33	10	2
21	1942	43	21	24	13	0

Continued on next page

TABLE 4-4 CONTINUED
IMPERIAL AND NATIONAL DIET
PROFESSIONALISM
Number of Times elected by Election

Election	Year	Times Elected (% of those elected each year)				
		1	2-3	4-6	7-10	More than 10
22	1946	82	9	8	0	0
23	1947	47	42	7	2	1
24	1949	42	51	5	2	0
25	1952	23	46	25	6	0
26	1953	10	48	34	7	0
27	1955	12	38	43	7	0
28	1958	14	22	49	13	3
29	1960	13	22	43	19	2
30	1963	15	19	36	28	2
31	1967	21	20	25	28	7
32	1969	20	28	20	27	4
33	1972	19	29	22	23	6
34	1976	24	29	26	14	7
35	1979	15	33	32	12	9
36	1980	7	33	36	14	9
37	1983	16	20	36	20	7
38	1986	13	20	36	24	7
39	1990	26	22	26	22	4

TABLE 4-5
PROFESSIONALISM
POSTWAR DIET MEMBERS
Average Number of Times Elected by Party

| | LDP | | JSP | | JCP | | DSP | | Komeito | |
	all	new	all	new	all	new	all	new	all	new
Avg. no. of times elected	4.44	4.12	4.03	3.91	—	2.96	3.72	3.76	—	3.97
No. of members	1337	1162	552	521		96	85	84		103

which were "safest" or promoted professionalism most clearly, there is no obvious pattern. One cannot say, either for prewar or postwar times, that urban prefectures were more likely to have high rates of professionalism. Nor can the same be argued for the rural prefectures, presumably more impervious to change. In fact, what Table A-7 does not show, but nevertheless implies, is that a few prefectures (Miyagi, Mie, Okayama, for example) produced a few extraordinarily long-lived professional politicians.[14] There is also wild fluctuation in the professionalism ranking of prefectures between prewar and postwar time periods. For example, Oita, which had the fifth highest average in the prewar period, has fallen to last place in the postwar years.

The conclusion I draw here is that, except for Tokyo where more professional politicians necessarily congregated in the early decades of the system, there is no particular region or prefecture of Japan which is or has been more heavily "politicized" to the electoral system and thus productive of a line of more successful professional politicians. There are also few areas where instability is reflected in a much lower rate of electability. In short, the entire nation seems to be represented at about the same rate by amateurs and professionals in national elective office. The absence of much disparity also suggests the high degree to which Japan has been politically integrated in modern times.

There are "safe" seats in the Japanese Diet and there have been some since the early days. They have been, for the most part, "safe" for individuals rather than parties. In the beginning "safe" seats were relatively rare, subject to the many changes in the election laws, the size of districts and weak party organizations. Only a few individuals with "iron jiban" were assured reelection on a regular basis.[15]   The multi-member districts in effect after 1920 favored high retention rates for individuals even in what amounted to a two-party system in the 1920s and early 1930s.[16] In postwar times, the "inheritance" of a support base (*jiban*) will naturally be accomplished among members of the same party and is most commonly found in the LDP. It is less common in other parties, although the Komeitō can count on a single "safe" seat in certain urban districts.[17] In the postwar period there have been no swing districts which could go either way, though there have been some swing slots within a district. The absence of swing districts has, to be sure, promoted stability, continuity and reelectability. On the other hand, unnatural factors, such as the postwar purge and depurge, as well as the steady increase in the number of seats, have also affected the statistical outcome revealed in these figures.

The thumbnail biography section of this chapter capsulizes the careers of three professionals, one amateur and two "wartime recommended" candidates who were successful.

Ōtsu Jun'ichirō was a professional politician with a long and consistent career spanning the first forty-two years of the representative system. Born in Ibaraki in 1856, he was attracted to the popular rights movement and began publishing the *Ibaraki Nichi Nichi Shimbun* in Mito as early as 1879. He became a follower of Ōkuma Shigenobu, joined the Kaishintō and was elected to the Ibaraki Prefectural Assembly. He then became a contestant for the first Imperial Diet as a thirty-four year old candidate. He remained faithful to the Ōkuma-Kaishintō line, staying with this party through its many name changes until 1927 when he was appointed to the House of Peers. All in all, he was elected thirteen times, failing only in 1892 (second election) and 1912 (twelfth). In view of this longevity, he naturally occupied high party positions, including sōmu (director) and komon (advisor).

In 1927 Ōtsu published a ten volume *Constitutional History of Japan* .[18] It was a solid scholarly study which remained a standard treatment, except for the ultranationalist thirties, for many years.

Otsu was representative of the loyal party man of prewar times who was brought into the popular rights movement at its inception and was faithful to its ideals as a practicng politician in the Diet. His career was less colorful than many of his compatriots. If he was unusual it was his consistency in an era of uncertainty in Japan's parliamentary history.

Inukai Takeru (Ken) grew up in Japanese politics as the eldest son of Inukai Tsuyoshi. Like his father he was a parliamentary professional, winning election eleven times: consecutively from the 17th (1930) to the 22nd (1936) and, after being purged, again from 1949 to 1958. He died in 1960 while still serving in the Diet.

Originally, Inukai, a Todai drop-out, was a novelist, publishing several well received topical works often with Chinese themes in the 1920s. Once he entered the political world, however, he was hooked and he never returned to serious fiction. In 1939 and 1940 he was Japan's chief negotiator with Wang Ching-wei to set up a puppet government in Nanking. Because, however, of his friendship with Ozaki Hotsumi, Inukai was arrested when Ozaki was apprehended for treason in 1941 in connection with the Sorge spy ring.[19]

After the war Inukai was one of the principal actors in the politics of the Shimpotō in 1946 and 1947. When the Shimpotō was dissolved and replaced by the Minshutō in March 1947 he was a leading member. Just at this point, however, he was purged by Occupation authorities, accounting for his ineligibility in that year's general election. He was released in 1948 and he immediately returned to politics in the conservative camp. He was Minister of Justice in the 4th and 5th Yoshida Cabinets from 1952 to 1954. In this capacity he intervened to save the careers of Satō Eisaku and Ikeda Hayato (both future prime ministers) in the Shipbuilding Scandal of 1954, a major early postwar bribery case. It contributed to the fall of the 5th Yoshida Cabinet in late 1954, though Inukai himself was obliged to resign earlier. Inukai was considered a possible prime minister at various times and clearly stands out as a good example of the professional politician.

Saitō Takao is included as a long-term professional. I also regard him as a kind of personal hero - a "profile in courage" among elected politicians in Japan.

Saitō was born in Hyogo in 1870, graduated from Tokyo Semmon Gakkō (later Waseda University) in 1894 and also attended Yale. Back in Japan in the 1900s he practiced law and then turned to politics, winning his first election as a Kokumintō candidate in 1912. He was subsequently reelected 12 times, the last in 1949, failing only in 1920 when his party (Kenseikai) was overwhelmed by Hara's Seiyūkai. He died in late 1949 as a sitting Diet member.

Saitō was more prominent in opposition than as a government spokesman. Although he held ministerial appointments (Parliamentary Vice-Minister in the Hamaguchi and Saitō Makoto cabinets) and extensive party posts in the Kenseikai-Minseitō, he is best known for his rousing opposition to militarism in the 1930s and 1940s.

He embodied the liberal tradition of Taishō democracy, but went much father than most of his colleagues in denouncing the encroachments of the military in state affairs. In 1936 he introduced a resolution condemning the participation in politics of military officers. He also blamed the Army for the February 26 incident of that year. In 1938 he took the lead in denouncing the General Mobilization Law of the Konoe government. But his most spectacular foray of this sort was a Diet speech delivered in February 1940 in which he condemned the hypocrisy of the military in its moralistic contention regarding China. This was regarded as virtual un-Japanese heresy. The Army high command was so angered by this attack that it was able to persuade the pusillanimous Diet members to vote Saitō's expulsion from the Diet in March 1940.[20]

Despite his removal from the Diet, Saitō refused to shut up. He campaigned for reelection in 1942, obviously without government endorsement. During the campaign the police confiscated some of his campaign literature, but he prevailed nonetheless. By war's end Saitō was aging, but he participated in the revival of the conservative line political parties and was elected in 1946, 1947 and 1949. He wound up his distinguished career with cabinet posts in the first Yoshida and Katayama cabinets. He also wrote several books on constitutional law and on elections.

Some members of the Diet had short careers therein, earning them the description of "amateurs" according to my definition. Of these, however, some were illustrious figures who influenced the political history of Japan from outside the walls at Nagata-chō. One such was Ōyama Ikuo.

Ōyama was born in 1880, the second son of a physician in Hyogo Prefecture. He was adopted in his teens by the Ōyama family. He was educated at Waseda where he was in the first graduating class of that institution as a university. This was in 1905 and he was immediately offered a post as lecturer at Waseda. From 1910 to 1914 he conducted advanced studies at the University of Chicago and in Munich after which he returned to his professorship at Waseda. In 1917 he resigned to protest the firing of a colleague and joined the *Osaka Asahi Shimbun* as an editorial writer.

Ōyama was continuously active in political causes, gradually moving more and more to the left. In 1918 he left the newspaper along with Hasegawa Nyōzekan and Torii Sosen when the Terauchi government objected to its coverage of the rice riots. He then joined Yoshino Sakuzō and others to form the Reimeikai which promoted *"minponism"*. The following year, Ōyama, Kawakami Hajime and others began publication of *Warera* which also advanced democratic ideals.

In 1920 he returned to Waseda where he became involved in several academic freedom incidents. After he became chairman of the left-wing Rōdō Nōmintō in 1926 he was asked to resign from Waseda. He did so under protest, but a general strike ensued at the university.

Ōyama first ran for the Diet in 1928 as a proletarian candidate of Rōdō Nōmintō. He lost and the party was dissolved only to be resurrected in 1929 under the simplified name of Rōnōtō. Ōyama's lone success in lower house elections came in 1930 when he was one of eight proletarian candidates to win. He ran in a Tokyo district, but soon began to receive death threats. He thus left Japan for exile in the U.S. in early 1933. He remained there, working as a research associate at Northwestern University for Kenneth Colegrove, until after the war. He then returned to Japan in 1947, was reinstated at Waseda for the fourth time, and was elected to the House of Councillors in 1950. He became active in peace movements and in 1951 was awarded the Stalin Peace Prize which was highly regarded then in Japanese left-wing circles. Ōyama died in 1955.

Ōyama typifies the "liberal" professor, from Waseda, who, instead of turning more conservative with age, steadily moved to the left throughout his career both as a scholar and as a political activist. He once used a Japanese version of the snake oil salesman line by contending that "the confused opinions of politicians are nothing more than advertisements for patent medicines."[21] He also exemplified outstanding moral courage on more than one occasion. His exile to the U.S. was singular as most others on the left were either imprisoned or fled to China in the late 1930s.

Ōishi Dai is included here as a wartime recommended candidate, but he also fits several other categories. He graduated from a major private university, held a position in the central government bureaucracy, and served apprenticeship in local government.

Ōishi graduated from the Meiji University Law faculty in 1903 and, after a brief stint as a primary school teacher, he entered government service in the police agency. He eventually became head of the Police Department of Kagawa Prefecture and of the Secret Service Police (Kōtō Keisatsu Kachō). After a distinguished career here, he entered politics, securing first a position in the Kōchi City Assembly and council. He then stood for the Imperial Diet from Kōchi under the Seiyūkai in 1920, one of many new faces recruited by Hara from the Home Ministry and its police division. He was reelected in 1924, but followed Tokonami into the Seiyūhontō when that group split from the Seiyūkai in 1927. Ōishi was defeated in 1928.

In the late 1920s and 1930s Ōishi turned his attention to the business world. He became managing director of several railroad companies and was also involved in other enterprises, mostly local in Shikoku. In 1936 he was enticed back into national politics, running on the Tōhōkai ticket led by Nakano Seigō. By this time Ōishi had become a strident nationalist and restorationist, favoring an aggressive foreign policy and major changes in the political system at home. He was reelected as a Nakano supporter in 1937 and 1942, joined the IRAA with some reluctance, and disappeared from politics after the war. He stands as a minor super-patriot of which there were many in 20th century Japan, both in and out of the Diet.

Shiōden Nobutaka was not a quintessential Diet member, but he was interesting. He was typical of something else in Japanese life. He was a military man, by profession and outlook. As pointed out by Mellors, retired military persons were quite normal in the British House of Commons, especially in the early years following the Second World War. Despite the prestige of a military occupation in Japan, however, very few professional soldiers or sailors entered politics in the first fifty years of the system. This was due, in part, to Yamagata's early dictum ordering the military to abjure politics. It was also the result of the general disdain with which the services regarded the system of representation.

By the time of the struggle in World War II things had changed. In the 1942 election the government sought strong nationalists and recruited several to run as endorsed candidates. One such was Shiōden. At 63 it was his only campaign.

Shiōden was born in Tokyo in 1879, attended the Army Officers School and graduated from the Army College in 1909. He served as Military Attache in Paris during the First World War and was sent to Siberia in the Siberian Expedition. He returned a ferocious anti-communist. He retired in 1928 with the rank of Lieutenant General.

In the late 1930s Shiōden became perhaps Japan's most famous anti-semite, although Japan had no history of anti-semitism and most of the small group so defined were "second rate figures".Claiming to have lived for over a year with a Jewish family, Shiōden wrote several books on Jews and Judaism. *Yudaya Minzoku no Kenkyū* contains much of the same nonsense attributed to the Jews by rabid European anti-semites, plus some particular Japanese twists. In another book, *Kyōsan Shugi Shakai Shugi Undō no Jissai,*[22] he compared Japanese exclusiveness to Jewish exclusiveness in mean-spirited terms. He also edited a monthly journal, *Yudaya Kenkyū,* begun in 1940.   In the 1942 election, running in a Tokyo district on an anti-Jewish theme, Shiōden received the largest number of votes of any candidate nationwide.[23]   At the end of the war, Shiōden was arrested as a war criminal. This was, of course, based mainly on his military occupation and rank. He was not depurged until Occupation recommendation on March 24, 1952.

NOTES

1 Mellors, *The British M.P.* , P.W. Buck, *Amateurs and Professionals in British Politics* (1963); Donald Matthews, *U.S. Senators and Their World* (1960).

2 Mellors, *The British M.P.*, p. 82.

3 Mellors says that about two-thirds of British MPs in the 1945-1974 period did become professionals. (*The British M.P.*, p. 83).

4 Tsuji Kan'ichi, *Seijika to Iu Mono* (1955), pp. 74-75.

5 Tsurumi, "The Liberal Movement in Japan", p. 75.

6 Tsurumi, "The Liberal Movement in Japan", p. 77.

7 See, for example, George R. Packard III, *Protest in Tokyo. The Security Treaty Crisis of 1960* (1968), pp. 190-191 on why Prime Minister Kishi was reluctant to dissolve the Diet in early 1960.

8 Hoshi Hajime, *Senkyō Daigaku* (1924).

9 The election campaign of April 1942 is described in great detail by Edward J. Drea, *The 1942 Japanese General Election: Political Mobilization in Wartime Japan* (1979). In summary form, it is also described by Ben-Ami Shillony, *Politics and Culture in Wartime Japan* (1981), pp. 22-26.

10 On "continuity" versus "discontinuity" during the Occupation, see Ishikawa, *Sengo Seiji*, pp. 4-9.

11 Curtis, *The Japanese Way of Politics*, pp. 90-91. Curtis points out that about sixty percent of the Dietmen appointed to cabinet posts serve only once in that capacity.

12 On June 27, 1950 seven JCP Diet members were purged in accordance with a memorandum originally drawn up in 1947 when it had been designed to eliminate ultranationalist and right-wing individuals and groups. One additional JCP member was purged on July 19, 1950 and three more on September 27, 1951 on the same grounds. See Japan. Kokkai. Shūgiin, *Shūgiin Giin*

Tōreki Roku (1957), p. 64 et.seq. See also Baerwald, *The Purge of Japanese Leaders*, pp. 18-19.

13 Okinawa represents an abnormal prefecture as well as a separate region. Okinawa had no representation in the Imperial Diet until 1912, missing the first ten elections; none from 1946 to 1972, missing the first eleven postwar elections.

14 Ozaki Yukio, for example, was elected twenty-five consecutive times from Mie and is the all-time champion. Inukai Tsuyoshi was chosen eighteen consecutive times from Okayama.

15 Tetsuo Najita, *Hara Kei in the Politics of Compromise, 1905-1915* (1967), pp. 59-60.

16 See Gordon Mark Berger, *Parties Out of Power in Japan, 1931-1941* (1977), pp. 18-21. Prewar politicians frequently shifted party allegiance. If they were well established this had little effect on their electoral fortunes.

17 See Gerald Curtis, *Election Campaigning Japanese Style* (1971) on inheriting *jiban*. See also Baerwald, *Party Politics*, pp. 35-58, *passum*.

18 Ōtsu Jun'ichirō, *Dai Nihon Kensei Shi*, 10 vol. (1927-28).

19 See Chalmers Johnson, *An Instance of Treason. Ozaki Hotsumi and the Sorge Spy Ring* (1964), p. 180.

20 The question of Saitō's expulsion bitterly divided the existing parties and factions, weakening them overall in contending for influence. It also led to the disappearance of serious debate in the Diet on major national issues. Later, a yea or nay vote on Saitō's expulsion was used by some as a litmus test of "liberalism".

21 Ōyama Ikuo, *Gendai Nihon no Seiji Katei* (1925), p. 13.

22 Shiōden Nobutaka,, *Kyōsan Shugi Shakai Shugi Undō no Jissai* (1941), pp. 12-13.

23 Ben-Ami Shillony, *Politics and Culture in Wartime Japan*, pp. 158-159.

Chapter 5

Age

■

In his study of the British MP, Colin Mellors comments that "politics is very much a middle-aged occupation."[1] Mellors confined his examination to the British House of Commons for the period from 1945 to 1974 where he found that most persons were in their thirties and forties when first elected (about seventy-five percent were in these age groups) and that the average age of all those elected in this period was 41.7 on the occasion of their first election. Mellors also discovered that the Conservative Party generally selected younger persons as candidates than did the Labour Party.[2]

In the Japanese case the middle-aged quality is even more apparent and probably for the same reasons. To be sure, at the beginning of the electoral system in 1890 almost half of those elected were in their thirties and the average age was under forty. As is clear from Graph 5-1 and Tables 5-1 and 5-2, the average age climbed steadily and swiftly until it exceeded fifty by the election of 1932. Simultaneously, the percentage of those in their thirties dwindled to less than ten by the beginning of the 1930s. The age distribution of new members fluctuated moderately, but also rose regularly during the days of the Imperial Diet. By the wartime election of 1942 only 9.9% of the new members were under forty and the average age of new members had reached 48.97, the second highest figure on record.

After the war the age distribution pattern indicates a return to the ascending curve of the late 1920s. This is to say, the average age figure for the election of 1946 closely resembles the figures for 1924, 1928, and 1930. There was little variation in the age patterns for these three elections. The age pattern thus supports the contention that, in electoral politics as in other features of political life in Japan, the 1930s and early 1940s represented an aberration (the "dark valley") which interrupted the steady development of trends begun in the Meiji era.

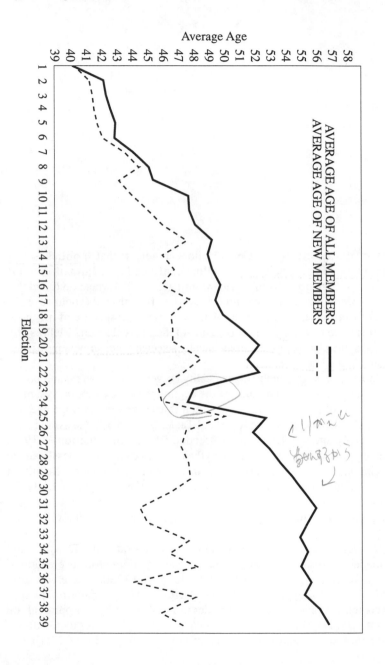

GRAPH 5-1
AGE

Proponents of this "aberration" theory ordinarily stress that the trend was in the direction of greater power for parliament and that the political drive commenced in Meiji but arrested by "fascism" was a march toward democracy.3 It is certainly questionable that the resumption of an age distribution cycle indicates the growth of democracy, whatever the word may mean. It is undeniable, however, that the first postwar election, when 385 persons (82% of all those elected) were rookies, saw the age level fall back to what it had been at the onset of the 1930s.

In the two subsequent elections held under the Occupation, in 1947 and 1949, the average age dropped further, no doubt as a result of continued purges which deprived additional old timers of the right to run for elective office. It was also due to the high turnover in these elections. A postwar low average of 47.83 was reached in 1949 when more than eighteen percent of those elected were under forty. This was the lowest average figure since 1912. It is relevant to note that there were 225 newcomers (47.5%) in 1947 and 195 (41.7%) in 1949. These are, by far, the highest figures of the entire postwar era, except of course, for the initial postwar election of 1946. The high percentages of first timers reflects not only Occupation policy, but also the relative political instability of early postwar Japan.

When the Occupation came to an end what happened in Japanese electoral politics typefies circumstances when emergency conditions arrest an earlier course of development. The Occupation represented extraordinary or emergency conditions. If the Occupation itself led to the resumption of a line of movement cut off by the depression and the emergence of "fascism" (also marked by the decline of party government), so did the end of the Occupation see the return of the pattern which the loss of the war brought to an end. Graph 5-1 shows that the average age for all members and for new members in 1952 had shot back up to and exceeded the figures for 1942 which were the previous all time highs. Thereafter, age distribution has shown a gradual upward movement with the average age reaching 56.59 in the general election of 1986 and 56.11 in February 1990. The average age of newcomers has not changed much, but the overall distribution (Table 5-1) shows sixty-five percent of all members in their fifties and sixties with less than ten percent under forty on every occasion since 1952.

Obviously, this kind of age pattern implies stability within the system, with incumbency on the rise and reelection a sure thing for many. It also suggests that very few politicians, once elected at the national level, choose voluntarily to resign or retire, something that was quite common in the prewar Diet. Since 1952 the percentage of newcomers among all electees has ranged between 7.0% (1980) and 34.5% in 1976. These are low percentages, despite the increase in membership from 466 to 512 seats during that period of time. Forty-six new seats have been added: twenty in 1967, five in 1972 (due to the recovery of Okinawa), twenty in 1976, and one in 1986.

TABLE 5-1
IMPERIAL AND NATIONAL DIET
Age Distribution: All Members

Election	Year	20-29 No.	20-29 %	30-39 No.	30-39 %	40-49 No.	40-49 %	50-59 No.	50-59 %	60-69 No.	60-69 %	70+ No.	70+ %	Avg. age
1	1890			152	47.5	123	38.4	35	10.9	10	3.1			39.95
2	1892			151	46.7	119	36.8	44	13.6	9	2.8			42.03
3	1894-1			134	44.7	117	39.0	40	13.3	9	3.0			42.04
4	1894-2			129	39.3	132	40.2	55	17.0	11	3.4	1	0.3	42.49
5	1898-1			108	36.0	139	46.3	44	14.7	8	2.7	1	0.3	42.97
6	1898-2			105	32.0	164	50.0	51	15.5	7	2.1	1	0.3	43.05
7	1902			100	26.6	186	49.5	75	19.9	15	4.0			44.45
8	1903			100	26.3	189	49.7	74	19.5	16	4.2	1	0.3	45.05
9	1904			103	25.6	201	49.9	82	20.3	16	4.0	1	0.2	45.21
10	1908			65	15.4	196	46.4	145	34.4	14	3.3	2	0.5	47.61
11	1912			67	16.3	194	47.1	125	30.3	25	6.1	1	0.2	47.65
12	1915			46	11.6	176	44.3	141	35.5	33	8.3	1	0.3	48.12
13	1917			53	12.8	166	40.2	148	35.8	46	11.1			49.31
14	1920			86	17.1	177	35.1	183	36.3	51	10.1	7	1.4	49.17
15	1924			74	14.4	196	38.2	194	37.8	45	8.8	4	0.8	49.32
16	1928			50	10.7	183	39.2	160	34.3	71	25.0	3	0.6	49.94
17	1930			40	8.5	192	41.0	145	31.0	84	17.9	7	1.5	49.55
18	1932			37	7.8	197	41.7	163	34.5	69	14.6	6	1.3	50.16
19	1936			33	6.9	157	32.7	191	39.7	85	17.7	15	3.1	52.34
20	1937			43	8.7	170	34.4	184	37.2	81	16.4	16	3.2	51.75
21	1942			28	5.9	157	33.2	200	42.3	77	16.3	11	2.3	52.44

Continued on next page

TABLE 5-1 CONTINUED
IMPERIAL AND NATIONAL DIET
Age Distribution: All Members

Election	Year	20-29		30-39		40-49		50-59		60-69		70+		Avg. age
		No.	%	No.	%	No.	%	No.	%	No.	%	No.	%	
22	1946	6	1.3	56	12.0	179	38.2	172	36.8	49	10.5	6	1.3	49.43
23	1947	8	1.7	81	17.1	198	41.8	141	29.7	40	8.4	6	1.3	48.16
24	1949	2	0.4	84	17.9	198	42.3	138	29.5	39	8.3	7	1.5	47.83
25	1952	1	0.2	24	5.1	142	30.4	201	43.0	82	17.6	17	3.6	52.56
26	1953	1	0.2	28	6.0	159	34.0	198	42.4	74	15.8	7	1.5	51.87
27	1955			31	6.5	135	28.5	195	41.1	98	20.7	15	3.2	53.08
28	1958	1	0.2	21	4.5	130	27.6	205	43.5	94	20.0	20	4.2	54.14
29	1960	1	0.2	15	3.2	104	22.3	198	42.4	120	25.7	29	6.2	55.46
30	1963	4	0.9	14	3.0	91	19.5	189	40.5	134	28.7	35	7.5	56.10
31	1967	5	1.0	26	5.3	112	23.0	171	35.2	134	27.6	38	7.8	55.34
32	1969	4	0.3	40	8.1	107	21.8	162	33.0	138	28.1	40	8.1	55.06
33	1972	2	0.4	28	5.7	117	23.8	157	32.0	141	28.7	46	9.4	55.23
34	1976	4	0.3	35	6.8	111	21.7	194	38.0	125	24.5	42	8.2	54.97
35	1979	1	0.2	25	4.9	104	20.4	193	37.8	146	28.6	42	8.2	55.56
36	1980	1	0.2	35	6.8	107	20.9	194	38.0	135	26.4	39	7.6	55.12
37	1983			27	5.3	104	20.4	209	40.9	118	23.1	53	10.4	56.08
38	1986	1	0.2	19	3.7	102	19.9	174	34.0	161	31.4	55	10.7	56.59
39	1990			26	5.1	123	24.0	161	31.4	163	31.8	39	7.6	56.11

TABLE 5-2
IMPERIAL AND NATIONAL DIET
Age Distribution: New Members

	Election Year	20-29 No.	20-29 %	30-39 No.	30-39 %	40-49 No.	40-49 %	50-59 No.	50-59 %	60-69 No.	60-69 %	70+ No.	70+ %	Avg. age
2	1892	166		80	48.2	60	36.1	22	13.3	4	2.4			41.22
3-4	1894	265		113	42.6	100	37.7	46	17.4	5	1.9	1	0.4	41.66
5-6	1898	258		106	41.1	109	42.2	37	14.3	6	2.3			42.28
7	1902	228		82	36.0	90	39.5	44	19.3	12	5.3			43.88
8	1903	93		31	33.3	40	43.0	17	18.3	4	4.3			44.48
9	1904	120		42	35.0	57	47.5	15	12.5	6	5.0	1	1.1	43.51
10	1908	206		60	29.1	104	50.5	34	16.5	8	3.9			44.65
11	1912	195		53	27.2	97	49.7	33	16.9	11	5.6	1	0.5	45.43
12	1915	153		33	21.6	64	41.8	49	32.0	7	4.6			48.10
13	1917	151		31	20.5	69	45.7	43	28.5	8	5.3			46.54
14	1920	277		65	23.5	123	44.4	74	26.7	15	5.4			46.29
15	1924	252		59	23.4	111	44.0	68	27.0	13	5.2	1	0.4	46.67
16	1928	173		32	18.5	81	46.8	53	30.6	7	4.0			46.42
17	1930	127		22	17.3	60	47.2	28	22.0	16	12.6	1	0.8	47.66
18	1932	128		21	16.4	66	51.6	33	25.8	8	6.3			46.66
19	1936	127		26	20.5	56	44.1	35	27.6	10	7.9			46.62
20	1937	93		18	19.4	44	47.3	24	25.8	7	7.5			46.66
21	1942	202		20	9.9	90	44.6	78	38.6	14	6.9			48.97

Continued on next page

TABLE 5-2 CONTINUED
IMPERIAL AND NATIONAL DIET
Age Distribution: New Members

	Election Year	No.	20-29 No.	%	30-39 No.	%	40-49 No.	%	50-59 No.	%	60-69 No.	%	70+ No.	%	Avg. age
22	1946	385	6	1.6	55	14.3	162	42.1	131	34.0	31	8.1			48.01
23	1947	225	6	2.7	45	20.0	100	44.4	63	28.0	10	4.4	1	0.4	45.97
24	1949	194	1	0.5	33	17.0	104	53.6	50	25.7	7	3.6			46.08
25	1952	109	1	0.9	5	4.6	50	45.9	38	34.9	14	12.9	1	0.9	49.98
26	1953	48			6	12.5	18	37.5	16	33.3	8	16.7			48.23
27	1955	57			11	19.3	17	29.8	22	38.6	7	12.3			47.98
28	1958	68	1	1.5	8	11.8	27	39.7	27	39.7	5	7.4			48.18
29	1960	59	1	1.7	6	10.2	29	49.2	19	32.2	4	6.8			48.10
30	1963	72	4	5.6	8	11.1	32	44.4	22	30.6	6	8.3			46.93
31	1967	102	3	2.9	16	15.7	53	52.0	29	28.4	1	1.0			45.11
32	1969	99	3	3.0	23	23.2	40	40.4	26	26.3	7	7.1			45.66
33	1972	95	1	1.1	12	12.6	39	41.1	35	36.8	8	8.4			48.22
34	1976	125	3	2.4	19	15.2	46	36.8	48	38.4	9	7.2			47.80
35	1979	76	1	1.3	8	10.5	29	38.2	32	42.1	6	7.9			48.64
36	1980	36			8	22.2	15	41.7	13	36.1					45.27
37	1983	84			13	15.5	28	33.3	38	45.2	5	6.0			48.69
38	1986	64	1	1.6	10	15.6	24	37.5	27	42.2	2	3.1			46.88
39	1990	133			21	15.8	55	41.4	39	29.3	18	13.5			48.25

Two other factors that the age trends signalize have already been noted and will be amplified in the concluding chapters. These are the discontinuity provided respectively by the descent into "fascism" in the 1930s and the loss of the war/Occupation beginning in 1945.

The average age of all persons elected to the House of Representatives in the Japanese Diet was 45.64 at the time of their first election. It was 44.76 for the prewar members and 47.28 for those elected for the first time after the war. This latter figure, incidentally, is about five and one-half years greater than the average age of the members of the British House of Commons at the time of their first election in the 1945-1974 period studied by Mellors. This discrepancy can be accounted for, in part, by the fact that far fewer Japanese in their twenties and far more Japanese in their fifties were recruited by political parties as first time candidates.

The significance of the age patterns for parliamentary government in Japan is worth pondering. Does the pattern signify that a gradually aging set of representatives parallels the "graying" of society at large and is, therefore, truly representative and hence "democratic"? Does it simply mean that politics is properly a middle-aged profession and that the parameters of middle age like those of the middle class are stretching to meet new conditions? Or, does it indicate a retreat from participatory democracy toward "spectator democracy", a charge sometimes levelled within Japan these days? Whatever the answer, we should evaluate these data against the criteria set up at the outset and which were designed to test the validity of the hypothesis of Japan as a stable, gradually evolving state. Looked at from this perspective, the age distribution patterns again suggest that, except for the Occupation, Japanese politics has been the scene of gradual and steady trends featuring incremental change rather than violent or eratic fluctuations.

Of course, when dealing with as many individuals as we are here, averages would not be expected to fluctuate greatly from one time to the next. Nevertheless, the movement is constant, election by election, in a steady upward direction, except for the immediate postwar period. In terms of age distribution, in fact, the Occupation, not the fascist "dark valley" represents the aberration, the period of most obvious discontinuity.

In the postwar House of Commons Mellors found that the Labour Party generally recruited slightly older persons to run as candidates than did the Conservative Party. He attributed this to Labour's attachment to the labor unions wherein status had first to be attained before the party could approve of an individual's candidacy. The average age for Britain was 40.9 for new Conservative Party candidates and 42.5 for new candidates representing Labour.

In the Japanese case, the Japan Socialist Party is and has been similarly dependent upon organized labor for both support and candidates. Until recently, however, JSP members have averaged about three years younger than conservative (LDP) members. Beginning with the 1979 election the Socialist average has been higher than that of the LDP in each election except one. (See Graph 5-2). More revealing are the data in Table 5-3 showing that the LDP has been able to recruit younger persons than the LDP in every election but one (1969) since 1963. The average age of Socialist members has been over fifty for the last five elections. This is due, no doubt, to circumstances similar to those prevailing in Britain. With its overall support base shrinking, the JSP has apparently had to turn increasingly to veteran union leadership and its sponsorship to provide candidates. This is despite the fact that the percentage of persons with union background has been declining for some time. (See Chapter Eight).

TABLE 5-3
NATIONAL DIET
Average Age of New Members by Party

JSP No.	JSP Avg. age	+/- LDP	YEAR	LDP No.	LDP Avg. age	+/- JSP
84	46.73	-1.61	1946	291	48.34	+1.61
73	43.97	-2.91	1947	138	46.88	+2.91
11	42.45	-4.17	1949	153	46.62	+4.17
34	41.26	-11.17	1952	72	52.43	+11.17
21	47.86	-2.53	1953	23	50.39	+2.53
21	44.62	-7.45	1955	30	52.07	+7.45
25	46.56	-3.85	1958	32	50.41	+3.85
26	46.65	-1.09	1960	31	47.74	+1.09
24	49.00	+4.09	1963	43	44.91	-4.09
33	47.42	+2.60	1967	33	44.82	-2.60
12	41.50	-5.39	1969	47	46.89	+5.39
28	49.43	+2.94	1972	37	46.69	-2.94
28	50.43	+2.80	1976	51	47.63	-2.80
13	53.31	+10.32	1979	35	42.49	-10.32
7	51.29	+7.37	1980	25	43.92	-7.37
22	50.73	+3.66	1983	30	47.07	-3.66
10	52.60	+5.30	1986	44	47.30	-5.30
56	52.11	+6.72	1990	48	45.39	-6.72

The figures in the LDP column for 1946-1953 include members of all conservative parties. In the JSP column are included for the same years those who switched to the DSP in 1960.

Continued on next page

TABLE 5-3 CONTINUED
NATIONAL DIET
Average Age of New Members by Party

Average Age of All New Members at the Time of the First Election
By Party

Postwar

LDP	47.54
JSP	50.08
JCP	47.08
DSP	49.46
KOMEITO	42.93

GRAPH 5-2

AGE BY PARTY

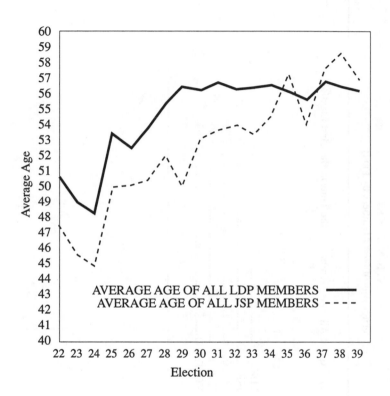

NOTES

1   Mellors, *The British M.P.*, p. 27.

2   Mellors, *The British M.P.*, pp. 27-35.

3   The "aberration" theory or "dark valley" concept is taken up in a section of a recent book in English, *Japan Examined* (1983), edited by Harry Wray and Hilary Conroy. There is a chapter entitled "The 1930s. Aberration or Logical Outcome?" which features articles by Robert M. Spaulding and George O. Totten essentially arguing in favor of the "aberration" theory. Also presented are dissenting views, particularly that of Kisaka Jun'ichirō who describes the aggression of the 1930s as a "logical outcome of Meiji policy". The positions expressed in this book are not new, having been developed by others some-what earlier. See, for example, Ōuchi Tsutomu, *Fuashizumu e no Michi* (1967), pp. 422-450; Richard Storry, *A History of Modern Japan* (1960), Chapter 8, pp. 182-213; Thomas R. Havens, *Valley of Darkness: the Japanese People and World War Two* (1978), especially Chapter 1, pp. 6-9. The very title of the last named book suggests, if not aberration, the concept of a trough or valley which implies heights on either side.

Chapter 6

Regions and Prefectures

■

Analysis of regional differences in the characteristics of Diet members reveals no startling statistical discrepancies. Individual prefectures, on the other hand, present a different story, one that permits analysis based on certain historical factors. This chapter, thus, examines the forty-seven prefectures according to the same charcteristics used in the previous chapters, following the same four-fold division. In Chapters Two, Three and Four national averages for these four cohort groups have been indicated respectively for occupation (Chapter Two), education (Chapter Three), and length of service or professionalism (Chapter Four). Chapter Eight deals with apprenticeship. The earlier chapters dealt frequently with "A" and "B" types statistically and the Introduction explained a formula for determining "elite status" of a particular cohort group. This chapter applies this formula to the representatives from each prefecture. It is also used in the next chapter and in Chapter Nine which deals with women representatives.

In the following tables using the four-fold division Table 6-1 lists the prefectures in their north to south regional order along with the plus or minus elite rating for all of the members. Table 6-1 also indicates the rank in elite status from one to forty-seven. Table 6-2 lists the prefectures in rank order for each of the four time divisions.

The first thing apparent in looking over the figures in these tables is the absence of a correlation between a high elite rating and economic development in any of the time periods. That is to say, the most highly developed, urbanized and "modernized" prefectures do not have the higher elite ratings. In fact, such prefectures tend to rest at points below the median.

In the case of a few prefectures there were dramatic changes from high elite ratings before the war to low ratings in the postwar period. The most notable of these was Kōchi which had the highest prewar elite rating, but fell to thirty-second place (thirtieth for new postwar) for the postwar era. Ehime, Fukuoka and

TABLE 6-1
IMPERIAL AND NATIONAL DIET
Membership Elite Status by Prefecture

Prefecture	All members		Prewar		All Postwar		New Postwar	
	ratio	rank	ratio	rank	ratio	rank	ratio	rank
HOKKAIDŌ	-27.1	42	-42.5	44	-46.4	46	-70.3	47
AOMORI	-23.7	38	-18.3	37	-52.5	47	-61.4	46
IWATE	+16.5	10	+18.0	9	+6.5	21	+11.6	17
MIYAGI	+38.4	3	+30.7	7	+51.1	1	+52.5	1
AKITA	-3.6	26	-13.9	32	+0.9	25	-1.8	26
YAMAGATA	+10.0	14	+5.7	22	+26.2	7	+27.5	6
FUKUSHIMA	-4.8	27	-19.5	38	-12.3	34	-12.3	33
IBARAKI	+8.7	15	+13.6	13	-4.7	30	-9.1	31
TOCHIGI	+0.2	24	+1.8	25	+14.1	14	+5.7	23
GUMMA	-8.5	33	-8.6	29	-36.2	43	-16.3	37
SAITAMA	+1.4	22	+7.6	18	-20.0	37	-23.9	41
CHIBA	-1.9	25	+7.6	18	-22.6	38	-21.6	39
TOKYŌ	+37.1	4	+41.1	5	+19.7	10	+20.4	11
KANAGAWA	+1.2	23	-7.2	26	-4.3	29	-8.1	29
NIIGATA	-26.1	41	-36.3	42	-2.9	27	+9.1	20
TOYAMA	-25.7	40	-18.1	36	-10.7	33	-17.3	38

Continued on next page

TABLE 6-1 CONTINUED
IMPERIAL AND NATIONAL DIET
Membership Elite Status by Prefecture

Prefecture	All members		Prewar		All Postwar		New Postwar	
	ratio	rank	ratio	rank	ratio	rank	ratio	rank
ISHIKAWA	-7.5	32	-14.0	33	+28.6	6	+21.8	10
FUKUI	-54.5	47	-55.3	46	-9.3	31	-10.1	32
YAMANASHI	-40.3	46	-56.0	47	+0.1	26	+7.2	22
NAGANO	+6.4	17	+9.7	14	+1.8	23	+10.8	19
GIFU	-39.8	45	-44.7	45	+11.8	16	+17.4	12
SHIZUOKA	-6.0	29	-26.3	41	+3.9	22	+4.5	24
AICHI	-11.8	34	-9.9	30	-2.9	27	-12.8	34
MIE	+6.1	18	+6.6	21	+11.4	17	+16.6	14
SHIGA	-36.5	44	-37.1	43	-22.6	38	-5.6	28
KYŌTO	-15.1	36	-16.6	35	+15.5	12	+2.6	25
ŌSAKA	-5.3	28	+6.9	20	-24.4	42	-27.3	42
HYŌGO	+10.5	13	+4.3	23	+10.0	19	+24.7	7
NARA	-34.7	43	-25.0	40	-40.2	44	-39.7	44
WAKAYAMA	+32.7	6	+35.8	6	+13.6	15	+24.3	8
TOTTORI	-24.2	39	-13.8	31	-42.4	45	-40.8	45
SHIMANE	-15.6	37	-15.3	34	+21.6	9	+23.9	9

Continued on next page

TABLE 6-1 CONTINUED
IMPERIAL AND NATIONAL DIET
Membership Elite Status by Prefecture

Prefecture	All members ratio	All members rank	Prewar ratio	Prewar rank	All Postwar ratio	All Postwar rank	New Postwar ratio	New Postwar rank
OKAYAMA	+43.1	1	+50.1	4	+45.5	2	+37.4	4
HIROSHIMA	+12.3	12	+9.3	16	+16.5	11	+11.8	16
YAMAGUCHI	-6.2	30	-7.9	27	+11.3	18	+8.3	21
TOKUSHIMA	+5.3	19	+8.3	17	+9.3	20	+12.9	15
KAGAWA	-14.3	35	-21.8	39	+15.5	12	+11.4	18
EHIME	+1.5	21	+14.1	11	-23.2	41	-21.7	40
KOCHI	+42.3	2	+73.0	1	-9.6	32	-8.7	30
FUKUOKA	+4.9	20	+14.0	12	-13.4	36	-16.2	36
SAGA	+16.8	9	+14.7	10	+30.5	4	+31.1	5
NAGASAKI	+6.6	16	+3.8	24	-12.4	35	-13.3	35
KUMAMOTO	+6.6	16	+9.5	15	+25.6	8	+17.4	12
OITA	+31.3	7	+50.4	3	+1.2	24	-4.7	27
MIYAZAKI	+13.4	11	-8.4	28	+30.0	5	+45.0	3
KAGOSHIMA	+30.6	8	+26.4	8	+41.1	3	+48.3	2
OKINAWA	+34.3	5	+59.6	2	-22.8	40	-30.0	43

Ōita also displayed this tendency as did Okinawa. The latter, however, may be dismissed in this analysis as its circumstances were irregular in both prewar and postwar times.

The reverse phenomenon, where the change from low prewar to high postwar elite ratings was apparent, is seen for Shimane (-15.3 to +23.9), Miyazaki (-8.4 to +45.0), Kagawa (-21.8 to +11.4) and Gifu (-44.7 to +17.4).

Prefectures with high elite ratings in both prewar and postwar periods are Miyagi, Tokyo, Wakayama, Okayama, Saga and Kagoshima.

A close examination reveals that, on the whole, Kyūshū prefectures had high prewar elite ratings. Only Miyazaki had a negative rating and only Nagasaki was on the negative side for all members, prewar and postwar. In the postwar era three of the top five elite ratings were for Kyūshū prefectures: Kagoshima, Miyazaki and Saga. Consistent negative ratings are found for Hokkaidō (an abnormal local unit), Aomori, Gumma, Toyama, Fukui, Nara and Tottori.

The most significant analytical element I can find here is that eight of the ten highest rated prefectures were in territories formerly ruled by tozama daimyō. To be sure, Okinawa should be eliminated from consideration, but the difference is startling even without Okinawa. The only prefectures with high prewar elite ratings that were in lands formerly in the hands of shimpan or fudai daimyō were Tokyo (ranked fifth) and Wakayama (sixth). This does not indicate that tozama realms were more politicized by the beginning of the constitutional era. Rather, it suggests that political parties were better organized in these prefectures and better able to recruit individuals with the kinds of backgrounds that I call "elite"; namely, those with university education and "modern" occupations, like government service, law and journalism. These were persons, in short, whose outlook was more national than provincial.

Now, in contrast, the ten lowest ranked prefectures were all in territories ruled by shimpan or fudai daimyo or else directly controlled by the Bakufu before the Meiji Restoration. There are two partial exceptions to this. Hokkaidō was not entirely or consistenty under direct Bakufu administration before 1868; much of it was classified as Tozama. Fukushima, a large prefecture, consisted of several daimiates , some of which were tozama before the Restoration. Again, however, the pattern is clear that pre-restoration affiliation with the Bakufu meant fewer elites among the elected representatives under the constitution. This historical association appears to be the only clear factor differentiating prefectures with high and low elite ratings in the prewar period.

Any carry-over from the feudal period, whatever form it might take, could be expected to be stronger in the 19th and early 20th centuries. It was, after all, individuals from tozama domains who led the overthrow of the Bakufu. That the most active areas should provide the most "modern" and "elite" representatives in the electoral system is not, perhaps, surprising. Not all restoration leaders, however, favored elected representation and agitation for a constitution and representative government was strongest in areas neglected by the Meiji oligarchy. Significantly, the one prefecture with the highest prewar rating - Kōchi - is that of Tosa han, home of Itagaki and other early advocates of a constitution. Saga, the home prefecture of Ōkuma (Hizen) and Ōita (Bungo and Bizen), original home of Fukuzawa, also had higher than average prewar elite status ratings.

A pattern of this sort does not hold up for the postwar. In fact, it is impossible to see much in common for the ten highest rated postwar prefectures. The top five were also former tozama realms, but only six of the top ten. Miyagi (ranked first for postwar elite status), Kagoshima (second), Okayama (fourth), and Hyōgo (seventh) contain large cities, though not immense ones. The others do not have large urban aggregations within their borders. Perhaps it is worthy of comment that only two of the highest rated postwar ten (Hyōgo and Okayama) are part of the postwar economic core area of Japan - the Pacific Belt.

Prefectures with low postwar elite ratings also display little in common with one another, although the lowest five (Hokkaidō, Aomori, Tottori, Nara and Okinawa) are all located outside the core area and are rather low in population density. The other low rated prefectures include Ōsaka, Saitama and Chiba, all core areas where the population has grown substantially in postwar times. The figures for prefectural elite status signify that Japan has become increasingly integrated, homogenized and structured. The result is that the recruitment of politicians, regardless of region or party, is likely to focus on individuals with elite credentials. The national educational system has long made it possible for persons from outlying areas to gain access to the center through university attendance. This, in turn, contributed to their "national" rather than "provincial" orientation, an attractive attribute for political recruitment. Thus, sophisticated "elite" politicians in Japan are as likely to come from any one area as from another in recent times.

TABLE 6-2
IMPERIAL AND NATIONAL DIET
Membership Elite Status by Prefecture

	All Members			Prewar Members			All Postwar Members			New Postwar Members	
Rank	Prefecture	ratio	Rank	Prefecture	ratio	Rank	Prefecture	ratio	Rank	Prefecture	ratio
1	OKAYAMA	+43.1	1	KOCHI	+73.0	1	MIYAGI	+51.1	1	MIYAGI	+52.5
2	KOCHI	+42.3	2	OKINAWA	+59.6	2	OKAYAMA	+45.5	2	KAGOSHIMA	+48.3
3	MIYAGI	+38.4	3	OITA	+50.4	3	KAGOSHIMA	+41.1	3	MIYAZAKI	+45.0
4	TOKYO	+37.1	4	OKAYAMA	+50.1	4	SAGA	+30.5	4	OKAYAMA	+37.4
5	OKINAWA	+34.3	5	TOKYO	+41.1	5	MIYAZAKI	+30.0	5	SAGA	+31.1
6	WAKAYAMA	+32.7	6	WAKAYAMA	+35.8	6	ISHIKAWA	+28.6	6	YAMAGATA	+27.5
7	OITA	+31.3	7	MIYAGI	+30.7	7	YAMAGATA	+26.2	7	HYOGO	+24.7
8	KAGOSHIMA	+30.6	8	KAGOSHIMA	+26.4	8	KUMAMOTO	+25.6	8	WAKAYAMA	+24.3
9	SAGA	+16.8	9	IWATE	+18.0	9	SHIMANE	+21.6	9	SHIMANE	+23.9
10	IWATE	+16.5	10	SAGA	+14.7	10	TOKYO	+19.7	10	ISHIKAWA	+21.8
11	MIYAZAKI	+13.4	11	EHIME	+14.1	11	HIROSHIMA	+16.5	11	TOKYO	+20.4
12	HIROSHIMA	+12.3	12	FUKUOKA	+14.0	12	KAGAWA	+15.5	12	GIFU	+17.4
13	HYOGO	+10.5	13	IBARAKI	+13.6	12	KYOTO	+15.5	12	KUMAMOTO	+17.4
14	YAMAGATA	+10.0	14	NAGANO	+9.7	14	TOCHIGI	+14.1	14	MIE	+16.6
15	IBARAKI	+8.7	15	KUMAMOTO	+9.5	15	WAKAYAMA	+13.6	15	TOKUSHIMA	+12.9
16	KUMAMOTO	+6.6	16	HIROSHIMA	+9.3	16	GIFU	+11.8	16	HIROSHIMA	+11.8

Continued on next page

TABLE 6-2 CONTINUED
IMPERIAL AND NATIONAL DIET
Membership Elite Status by Prefecture

	All Members			Prewar Members			All Postwar Members			New Postwar Members	
Rank	Prefecture	ratio	Rank	Prefecture	ratio	Rank	Prefecture	ratio	Rank	Prefecture	ratio
17	NAGANO	+6.4	17	TOKUSHIMA	+8.3	17	MIE	+11.4	17	IWATE	+11.6
18	MIE	+6.1	18	SAITAMA	+7.6	18	YAMAGUCHI	+11.3	18	KAGAWA	+11.4
19	TOKUSHIMA	+5.3	18	CHIBA	+7.6	19	HYOGO	+10.0	19	NAGANO	+10.8
20	FUKUOKA	+4.9	20	OSAKA	+6.9	20	TOKUSHIMA	+9.3	20	NIIGATA	+9.1
21	EHIME	+1.5	21	MIE	+6.6	21	IWATE	+6.5	21	YAMAGUCHI	+8.3
22	SAITAMA	+1.4	22	YAMAGATA	+5.7	22	SHIZUOKA	+3.9	22	YAMANASHI	+7.2
23	KANAGAWA	+1.2	23	HYOGO	+4.3	23	NAGANO	+1.8	23	TOCHIGI	+5.7
24	TOCHIGI	+0.2	24	NAGASAKI	+3.8	24	OITA	+1.2	24	SHIZUOKA	+4.5
25	CHIBA	-1.9	25	TOCHIGI	+1.8	25	AKITA	+0.9	25	KYOTO	+2.6
26	AKITA	-3.6	26	KANAGAWA	-7.2	26	YAMANASHI	+0.1	26	AKITA	-1.8
27	FUKUSHIMA	-4.8	27	YAMAGUCHI	-7.9	27	AICHI	-2.9	27	OITA	-4.7
28	OSAKA	-5.3	28	MIYAZAKI	-8.4	27	NIIGATA	-2.9	28	SHIGA	-5.6
29	SHIZUOKA	-6.0	29	GUMMA	-8.6	29	KANAGAWA	-4.3	29	KANAGAWA	-8.1
30	YAMAGUCHI	-6.2	30	AICHI	-9.9	30	IBARAKI	-4.7	30	KOCHI	-8.7
31	NAGASAKI	-6.6	31	TOTTORI	-13.8	31	FUKUI	-9.3	31	IBARAKI	-9.1
32	ISHIKAWA	-7.5	32	AKITA	-13.9	32	KOCHI	-9.6	32	FUKUI	-10.1

Continued on next page

TABLE 6-2 CONTINUED
IMPERIAL AND NATIONAL DIET
Membership Elite Status by Prefecture

All Members			Prewar Members			All Postwar Members			New Postwar Members		
Rank	Prefecture	ratio	Rank	Prefecture	ratio	Rank	Prefecture	ratio	Rank	Prefecture	ratio
33	GUMMA	-8.5	33	ISHIKAWA	-14.0	33	TOYAMA	-10.7	33	FUKUSHIMA	-12.3
34	AICHI	-11.8	34	SHIMANE	-15.3	34	FUKUSHIMA	-12.3	34	AICHI	-12.8
35	KAGAWA	-14.3	35	KYOTO	-16.6	35	NAGASAKI	-12.4	35	NAGASAKI	-13.3
36	KYOTO	-15.1	36	TOYAMA	-18.1	36	FUKUOKA	-13.4	36	FUKUOKA	-16.2
37	SHIMANE	-15.6	37	AOMORI	-18.3	37	SAITAMA	-20.0	37	GUMMA	-16.3
38	AOMORI	-23.7	38	FUKUSHIMA	-19.5	38	CHIBA	-22.6	38	TOYAMA	-17.3
39	TOTTORI	-24.2	39	KAGAWA	-21.8	38	SHIGA	-22.6	39	CHIBA	-21.6
40	TOYAMA	-25.7	40	NARA	-25.0	40	OKINAWA	-22.8	40	EHIME	-21.7
41	NIIGATA	-26.1	41	SHIZUOKA	-26.3	41	EHIME	-23.3	41	SAITAMA	-23.9
42	HOKKAIDO	-27.1	42	NIIGATA	-36.3	42	OSAKA	-24.4	42	OSAKA	-27.3
43	NARA	-34.7	43	SHIGA	-37.1	43	GUMMA	-36.2	43	OKINAWA	-30.0
44	SHIGA	-36.5	44	HOKKAIDO	-42.5	44	NARA	-40.2	44	NARA	-39.7
45	GIFU	-39.8	45	GIFU	-44.7	45	TOTTORI	-42.4	45	TOTTORI	-40.8
46	YAMANASHI	-40.8	46	FUKUI	-55.3	46	HOKKAIDO	-46.4	46	AOMORI	-61.4
47	FUKUI	-54.5	47	YAMANASHI	-56.0	47	AOMORI	-52.5	47	HOKKAIDO	-70.3

Chapter 7

Party

■

This chapter examines the membership of the House of Representatives according to party affiliation, but for the postwar period only. There have been some previous attempts to analyze statistically the party membership for portions of the prewar era.[1] For the most part, however, the prewar parties were all bourgeois in nature, hence similar in quality. Moreover, there were numerous party crossovers, defections and reaffiliations so that a serious analysis of the overall pattern by party is next to impossible.[2] In the previous sections of this work there has been frequent reference to association with political parties. Hence, here is broken down the party membership in simplified fashion for the postwar period. Although this kind of thing has been done elsewhere[3], a new approach is followed here.

In the following lists are grouped all members of conservative parties, including those in existence before 1955, under the heading of the LDP. The number of postwar Diet members who switched parties is not great, but there have been some. Since, when evaluating the entire membership, they cannot be counted under both columns, such individuals have been placed under the party to which they switched.

The party by party comparison of all postwar members contains few surprises. In the occupational realm business and government service dominate among conservative (LDP) members. Almost half of all LDPers came from these two occupational backgrounds. By contrast, all of the opposition parties have low percentages in these categories. The JSP and DSP both have fairly high percentages coming from the labor movement while all of the opposition parties recruited many whose occupations can be called "politics" before they entered the Diet. This is especially true of DSP and Kōmeitō assemblymen, many of whom served as party functionaries before winning endorsement and election. The JSP membership attained double digit percentages in only one occupational field other

TABLE 7-1
COMPARISON BY PARTY OF ALL POSTWAR MEMBERS

Occupation	LDP(1337) no.	%	JSP(552) no.	%	JCP(96) no.	%	DSP(85) no.	%	KOMEI(103) no.	%
Agriculture	74	5.5	29	5.3	0	-	5	5.9	1	1.0
Business	379	28.3	31	5.6	0	-	5	5.9	6	5.8
Education	78	5.8	59	10.7	9	9.4	5	5.9	3	2.9
Higher Ed.	27	2.0	15	2.7	4	4.2	2	2.4	2	1.9
Govt. (Central)	178	13.8	16	2.9	1	1.0	2	2.4	3	2.9
Govt. (Home Min.)	81	6.1	2	0.4	0	-	0	-	1	1.0
Total C. Govt.	259	19.4	18	3.3	1	1.0	2	2.4	4	3.9
Local Govt.	38	2.8	11	2.0	4	4.2	1	1.2	6	5.8
Journalism	111	8.3	31	5.6	8	8.3	3	3.5	6	5.8
Law	89	6.7	58	10.5	20	20.8	5	5.9	9	8.7
Labor/Soc.	0	-	91	16.5	7	7.3	14	16.5	1	1.0
Medicine	32	2.4	14	2.5	3	3.1	1	1.2	5	4.9
Military	6	0.4	0	-	0	-	0	-	0	-
Politics	156	11.7	106	19.2	22	22.9	31	36.5	39	37.9
Religion	5	0.5	5	0.9	0	-	0	-	0	-
Women's Orgs.	2	0.1	2	0.4	2	2.1	0	-	1	1.0
Writing	5	0.5	4	0.7	5	5.2	0	-	0	-
Blue Collar	0	-	42	7.6	7	7.3	0	-	0	-
White Collar	75	5.6	33	6.0	3	3.1	11	12.9	10	9.7
Soka Gakkai	0	-	0	-	0	-	0	-	10	9.7
Other/None	1	0.1	3	0.5	1	1.0	0	-	0	-

Continued on next page

TABLE 7-1 CONTINUED
COMPARISON BY PARTY OF ALL POSTWAR MEMBERS

Education	LDP(1337) no.	%	JSP(552) no.	%	JCP(96) no.	%	DSP(85) no.	%	KOMEI(103) no.	%
University	971	72.6	291	52.7	65	67.7	56	65.9	67	65.0
Major Univ.	837	62.6	216	39.1	48	50.0	43	50.6	35	34.0
TODAI	317	23.7	69	12.5	18	18.8	13	15.3	3	2.9
KYODAI	58	4.3	14	2.5	7	7.3	9	10.6	3	2.9
WASEDA	153	11.4	46	8.3	6	6.3	5	5.9	8	7.8
KEIO	66	4.9	5	0.9	2	2.1	6	7.1	7	6.8
MEIJI	62	4.6	11	2.0	4	4.2	1	1.2	3	2.9
CHUO	74	5.5	31	5.6	6	6.3	4	4.7	4	3.9
NIHON	63	4.7	23	4.2	4	4.2	5	5.9	4	3.9
HOSEI	19	1.4	7	1.3	0	-	0	-	0	-
TOHOKU	18	1.3	8	1.4	1	1.0	0	-	3	2.9
HOKUDAI	7	0.5	2	0.4	0	-	0	-	0	-
High(er) School	19	1.4	35	6.3	10	10.4	2	2.4	5	4.9
Middle School	48	3.6	23	4.2	4	4.2	2	2.4	5	4.9
Elementary	8	0.6	14	2.5	1	1.0	5	5.9	2	1.9
Private Educ.	2	0.1	0	-	0	-	0	-	0	-
Other Schools	189	14.1	129	23.4	9	9.4	20	23.5	23	22.3
None Listed	100	7.5	60	10.9	7	7.3	0	-	1	1.0

Continued on next page

TABLE 7-1 CONTINUED
COMPARISON BY PARTY OF ALL POSTWAR MEMBERS

	LDP(1337) no.	%	JSP(552) no.	%	JCP(96) no.	%	DSP(85) no.	%	KOMEI(103) no.	%
Local Assy. Mem.	430	32.2	196	35.5	17	17.7	30	35.3	40	38.8
Co. Directors	583	43.6	54	9.8	0	–	3	3.5	5	4.9
Union Background	4	0.3	233	42.2	20	20.8	27	31.8	1	1.0
Female members	33	2.5	28	5.1	14	14.6	3	3.5	3	2.9
Avg. no. of times elected	4.44		4.03		2.92		3.72		3.97	

than labor or politics - education. They did, however, come very close in law at 9.9%. In fact, in education and law, which I have described as "elite" type "modern" occupations, the JSP and the JCP both topped the conservative LDP. Indeed, 20.7% of all successful Communist candidates were attorneys, a figure far higher than for any other party.

In educational background the LDP collectively has the most prestigious pedigree, followed by the JCP and the DSP. The JSP and Kōmeitō bring up the rear. It is mildly surprising that the JCP and DSP have university attendance figures so close to those of the LDP. The figures confirm statistically, however, the common belief that these two opposition parties have attracted intellectuals. Although sixty-five percent of Kōmeitō members have attended universities, only about half of them attended the more prestigious ones and only three (2.9%) are graduates of Todai. Kōmeitō's educational profile is the least elite in composition.

It is worth noting and perhaps significant that the JCP has the highest percentage of female members. This will draw more detailed comment in a later chapter. Professionalism, measured by times elected as covered in Chapter Four, is nearly equal for all parties except the JCP whose fortunes have been subject to more violent fluctuations than any other postwar political association.

In the introduction I explained a formula for determining the elite status ratings of cohort groups of Diet members. I applied this to various prefectures in the previous chapters. Applying the same formula to the postwar membership by party, I come up with the following elite ratings:

	All Postwar	New Postwar
LDP	+8.1	+6.0
JSP	-10.9	-8.2
JCP	*	+27.9
DSP	-8.5	-9.6
KOMEITO	*	-26.5

* No members elected before 1946

These figures are rather interesting. The disparity between the two major parties is about what one would expect. The LDP is more elite oriented, but not to an overwhelming degree. The JSP is non-elite, but not excessively. Despite higher educational levels, the non-elite rating of the DSP is very close to that of the JSP. The two outstanding features are the very high rating of the JCP and the very low rating of the Kōmeitō. This confirms, but more pointedly than expected, the common notion that the JCP has drawn heavily from elite background individuals and that the Kōmeitō is representative of a portion of the urban under-class in the 1960s and after.[4]

Table 7-2 compares the two major parties election by election in selected occupational and educational categories. A close inspection of the figures reveals some trends in both parties. There are several classifications where significant percentage changes occurred over the course of the last forty years.

With its strong support base in the teachers union, the JSP had consistently high percentages of its members drawn from the field of education. The percentage of JSP Diet members who had teaching careers dropped below ten only three times (to 9.0% in 1947, 9.1% in 1986 and 9.5% in 1990). The rest of the time it hovered between 10.8% and 13.7%. The LDP, on the other hand, recruited educators heavily only in the early postwar years. Of the successful conservative candidates in 1946 14.9% listed education as their primary occupation. This figure fell to 10.6% in 1947 and has been under five percent ever since 1949.

Chapter Two covered the central government bureaucracy as a source of recruitment for membership in general. The decline in the overall figures for that occupational category is due largely to what happened in the ranks of the LDP. The pattern, however, is rather like the familiar bell-shaped curve. During the Occupation , ex-bureaucrats were often *personae non gratae*. Hence, few stood for election. Then, however, their numbers shot up before falling again. In the 1963 election over thirty percent of the successful LDP candidates were former bureaucrats. This figure has now dwindled to between twelve and fourteen percent as the dominant party has emphasized persons whose entire careers may be described as political. Many of these are proteges of LDP members whom they served as secretaries or legislative assistants.[5]

As noted in Chapter Two the ranks of former journalists in the House of Representatives have diminished since the 1950s. Both major parties have apparently stopped serious recruiting from that source. The same decline is seen in law where, the fall off of JSP attorneys has been much more dramatic.

Although the percentage of "pure politicians" among all postwar members is higher for the JSP than the LDP, the figures have been nearly identical in each election since the late 1970s. Many of the socialists had labor union affiliations without, however, considering union work as their primary occupation. For this reason, JSP recruitment of "pure politicians" from the ranks of the unions began somewhat sooner than in the LDP.

Among members with university education, the percentage in the JSP was actually higher than in the LDP in the first postwar election of 1946. This is largely due to the purging of the "best and the brightest." Thereafter, JSP figures for university educated rose into the sixty percentile range, but dropped back again to settle at around fifty percent of the Diet membership. LDPers with university training, however, increased steadily as the general population of the nation became better educated.. The LDP rate of university educated stood in 1990 at 91.2%, the highest level ever.

TABLE 7-2
NATIONAL DIET
Comparison, by Election, of Selected Occupational and Educational Categories
Conservatives (LDP) vs Socialists (JSP)

	Education		C. Govt.		Journalism		Law		Politics		University		TODAI	
	LDP	JSP	LDP	JSP	LDP	JSP	LDP	JSP	LDP	JSP	LDP	JSP	LDP	JSP
1946	14.9	11.9	9.8	5.0	8.4	11.9	7.3	17.8	3.7	3.0	53.7	55.4	10.4	18.8
1947	10.6	9.0	15.4	3.5	12.3	11.7	9.0	13.8	1.9	4.1	68.7	56.6	12.6	17.2
1949	3.9	10.8	20.3	1.5	12.2	4.6	7.8	18.5	1.7	4.6	70.6	56.9	19.4	10.8
1952	4.4	12.2	27.8	3.4	11.7	9.6	10.2	20.0	2.3	3.5	77.2	63.5	29.5	15.7
1953	4.4	12.0	29.6	4.5	13.5	9.8	9.1	16.5	2.5	6.0	78.6	60.9	28.3	17.3
1955	4.5	12.4	29.8	5.5	10.4	7.6	9.7	15.2	2.6	4.8	78.3	59.3	30.7	13.8
1958	4.6	12.1	29.8	6.4	12.6	7.1	7.6	10.0	3.3	5.0	78.8	57.4	30.5	11.3
1960	4.0	13.4	28.1	5.4	13.5	7.4	7.9	10.1	4.3	6.7	81.2	53.7	32.3	14.1
1963	3.1	13.7	30.8	5.9	10.6	6.5	5.5	6.5	7.2	13.1	82.9	52.9	34.9	12.4
1967	3.2	12.3	29.1	2.1	11.3	4.8	5.7	5.5	10.3	17.8	84.4	49.3	34.8	9.6
1969	3.0	13.5	24.2	4.2	9.9	2.1	5.0	7.3	11.3	15.6	83.1	51.0	33.4	9.4
1972	2.8	12.7	22.2	1.7	8.1	1.7	4.9	3.4	17.3	22.9	83.0	52.5	32.2	8.5
1976	1.9	12.2	18.2	0.8	8.9	1.6	3.3	5.7	25.2	29.3	85.9	49.6	31.5	10.6
1979	1.5	11.7	14.1	0.9	7.6	0.9	4.2	4.5	31.6	32.4	84.8	52.3	28.1	6.3
1980	1.7	10.9	12.7	0.9	7.0	0.9	4.0	6.4	34.6	30.0	85.9	50.0	28.9	8.2
1983	2.3	11.3	12.6	0.9	6.9	0.9	4.2	4.3	37.8	34.8	85.9	50.4	29.0	4.3
1986	2.0	9.1	12.4	1.1	5.6	1.1	4.3	4.5	36.1	37.5	87.9	52.3	28.9	4.5
1990	1.1	9.5	13.8	0.7	6.4	2.9	3.2	8.8	35.0	38.7	91.2	52.6	27.2	7.3

For Todai matriculants, the pattern is similar. In the first two postwar elections a higher percentage of socialist candidates were Todai alumni. When the Occupation ended, however, and depurging took over, many prewar elites with Todai backgrounds reentered the conservative parties and won election to the Diet. LDP Todai representation reached its zenith in 1963 at 34.9%. Since then, it has fallen back slightly to about the level of 1952. JSP Todai affiliates have dropped precipitously from double digit percentages to less than five percent in the last two elections. The JSP appears to be on an ever so gradual course of de-intellectualizing itself over the past forty years.

Chapter Five noted the age differentials between the two most important parties. Graph 5-2 is illustrative. Successful socialist candidates averaged about three years younger than their conservative counterparts until the 35th election in October 1979. In that election, however, the average age of JSP members exceeded that of the LDP, a situation that was repeated in 1983, 1986 and 1990. That this was not the case in 1980 is due to the very poor showing of the party in which many veterans were unseated. The average age of new members of the JSP has been higher than that of LDP newcomers in every election since 1972.

For thumbnail biographies have been selected three prewar party members and five from the postwar, each in one way or another representative. Nemoto Tadashi (Shō) was a Seiyūkai representative who was elected ten consecutive times from Ibaraki prefecture. His first successful campaign was in March 1898 when he was 46 and his last was in May 1920. I have classified him occupationally as a professional politician, but he also worked briefly in the central government, for the Foreign Ministry and the Ministry of Agriculture and Commerce. In addition, he was an agricultural entrepreneur, a reporter for *Kuni no Hikari* and served several private corporations. He was typical in the variety of experience which he brought to politics.

In other ways, however, Nemoto was quite unusual. After private schooling, he was sent to the United States in 1877 when he was twenty-six years of age. He eventually attended Vermont University, graduating in 1889. Upon his return to Japan in 1890 he organized the Japan Prohibition League (Nihon Kinshū Dōmei). He is best known as a temperance leader. His most notable success was the passage of a law in 1922 prohibiting the consumption of alcoholic beverages by minors. Few observers would feel that this law has been followed very closely in subsequent years. Nemoto was also a strong advocate of compulsory free education for ordinary elementary schools.

It is more than obvious where Nemoto acquired his temperance views. It is likely that only in the U.S. could a Japanese have gained such an aversion to alcohol. His attempts to transfer such attitudes to a sake-soaked Japan may now be regarded as comical. Nemoto, like most temperance figures, was no comedian.

He was deadly serious. He also wrote popular books about the United States and travelled widely. He was a reliable though unspectacular member of the Seiyukai in the Diet until his retirement in 1924. He died in 1933.

A second Seiyūkai politician of note was Takekoshi (also Takegoshi) Yosaburō, elected five consecutive times from 1902 through 1912. The first four times he ran from Niigata, but the last time he switched to run in Maebashi city, a municipal district in Gunma Prefecture.

Takekoshi, however, was born in Saitama in 1865 and, after attending both Dōshisha and Keiō University, he started out as a journalist. Initially he worked as a reporter for *Jiji Shimpō* (Founded by Fukuzawa), *Kokumin Shimbun* (founded by Tokutomi Sohō and supportive of the government oligarchy) and, finally, *Yomiuri Shimbun*. He is best known as a serious historian. In 1891 and 1892 he published *Shin Nihon Shi*, a two volume work, and *Nisengohyakunen Shi* followed in 1896. Both investigated general world developments and popular trends.

These works attracted the attention of Saionji Kinmochi who recruited Takekoshi, first to serve as editor of his magazine, *Sekai no Nihon*, and then to government service in the Education Ministry when Saionji was its head in the 3rd Itō Cabinet (1898). In 1899 Takekoshi travelled to Europe and returned to enter politics.

In the Diet after 1902 Takekoshi was a moderate Seiyūkai supporter of Saionji. He differed from some of the other early legislators as he did not rise out of the popular rights movement, but was instead recruited from the literary world by a leading member of the Meiji establishment. Hence, he was not a critic of the oligarchy, but generally supported it.

He dropped out of electoral politics after 1912, but continued to write, producing his most respected work, *Nihon Keizai Shi*, in eight volumes in 1920. In 1922 he was appointed to the House of Peers. In the twenties and thirties he worked in the Editorial Board of the Imperial Household Ministry, eventually serving as head of that august agency. In 1940 he was appointed to the Privy Council, a testament to his conservatism. He survived the war to die in 1950 at the age of 85.

Takekoshi also wrote three books which appeared in English language versions: *The Economic Aspects of Japan*, in three volumes (1930), *Japanese Rule in Formosa* (1907), and a biography of Prince Saionji (1933).

The selection in the Kenseikai-Minseitō line is Shiba Shirō, a consistent member on that side of the aisle in the early years. He was born before the Restoration in 1852. His early life was colorful, but it is difficult to call it unconventional, for many early elected officials experienced interesting and varied lives. They hardly fit the contemporary stereotype of the stodgy, elderly politician with no ideas and little eclat. In 1868 (age 16) Shiba, the son of a prominent samurai from Aizu, served on the losing side in the Boshin War. In this battle his brother was killed, his father was wounded and his mother and sister both committed suicide. After that Shiba enrolled in Daigaku Nankō, the precursor of Todai, following which he travelled to the United States, attending Harvard and also the Wharton School at the University of Pennsylvania, majoring in political economy.

Back in Japan in 1887 he published a massive political novel under the pseudonym of Tōkai Sanshi. The work was entitled *Kajin no Kigū* (Chance Meetings with Beautiful Women). It was so immensely popular that Shiba produced eight parts in all, extending the life of the novel until 1897.[6] It was highly idealistic and very political, expressing admiration for the nationalistic aspirations of oppressed peoples, such as the Irish, Hungarians and others. It seems to have captured strongly the spirit of educated youth in Japan at this time.

Shiba also produced several other books (including a history of Egypt) and Chinese style poetry, but he turned to politics in the second general election of 1892. Succeeding in his first try, he was reelected five consecutive times until 1902. Defeated in 1903, he bounced back with wins in 1904, 1908, 1915 and 1917. In the Diet he was a loyal party man, rising to prominence primarily in matters having to do with economic issues. As a novelist, his work has not survived as significant and he was not really a rarity as a novelist-politician. One could perhaps note that Ishihara Shintarō seems like a more recent reincarnation.

There are many famous LDP members in the past forty years. Most have been the subject of full length biographies and some are well known outside Japan as well. It is unnecessary to repeat their careers here, however representative they may have been. Instead, as LDP members are briefly encapsulated the careers of two prominent but less well-known figures: Kosaka Zentarō and Mitamura Takeo.

Kosaka stands as typical in several respects, unusual in others. He was the son of a prewar Diet member (Kosaka Junzō) which is typical and the grandson of an early Diet member (Zennosuke) which is unusual. The family, from Nagano, had extensive local business interests and was active in political affairs as well. Kosaka Zentarō was eminently successful as a politician with sixteen wins in the first seventeen postwar elections beginning in 1946. His only loss was in the LDP disaster of December 1983. Like almost all LDP members with this kind of record, he rose to cabinet rank on several occasions: Labor Minister in the 5th Yoshida Cabinet (1953-54) when only 41 years of age; Chairman of the National Public Safety Commission (1954); and Foreign Minister in the first and second Ikeda cabinets (1960-62) and also in the Miki Cabinet (1976).

Kosaka graduated from Tokyo Commercial University in 1935. His first career was in the business world, serving in an advisory capacity for a Nagano chemical company. He was a candidate of the Shimpotō in the initial postwar election at the age of 34. Thereafter, as a continuous member of the Diet he held a long succession of party positions, served on all kinds of committees, rising as fast as he did largely because of the shortage of veteran members who survived the postwar purges. He has come to be regarded within the party as a theorist with competence in economic affairs and labor. In February 1990 his son (Kenji) became the fourth generation of the Kosaka family to be elected to the Diet.

The other LDP choice, Mitamura Takeo, is best known as a devoted follower of Nakano Seigō, the aggressive populist nationalist of the 1930s. Mitamura typifies the late prewar politician who was purged by the Occupation but returned later as a conservative. Many of the LDP members in its early years shared this experience, illustrating the sense of continuity.

From Gifu, Mitamura attended the Home Ministry Police Academy where he graduated in 1927. He then served as a police officer in Gifu, was attached to the Home Ministry and also to the Colonization Ministry. After the war, deprived of public office, he took up writing, turning out a succession of books on police enforcement, electoral politics and critiques of socialism and communism. Many of these writings also attempted to explain and justify the actions of his mentor, Nakano Seigō.

In fact, Mitamura entered politics as a Nakano disciple. A former outspoken member of the Kenseikai/Minseitō, Nakano had organized a party called the Tōhōkai in 1936 following the February 26 Incident. It was ultranationalist and reformist, calling for the liberation of Asia from Western dominance. Mitamura was one of twelve successful Tōhōkai candidates in the general election of 1937. Nakano and Mitamura challenged the Tōjō government in the 1942 election, endorsing 47 candidates. Only six, including Mitamura and Nakano, were elected. Nevertheless, they continued to attack the Tōjō government. Eventually, Mitamura and Nakano were both arrested in September 1943 on suspicion of planning to overthrow the government. Mitamura was released after questioning, but Nakano was kept under house arrest until he committed suicide in October 1943.

After the end of the Occupation, Mitamura returned to politics, winning election as a Minshutō candidate in 1955. He thus became an LDP member when the merger took place later that year. He was reelected under LDP endorsement in 1958.

Representative of early postwar socialists is Arahata Katsuzō (better known as Kanson) who had a fascinating and colorful career, in many ways typical of early socialists in Japan.

Arahata was born into humble circumstances in Yokohama in 1887 and attended school only until the age of fourteen. Like many leftists in Japan he was baptized a Christian (in 1902) after which he became an apprentice at the

Yokosuka Naval Shipyard Arsenal. Impressed by the anti-war (with Russia) movement of Sakai Toshihiko and others, he joined the Heiminsha, one of Japan's first specifically socialist societies.

His checkered career thereafter included a period of living with the famous anarchist Kanno Suga with whom he was arrested in the Red Flag incident of 1908. Although Kanno was released soon, Arahata remained in prison for a year and a half and he thus escaped implication in the High Treason Incident which cost Kanno her life. Arahata, nevertheless, remained active in left wing circles. In 1912 he began publication of *Kindai Shisō* with Ōsugi Sakae and others. Its objective was to promote anarcho-syndicalism.

In 1922 Arahata was among the founders of the Japan Communist Party under whose sponsorship he visited the Soviet Union. He also met with Comintern agents in China. In 1927 when the party was refounded he was denied membership because of his opposition to Fukumotoism. He then drifted into the Rōnō camp.

He was arrested for the fourth time in 1937. Released in 1939 he spent the remainder of the war years under house arrest. He participated in the founding of the JSP and was elected to the Diet from Tokyo in 1946 and 1947. In 1948 he opposed the budget proposals of the Ashida Cabinet (which included socialists) and was forced to resign from the party. He was defeated running as an independent in the 1949 election. Thereafter, he withdrew from politics, but continued writing until his death in 1981. He received several prestigious cultural awards and authored many books and countless articles on an incredible variety of social and political subjects.

The JCP choice here is Shiga Yoshio. It is fair to say that there are no "typical" Communist representatives in the Japanese House of Representatives. To be a Communist in Japan has meant alienation in the first place, a fact that is noted for the women Communist representatives in Chapter Nine.

I have chosen Shiga for the thumbnail sketch of a JCP member for several reasons. He is less well known than some of the luminaries like Nosaka Sanzō or Miyamoto Kenji, but he is prominent and has written extensively. He was also one of those Diet members subjected to the "Red Purge" by the Occupation in 1950.

Shiga was born in 1901 and attended Todai in the early 1920s. He was attracted at once to left-wing causes, organizing a student society, Gakusei Rengōkai, in 1922. He joined the JCP in 1923 before his graduation. He completed his university degree in Social Science in 1925 and spent the rest of his life as a professional politician, almost all of it as a communist.

Along with Tokuda Kyūichi, Shiga was instrumental in reviving the party in 1925 after its initial collapse. In the mid-1920s he edited *Marukusu Shugi*

(Marxism), the party organ and he became a member of the Central Committee in 1927. In March 1928 he was arrested along with many others of the left. He spent the next eighteen years in prison, steadfastly refusing to recant as so many others did. He and Tokuda wrote of their prison experience in *Gokuchū Jūhachi Nen*, published in 1947.

After release from prison in early 1946 Shiga immediately became active in reorganizing the JCP. He was the first postwar editor of the new party organ, *Akahata*. He stood for election to the Diet in 1946 and was one of only six Communists to succeed. At this time he and Tokuda publicly supported the Occupation as an "army of liberation." Defeated in 1947, he was elected again in 1949, but by now the "reverse course" had set in. In 1950 Shiga was expelled from the Diet by order of SCAP.

In 1955 he returned to electoral politics and won again in 1958. Like many Communists he was never a sure winner, usually finishing fourth or fifth in his Osaka district. He was active in the Security Treaty struggle of 1960, but, as a longtime admirer of the Soviet Union, he supported the Nuclear Test Ban Treaty in 1963. For this he was drummed out of the JCP the following year. He formed a society known as "Nihon no Koe" (The Voice of Japan) and continued to write polemically and profusely.

Nishio Suehiro was a prominent DSP member and leader with long and deep ties to the socialist and labor movements in 20th century Japan. Born in Osaka in 1891, Nishio attended school only as far as the elementary level and went to work in the Osaka Armory at the age of fourteen. He is one of the few major socialist political figures to rise through the union movement from the shop floor in the prewar period. While employed in the Sumitomo Steel factory in 1916 he began to assert leadership qualities and, in 1919, he joined the Yūaikai which began to show vigor following the First World War. In the 1920s he was involved in various labor disputes and was a leading member of Sōdōmei by 1924. In 1926, however, he withdrew from this organization, citing the influence of communism. This was also the year of the founding of Shakai Minshutō of which Nishio then became a leader. He was one of only eight proletarian candidates elected to the Diet in 1928.

As a member of the Diet, Nishio had a long and checkered career. Retaining his labor union connections, he was reelected to the Diet in 1930, but failed in 1932 and 1936. In 1937 he won again under the banner of the Shakai Taishutō which had adopted a moderate, even nationalistic stance. In March 1928 Nishio urged Premier Konoe to proceed boldly like Mussolini, Hitler and Stalin. His reference to Stalin caused the lower house to vote his expulsion from the Diet. However, he was restored to his seat in 1940 and was elected as an unrecommended candidate in 1942. During the war Nishio and associates adopted a position of hostility to the Tōjō government and, when the war ended, he immediately became active in reorganizing the moderate left. Along with Katayama Tetsu, Nishio organized the JSP in the fall of 1945. He was elected under that banner in 1946 and 1947, was Chief Cabinet Secretary in the coalition Katayama cabinet and then Deputy Premier in the Ashida cabinet in 1948. However, he was implicated along with many others in the Shōwa Denkō Scandal in 1948. This led to the resignation of the Ashida cabinet and the arrest of Nishio. He was eventually found innocent, but the Socialist Party never really recovered.

Because of the scandal Nishio was defeated in 1949, but he came back to the Diet in the election of 1952 and consecutively thereafter until 1969. He retired from active politics in 1972. In 1959 the JSP split mainly over the Security Treaty issue and Nishio left the party with a handful of followers to form the DSP. He was its unquestioned leader and chairman from 1960 until 1967. He was recognized throughout his career as a champion of labor and consistent opposition to communism. He died in 1981 at the age of 90.

NOTES

1 The most comprehensive breakdown by party of prewar representatives appears in Masumi Junnosuke, *Nihon Seitō Shiron* (1965-1980), Vols. 5 and 6.

2 It can, however, be done election by election. Masumi has accomplished this for the elections of the 1920s and 1930s in *Nihon Seitō Shiron*, Vol. 5, pp. 256-259.

3 For portions of the postwar period statistical breakdowns by party are found in, among others, Wakata, *Gendai Nihon Seiji*, pp. 42-52; Scalapino and Masumi, *Parties and Politics*, pp. 169-176; and Jung-suk Youn, "Candidates and Party Images", pp. 101-115. The latter study covers all candidates rather than confining itself to those elected.

4 Kōmeitō recruitment is explained rather generally in Ronald J. Hrebenar, "The Komeito: Party of 'Buddhist' Democracy", in Hrebenar, ed., *The Japanese Party System*, pp. 147-180. The JCP, which has fascinated American writers on Japanese politics, is examined all over the place. Its recruitment of candidates, however, has merited only passing attention in English language studies. The JCP is, nevertheless, often linked with the Kōmeitō as the two best organized political parties. In addition to the above, see Peter Berton, "The Japan Communist Party: the 'Lovable' Party", also in *The Japanese Party System*, pp. 116-141 and Cecil Brett, "The Komeito and Local Japanese Politics", *Asian Survey* (Apr. 1979), pp. 366-378.

5 Legislative assistants on the American model are very rare, although secretaries sometimes do research in preparation for legislation. The role of secretaries (*hisho*) is noted in Chapter Two and explained in Izumi, "Diet Members", pp. 74-75. Curtis, *The Japanese Way of Politics*, p. 97 also discusses it briefly.

6 See Keene, *Dawn to the West*, pp. 81-88 for a description of the story line.

Chapter 8

Apprenticeship

■

Local Assembly Membership

Apprenticeship through prior service in local assemblies was very important in the early years of the representative system. It must be borne in mind that elected assemblies at the prefectural level preceded the creation of the Imperial Diet by more than a decade. Hence, it was natural, perhaps inevitable, that local assembly members would serve as a valuable source of recruitment for candidates. This is particularly true for the political parties which had organized in anticipation of the new constitution. These parties encouraged their existing members to become active in electoral politics. In consequence, more than sixty-five percent of the successful Diet candidates in the first ten elections had previous experience in local government. (See Graph 8-1 and Table 8-1). The importance of this kind of apprenticeship then began to diminish. In elections 11 through 15 (1912 to 1924) the percentage with local assembly backgrounds was in the fifties. It fell to less than fifty percent in 1928 and remained in the forties (except for 50.4% in 1937) until after the war. In the second postwar election (1947) thirty-six percent of the winners had such experience. By 1958 the figure was in the high twenties where it has remained, though still falling very slightly most of the time until the present day.

For new members with local government experience (Table 8-2) the figure was always more than half (except for 49.2% in 1924) in the prewar period and consistently below fifty percent since the war. In neither era is there a clear pattern, except that the percentage of new members with local government background frequently was higher than usual when the number of new electees was small. Thus, before the war the highest percentage of new members with previous service in local assemblies was 74.2 in 1937 when only ninety-three (the low-

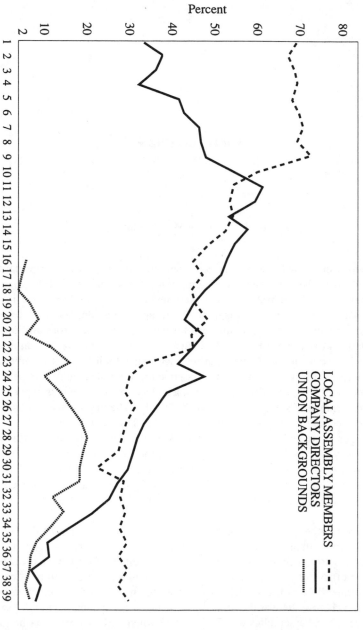

GRAPH 8 - 1
IMPERIAL AND NATIONAL DIET
APPRENTICESHIP

Percent

Election

LOCAL ASSEMBLY MEMBERS
COMPANY DIRECTORS
UNION BACKGROUNDS

TABLE 8-1
IMPERIAL AND NATIONAL DIET
APPRENTICESHIP
Local Assembly Members, Company Directors, Union Backgrounds

Election	Year	Local Assy.	Company Directors	Union Backgrounds
1	1890	67.9%	34.0%	
2	1892	66.9%	37.8%	
3	1894-1	69.3%	37.0%	
4	1894-2	69.6%	34.0%	
5	1898-1	68.3%	41.3%	
6	1898-2	70.4%	42.7%	
7	1902	71.3%	46.3%	
8	1903	70.5%	46.8%	
9	1904	72.5%	47.8%	
10	1908	65.2%	54.3%	
11	1912	56.2%	61.0%	
12	1915	55.3%	60.3%	
13	1917	55.8%	55.3%	
14	1920	56.3%	59.1%	
15	1924	50.1%	56.5%	
16	1928	46.3%	54.4%	0.6%
17	1930	48.1%	53.6%	0.4%
18	1932	46.1%	50.5%	0.2%
19	1936	47.8%	47.2%	3.1%
20	1937	50.4%	45.3%	6.1%
21	1942	46.5%	48.2%	2.1%

Continued on next page

TABLE 8-1 CONTINUED
IMPERIAL AND NATIONAL DIET
APPRENTICESHIP
Local Assembly Members, Company Directors, Union Backgrounds

Election	Year	Local Assy.	Company Directors	Union Backgrounds
22	1946	46.1%	44.8%	11.5%
23	1947	36.1%	43.0%	16.5%
24	1949	31.2%	48.3%	10.3%
25	1952	30.6%	40.3%	14.8%
26	1953	31.3%	38.1%	16.9%
27	1955	30.4%	35.7%	19.6%
28	1958	28.9%	34.0%	21.2%
29	1960	28.1%	33.2%	20.1%
30	1963	25.3%	30.6%	19.3%
31	1967	28.8%	25.9%	18.9%
32	1969	28.5%	27.5%	13.6%
33	1972	29.5%	21.8%	15.3%
34	1976	28.0%	17.4%	13.9%
35	1979	29.7%	14.9%	11.9%
36	1980	28.2%	14.9%	11.5%
37	1983	28.8%	11.1%	11.0%
38	1986	27.5%	11.5%	8.4%
39	1990	29.7%	10.2%	9.8%

est prewar figure) were elected. After the war, the relatively high percentages of new members with this experience are found in 1953, 1955, 1967, and 1980. Except for 1967, when an additional nineteen seats swelled the total, these were all years when the rookie class was small.

Since I have taken local assembly membership to represent a non-elite background quality, it may be argued that the steady drop in local assembly members who went on to the "big time" reflects the growing elite orientation of the National Diet. It also signifies, however, that political parties have increasingly recruited candidates with national rather than local outlook and experience and that they have sought successors from among their own proteges. This all coincides with the tremendous increase in "pure politicians" among candidates of all parties in the past thirty years. Obviously, apprenticeship in local assemblies is no longer of great importance. Chapter Six suggests, however, that it has been and continues to be more important in some prefectures than in others.

Local assembly membership as a background characteristic deserves to be classified as non-elite. Employing the same formula as elsewhere, but without incorporating local membership into the equation, I come up with the following elite ratings:

	Local Assembly Members	Non-Members
All members		
(prewar and postwar)	-43.3	+45.6
Prewar members	-32.5	+52.8
Postwar Only members	-50.0	+23.7

To summarize, local assembly members who went on to the national arena did play important roles in the political process, but mainly as members of the rank and file. On the whole, they tended to be less well educated, coming from less prestigious occupations with slightly poorer prospects for long term electoral success.

Company Directorships

Turning next to company directorship as an apprenticeship feature for Diet members, it can be seen from Table 8-1 that the highest level of such participation was during the "heyday" of bourgeois political parties - the 1910s and 1920s - the era of Taishō democracy. The prewar percentages of all members with such

TABLE 8-2
IMPERIAL AND NATIONAL DIET
NEW MEMBERS
Local Assembly Members, Company Directors, Union Backgrounds, Women

Elec.	Year	Local Assy.	Company Directors	Union Background	Women	Number
1	1890	67.9%	34.0%			300
2	1892	63.8%	34.9%			166
3-4	1894	71.3%	38.1%			265*
5-6	1898	71.3%	45.0%			158*
7	1902	69.3%	45.6%			228
8	1903	66.7%	55.9%			93
9	1904	71.7%	49.2%			120
10	1908	62.1%	56.3%			206
11	1912	55.1%	61.2%			196
12	1915	57.5%	58.8%			153
13	1917	55.6%	55.6%			151
14	1920	60.3%	62.5%			277
15	1924	49.2%	53.2%			252
16	1928	50.3%	54.3%	1.7%		173
17	1930	60.6%	53.5%	0.8%		127
18	1932	55.5%	49.2%	0.8%		128
19	1936	63.0%	40.2%	9.4%		127
20	1937	74.2%	41.9%	15.1%		93
21	1942	50.5%	52.5%	0.5%		202

Continued on next page

TABLE 8-2 CONTINUED
IMPERIAL AND NATIONAL DIET
NEW MEMBERS
Local Assembly Members, Company Directors, Union Backgrounds, Women

Elec.	Year	Local Assy.	Company Directors	Union Background	Women	Number
22	1946	42.7%	46.9%	10.6%	10.1%	386
23	1947	28.4%	44.4%	15.1%	1.3%	225
24	1949	24.6%	50.8%	9.2%	1.5%	195
25	1952	19.3%	34.9%	18.3%	—	109
26	1953	35.4%	37.5%	20.8%	4.2%	48
27	1955	42.1%	31.6%	29.8%	1.8%	57
28	1958	30.9%	26.5%	26.5%	5.9%	68
29	1960	28.8%	11.9%	25.4%	5.1%	59
30	1963	19.4%	16.7%	9.7%	1.4%	72
31	1967	39.2%	7.8%	11.8%	1.0%	102
32	1969	35.4%	21.2%	13.1%	4.0%	99
33	1972	32.6%	4.2%	9.5%	4.2%	95
34	1976	24.0%	4.0%	10.4%	0.8%	125
35	1979	27.6%	5.3%	5.3%	5.3%	76
36	1980	38.9%	5.6%	11.1%	2.8%	36
37	1983	26.2%	3.6%	10.7%	2.4%	84
38	1986	25.0%	10.9%	9.4%	1.6%	64
39	1990	31.6%	9.0%	12.0%	7.5%	133

Figures are percentages of all new members for each election.

*These figures are the combined totals of the two elections in the year indicated.

from
co. director

background ranged from a low of thirty-four percent in 1890 and 1894 to sixty-one percent in the election of 1912. By the late 1930s, however, the numbers had begun to fall, a trend that was continued after the war. Since the 1950s the recruitment of persons with this kind of experience has declined severely, hitting lows of 11.1%, 11.5% and 10.2% in the last three elections. Now, since nearly all (87.3%) of such persons belong to the LDP or its conservative precursors, the existence and continued presence of various socialist parties in the postwar era necessarily made the percentage figures drop. Nevertheless, it is also clear that this kind of apprenticeship has lost its importance in LDP recruitment. It bears mentioning, however, that the big business - LDP connection has remained strong[1], and a great many successful Diet members accept directorships after retirement (forced or voluntary) from the electoral wars. RTY

The trend referred to here is a further indication of the "professionalism"[2] of Diet politics in which more and more reliance is placed on "pure politicians" and less on the kinds of apprenticeship that were once so crucial. Business apprenticeship as an aspect of preparation for electoral politics obviously applies only to the "bourgeois" parties of prewar times and their postwar descendant - the LDP. However, the phenomenon of "professionalization" is also seen in the ranks of the JSP and its recruitment from the ranks of organized labor. This will be taken up shortly.

In the Introduction where the elite status formula was explained I indicated that company directorship should be considered a non-elite quality, but to a lesser degree than local assembly apprenticeship. That it belongs on the non-elite side is borne out by the application of the elite formula to all members, prewar and postwar, who had served as company directors.[3] All of the criteria used elsewhere to determine elite ratings have been used here, except company directorship itself.

	Company Directors	Non-Directors
All members		
(Prewar and postwar)	-24.8	+17.8
Prewar members	-8.5	+8.4
Postwar only members	-22.6	+8.7

These figures justify the decision to grant only half as many quality points to company directors as to local assembly members. As with the latter, moreover, company directorship was an important attribute for conservative recruits in Japanese electoral politics, especially before the war and in the immediate postwar period. It was never regarded as essential for leadership position, however, and it has dwindled in overall significance in the post-industrial society of Japan since the 1960s.

Labor Union Membership

The recruitment by socialist parties from the ranks of the labor unions has been referred to in Chapter Two on occupation. That section included in the column "Labor/Socialist movement" only those persons whose major careers were devoted to the labor or socialist cause. Identification with the socialist movement as an occupation was applicable only to a very small number of pre-war elected politicians. In this chapter, under the heading of "Union Background" (See Graph 8-1, Tables 8-1 and 8-2), I have included all members who belonged to labor unions prior to their election to the Diet. As explained in Chapter Seven, almost all of these persons were members of the JSP, DSP, or JCP.

Before the initial universal (manhood) suffrage election of 1928 there were no members with connections to organized labor. Surprisingly, however, as many as six percent of the entire membership in 1937 could claim such affiliation. The big surge in labor unionists came with the end of the war, the encouragement of the labor movement by the Occupation, and the establishment of a vigorous and viable Socialist Party. The percentages of all members with such apprenticeship naturally fluctuated with the fortunes of the left wing parties, especially the JSP. When the JSP faired poorly, as in 1949, labor union members declined as well. In periods of relative strength for the socialists in the 1950s and early 1960s, the percentage of unionists was also higher. Nevertheless, just as the recruitment of company directors by the LDP began to drop with national affluence in the late 60s, so did the socialist recruitment effort begin to tail off in the labor unions.[4] The fall is not as dramatic as with conservative business affiliated members, but both indices (company directors and union backgrounds) have declined as the process of "professionalization" has hit both major parties. Professionalism of this sort was already high in the minor parties: DSP, JCP, and Kōmeitō, many of whose candidates were professional politicians of long standing before succeeding in national elections.

The elite ratings for members with organized labor apprenticeship are revealed in a number of interesting ways.

Elite Rating for Members with Labor Union Background

	Number	Elite Rating
All members with Union backgrounds	283	+41.2
Prewar members	33	+67.0
Postwar members	250	-16.6

The prewar figures are derived from a mere thirty-three individuals, an insignificant proportion of the entire Diet membership. The few persons with labor union connections who entered the Diet before the war were individuals with elite educational credentials and prominent in the movement, sometimes as attorneys. With few exceptions they were not off the shop floor. They were also remarkably successful in winning elections. The average number of times elected for the thirty-three prewar union cohorts was 4.82 compared to the national average of 2.66.

It is these prewar figures that propell the overall elite status rating for union members into the positive column. The high ratings are based largely on reelectability, positive features for agriculture and teaching as occupations, and low levels for apprenticeship in local assembly membership and company directorships. In the postwar period the negative rating is based primarily on a very low figure for educational background. The only positive categories for postwar union members are education as an occupation, reelectability, and local assembly and company directorships. The one thing that can be said with assurance about union affiliated representatives is that they tend to have long lasting Diet careers. The average number of times elected for all union cohorts is 4.65 compared to the overall national average of 3.10. This, too, diminishes in significance when it is realized that the overall national average is pulled down greatly by the very low retention rates in the first thirty years of the system when there were no union members in the Diet because there were no unions and no left wing parties to recruit them.

Fujita Mokichi was a member of the first Imperial Diet, cited here as one who served a brief apprenticeship in a local assembly in the early years of the system. Fujita had other distinguishing characteristics as well. He was born in Edo in 1852 and was an early graduate of Keiō Gijuku. He immediately entered the world of journalism, befriending other Keiō grads and associates. Inukai Tsuyoshi, for example, stayed with him while attending Keiō a few years after Fujita.

Fujita was a charter member of Ōkuma's Rikken Kaishintō in 1882, joining

Inukai, Ozaki Yukio and other Keiō products in representing its most sophisticated wing. He was very active in the Kaishintō throughout the 1880s, serving on many boards and helping organize subgroups, such as the Meiji Kyōkai, a society of intellectuals. His principal occupation was journalism. For a while he and Inukai worked together for *Hōchi Shimbun* and Fujita became editor of *Yubin Hōchi Shimbun* in 1882. He seemed destined for a leadership role in the party and, indeed, the national government. His campaigns for election in 1890 and 1892 were marked by compelling liberal rhetoric. However, his career and life were cut short by an untimely death at the age of forty in August 1892.

In addition to serving in the Tokyo-fu Assembly and his role in party affairs, Fujita wrote prolifically, including a political novel and treatises on politics, history and travel in the West.

Sugita Teiichi was a long-time participant in the popular rights movement who used his position in the prefectural assembly of a small prefecture as a springboard to an elected seat in the Imperial Diet. He represents local government apprenticeship in the early years.

Sugita was from Fukui, born in 1851 the son of a wealthy farmer. He was educated privately, reading the Chinese classics, although he later studied abroad in China and England. In the 1870s he became associated with Itagaki Taisuke and the popular rights movement. As a member of the staff of *Hyōron Shimbun* he was a strident voice for the liberal cause. In 1881 he participated in the organizational planning of the Jiyūtō, Itagaki's first political party.

In the 1880s Sugita was elected to the Fukui prefectural assembbly, rising to the position of speaker by the end of the decade. Because of his stature throughout the region and his long standing identification with the national liberal movement, he was a natural choice as a candidate in 1890. He won handily and was reelected in 1892 and in March 1894. He lost in September 1894 when the government interfered heavily in the election, but he regained his seat in 1898 and kept it thereafter until 1912, winning nine elections in all. During this period he was a consistent supporter of liberal causes and a champion of parliamentary democracy. He never left the party founded by Itagaki, holding important posts in both the Kenseitō in 1898 and the Seiyūkai after 1900. In 1905 he became speaker of the House of Representatives, retaining that position until 1908. Well acquainted with Inukai and Hara, Sugita was the first party politician appointed to a seat in the House of Peers. This was engineered by Hara in 1912 as part of his effort to weaken the influence of the upper house.

Sugita was an important figure on the national stage, despite his background and lack of elite educational credentials. Coming as early as he did in Japan's parliamentary history, such credentials were less necessary than they later became. His career is also evidence that traditional Confucian education was not necessarily an impediment to a modern outlook and "liberalism" in the late 19th and early 20th centuries.

Hayashida Kametarō had an interesting and rather unusual apprenticeship. Born in Kumamoto in a samurai family in 1863, he graduated in politics from Todai in 1887 and went to work immediately in the central government. He was attached first to the Privy Council, then deliberating the constitution, and then to the Legislative Bureau. When the Imperial Diet came into being in 1890 Hayashida, at the age of 27, became the first Secretary (Shokikan) of the House of Representatives. In 1897 he was named Chief Secretary (Shokikan-chō) of that body. In the corporate world he was president of an electric company and a magazine and he also edited *Tokyo Maiyū Shimbun*.

After all that preparation, Hayashida finally tried his hand at elections in 1920 when he stood successfully as an independent from Tokyo. He was reelected in 1924, this time under the banner of the Kakushin Club, associated with Inukai Tsuyoshi. He obviously was very familiar with the operations of the national assembly. This was indicated in his two volume *Nihon Seitō Shi*, published in 1927, just before his death in December of that year. It was an encyclopedic, popular work, short on analysis, but containing some inside information.

I have listed Hayashida as a central government bureaucrat with apprenticeship as a company director. He is also representative in the heyday of the political parties as a Diet member with elite educational and bureaucratic connections. His type supports the contention that the Japanese parliament was a "committee of the bourgeoisie."

Hoshi Hajime was an interesting character who is included here for his business connections. But, he was much more than that. He was born in Fukushima in 1873 and, after attending Tokyo Commercial School, he went to the U.S. where he enrolled in Columbia University, majoring in political economy. After graduation he remained for a while in the U.S., publishing a bilingual journal *Japan and America*. He returned to Japan in 1901 and, after turning down an offer from Itō Hirobumi to work for the Government-general of Korea, he began a business making patent medicine with a start-up capital of 400 Yen. The business flourished and Hoshi opened a school for pharmaceutical salesmen. He joined the board of numerous other enterprises. He also wrote books on commerce, the bureaucracy, the history of China, and politics.

In 1908 he was elected to the Diet as an independent, but he soon became associated with Gotō Shimpei. Hoshi did not run again for the Diet until 1937, but he spent much of the 1910s and 1920s as a fund provider for Gotō and others. In 1921 he was arrested on a charge of violating regulations regarding opium production in Japan. He was ultimately found innocent of the charge, but his pharmaceutical business was damaged severely.

Meanwhile, he had become progressively more nationalistic. He re-entered politics in 1937 as a Seiyūkai candidate for the Diet. He was successful then and again as a recommended candidate in the wartime election of 1942. He survived the war and purges to be reelected in 1946 and, when the constitution created the House of Councillors he placed first in the national constituency in the initial election to that body in 1947. In 1937 he wrote a book in English, *Japan: A Country Founded by "Mother" : An Introductory History*. It was published by his alma mater, Columbia University Press and was a strongly nationalistic attempt to justify Japanese imperialism in Korea and Manchuria. He described Japan as possessing inherent "maternal" characteristics of compassion, kindness, sympathy and nurturing which were manifested in benevolent policies toward "backward" peoples such as those in the colonies. Hoshi stands as an example, a rather common one, whose education in the U.S. provided him with rhetorical justification for imperialism and the racism that went with it.

Hoshi died during his first term in the House of Councillors, in 1951. He was the father of Hoshi Shin'ichi, a well-known postwar science fiction writer.

Selected as a prewar parliamentarian with labor union apprenticeship is none other than Suzuki Bunji, one of the most famous labor leaders of modern Japan. Suzuki was born in Miyagi prefecture in 1885. His father was a sake brewer.[5] Despite what would appear to be a humble background, Suzuki attended Todai, graduating in law. While a university student he became a Christian, joined Ebina Danjō's Hongō Church and became interested in social problems under the influence of Yoshino Sakuzō, Kuwada Taizō and others.

After graduation he worked very briefly for *Tokyo Asahi Shimbun* which he quit to become Secretary (kanji) and head of the Social Welfare Department (Shakai Jigyō Buchō) of the Unitarian Church of Japan. In 1912 Suzuki was the driving force behind the organization of the Yūaikai, whose initial purposes were to enhance workers' welfare and promote industry-worker harmony. The society eventually developed into a nationwide labor organization, changing its name to Dai Nihon Rōdō Sōdōmei Yuaikai in 1919 and to Nihon Rōdō Sōdōmei in 1921. Suzuki served as the organization's president from its founding until 1930.

Suzuki was always seen as a moderate in the Japanese left wing. He consistently voiced opposition to communism, but he also called for better treatment of workers and for universal suffrage in the period immediately after the First World War. He was a regular representative of Japanese labor at international meetings in the 1930s.

In 1926 he participated in the organizational planning of the moderate Shakai Minshutō, was a charter member of its Central Executive Committee. In 1928 he was elected to the Diet from Osaka in the first election under universal manhood suffrage. He was beginning by now to lose some influence. He was unsuccessful in election bids in 1930 and 1932, but he transferred to Tokyo and won there in 1936 and 1937. After the war Suzuki was a JSP candidate from Miyagi in 1946, but he collapsed and died during a campaign swing in Sendai.

Suzuki Bunji was representative of Japan's labor/socialist movement before the war. He was a middle-class intellectual with no manual labor experience of his own. He was a Christian, so typical of Japanese socialists in the early 20th century. Finally, he was moderate and anti-communist. He enjoys a good, but not spectacular historical reputation today.

NOTES

1 All studies of the postwar LDP note, with varying degrees of emphasis, the strength of the connection to the business world. For relevant examples, see Mori Kishio, *Kokkai Giin no Himitsu* (1982); Nobuo Tomita, et.al., "The Liberal Democratic Party: the Ruling Party of Japan", in Hrebenar, ed., *The Japanese Party System*, pp. 235-282; Richardson and Flanagan, *Politics in Japan*, pp. 310-311; Gerald Curtis, "Big Business and Political Influence", in Ezra F. Vogel, ed., *Modern Japanese Organization and Decision-Making* (1975), pp. 33-70.

2 "Professionalization", as used here, should be distinguished from the matter of professionals versus amateurs as discussed in Chapter Four. There, length if service is used as a determinant of a "professional" politician. Here, I used "professionalization" to mean the growth of politics as a profession.

3 I include anyone who occupied any of the following posts in a private or public corporation: komon (advisor, consultant), riji (director), kanji (superintendent), torishimariyaku (director).

4 Curtis, *The Japanese Way of Politics*, pp. 212-220, has a good section on labor unions, their current status and relationship with the JSP.

5 Although I have not counted them, it seems to me that a good many politicians came from sake brewing or selling families. This is true in prefectural politics, but also at the national level. Two recent examples are Prime Ministers Takeshita Noboru and Uno Sosuke.

Chapter 9

Women in the House of Representatives
■

It has frequently been written that the enfranchisement of women at the end of the war opened the gates for female representation in the Diet.[1] A large number of women presented themselves as candidates in the first postwar election of April 10, 1946 with thirty-nine winning seats in the lower house.[2] This is, by far, the largest number elected at any one time and is, in fact, close to half of all the women ever elected to the House of Representatives. Women were newly eligible, had not been purged, and all competing political parties endorsed some women candidates. Many others ran as independents. By the second election in April 1947, the bloom had apparently faded despite the new constitution with its ERA provision. Only fifteen women secured election in 1947. The number and, of course, percentage of successful women candidates continued to drop and, since the end of the Occupation in 1952, there have been between six and twelve with percentages ranging from 1.2 (1976) to 2.3 (1958). There has been at least one new female winner in each election save one (1952), but no more than four such newcomers at any one time after 1946, until 1990 when an upsurge of candidates brought in ten.

It is not difficult to discern the reasons for the low percentage of women in elective positions, given the overwhelming conclusions that Japanese society, at least outwardly, has long been dominated by males. Nevertheless, a rather detailed analysis will be made of the women who have taken seats in the Japanese parliament, for the issue of female participation in politics is one of compelling current interest. This chapter will first offer some general observations based on the statistics followed by short biographies of twelve prominent female Diet members.

Table 9-1 breaks down the entire female membership into the several categories that have been taken up separately in the earlier chapters. The two most

TABLE 9-1
WOMEN REPRESENTATIVES: 84

	Occupation No.	%		Education No.	%
Agriculture	0	-	University	36	42.9
Business	5	6.8	Major Univ.	11	13.1
Education	25	29.8	TODAI	1	1.2
Higher Education	4	4.8	KYODAI	1	1.2
Govt. (Central)	1	1.2	WASEDA	3	3.6
Govt. (Home Min.)	0	-	KEIO	0	-
Total C. Govt.	1	1.2	MEIJI	2	2.4
Local Government	3	3.6	CHUO	2	2.4
Journalism	6	7.1	NIHON	2	2.4
Law	4	4.8	HOSEI	0	-
Labor/Soc.	3	3.6	TOHOKU	0	-
Medicine	6	7.1	HOKUDAI	0	-
Military	0	-	High(er) School	22	26.2
Politics	12	14.3	Middle School	0	-
Religion	0	-	Elementary	2	2.4
Women's Orgs.	7	8.3	Private Educ.	0	-
Writing	3	3.6	Other Schools	22	26.2
Blue Collar	0	-	None Listed	2	2.4
White Collar	3	3.6			
Soka Gakkai	1	1.2			
Other/None	1	1.2			

Apprenticeship

	No.	%
Local Assembly	4	4.8
Company Directors	5	5.9
Union Background	3	3.6

Party Affiliation

	No.	%
LDP	33	39.3
JSP	28	33.3
JCP	14	16.7
DSP	3	3.6
Komeito	3	3.6
2.29		
Independent	3	3.6

Electability

Avg. no. of times elected:

(Percentages figures are of total number of women elected: 84) common occupational categories are education and politics. Other relatively numerous occupations have been women's organizations, medicine and journalism. On the whole, the women representatives have not been as well educated as the men. Fewer attended universities, especially the elite ones, but many had high school or "other school" educations. The latter category includes normal schools and accounts for some who were educated before the war and entered politics after.

Otherwise, very few women served apprenticeships in any of the fields covered in the previous chapter: local assemblies, company directorships, or labor unions. Moreover, the rate of retention was very low in comparison to the national average which was 3.94 times elected for the postwar period. As noted in Chapter Seven women are more likely to be recruited by the opposition parties, especially since the end of the Occupation. The thirty-three conservative (LDP) women were elected mainly in the early years. Twenty-six of the thirty-three were elected for the first time in 1946. Twenty-two of the twenty-six female conservatives elected in 1946 served only one Diet term. Indeed, twenty-six of the total of thirty-nine in the "Class of 1946" enjoyed only one term (which lasted exactly twelve months) as representatives of the people. After 1946 the conservative parties elected two new women in 1947 and one each in 1958, 1960, 1963, 1967 and 1972. Since the LDP was formally organized in 1955 it has sent only five women to the House of Representatives. Two of the five were widows of recently deceased LDP members who, in effect, "inherited" their seats. At least three other LDP women also "inherited" their seats as did two JSP women.

The average number of times elected for conservative women has been 1.67, almost a full point lower than the overall retention rate for women. The inescapable conclusion here is that women have not been sought by the LDP and that this avoidance has become more and more pronounced as time elapsed. As of 1990 there were no LDP women in the lower house and the only one elected since 1972 was Yamaguchi Shizue, who switched parties after notable success as a Socialist. The LDP ran only one woman in 1990, the wife of another candidate against whom she competed in the same district.

The JSP and the JCP have recruited women much more vigorously. Of the twenty-eight JSP women, twelve were elected for the first time in 1946, but only four of those twelve were never reelected. Similarly, excluding the six new socialists elected in 1990, only nine JSP women served but one term and the average number of times elected (even counting the six first timers) is 3.04, nearly double the figure for LDP women. The most successful women elected representatives in Japan, measured by length of service, have all been JSP members. The all-time champion is Yamaguchi Shizue, just referred to, who was elected thirteen times, ten as a socialist and three as a member of the LDP. Next was Tokano Satoko, elected eleven times. And, of course, the recent president of the JSP is a woman - Doi Takako, who was first elected in 1969. Following the 1990 election there were seven women JSP members, plus one independent who votes socialist.

There is no denying that the opposition "reformist" parties have had greater appeal to feminist interests if not much to women as voters. The voting rates for women were about ten percentage points below men's rates in the first several elections. Beginning in 1969 they began to exceed the men, but there is no evidence to suggest that women vote more heavily for left wing candidates.[3]

The Japan Communist Party has had the highest percentage of women among its successful candidates. Fourteen out of ninety-six Communists in the Diet have been women. At 14.6% this is a much higher figure than for any other party. The JCP has regularly recruited female candidates, running as many as twenty-one in 1986 and twenty-six in 1990. At least one new JCP woman has won a seat in each lower house election since 1976, with four securing victory in 1979. Like other JCP representatives, however, their Diet careers have usually been short. The fourteen JCP women have been elected an average of 2.29 times. This includes some persons elected in recent times who may be reelectable in the future. In any event, it can readily be seen from the following table that most of the women elected for the first time since the late 1960s have been Communists. Since, women do not vote for Communists at a significantly higher level than do men, the large contingent of Communist women candidates is not due to the greater appeal of this most anti-establishment party, but rather to the conscious effort by the party to attract women candidates.

The Komeitō has the poorest record of selecting women candidates. Only three have served this party in the House of Representatives. Two were elected in 1969 and neither was reelected. The other was elected in 1990. Although there have not been very many Komeitō members, this low figure for women serves to substantiate the notion that the Komeitō, like its parent and sponsor, Sōka Gakkai, is organized along traditional male dominated lines and is inherently conservative in cast and outlook.

In the February 1990 election for the House of Representatives there were sixty-six women among 953 registered candidates for all seats. The breakdown by party was as follows:

LDP..............................1
JSP 9
JCP 29
DSP 2
Komeito.........................1
Independents 24

TABLE 9-2
NATIONAL DIET
New Women Representatives by Party

First Year elected	LDP	JSP	JCP	DSP	Komelto
1946	26	12	1		
1947	2	1			
1949			2	1	
1952					
1953		2			
1955		1			
1958	1	1		2	
1960	1	2			
1963	1				
1967	1				
1969		1	1		2
1972	1	1	1		
1976			1		
1979			4		
1980			1		
1983		1	1		
1986			1		
1990		6	1		1

One of the independents was a suporter of the JSP. One other was succesful and two or three others narrowly missed victory. The overwhelming majority of the independents, however, had no chance of winning in this election. Many of the JCP candidates were also without prospects for success, but of the female candidates who were endorsed by a political party or otherwise had a reasonable chance of winning, about seventy-five percent were Communists. The number of female Communist candidates, moreover, has been growing while the trend in the other parties, especially the LDP, has been in the opposite direction.

The Class of 1946

As noted, the initial postwar election featured thirty-nine successful women candidates of whom but thirteen were ever reelected. Six of these thirteen were reelected more than once, including the two most successful women in Diet history: Yamaguchi Shizue and Tokano Satoko. Yamaguchi's thirteen successful campaigns included ten consecutive wins as a Socialist (JSP) from Tokyo sixth district. She switched party affiliation in the 1969 election and won as an LDP candidate. She was defeated in 1972, but won again as a conservative in 1976 and 1979. She was unsuccessful in the elections of 1980 and 1983. On the whole she had better luck as a socialist than as a conservative. At the time of her first victory in 1946 she was twenty-nine years of age. She had a high school education and was active in women's organizations within the labor and socialist movements in the early postwar period.

Tokano Satoko ran as an independent in 1946, but joined the JSP soon after taking her Diet seat. She was then reelected ten consecutive times until 1969 from Tochigi first district. She was born in Matsumoto in 1908 and graduated from Kyoto Dōshisha Women's University in 1929 with a degree in English Literature. She served briefly as an English teacher in a girls school and then as a journalist in China for a Shanghai based newspaper. In 1950 she was one of ten women selected to tour the U.S. "to study the political, social, and economic activities of U.S. women." The group met with Eleanor Roosevelt and other prominent American women. In the Diet she was identified with the right wing of the JSP. Probably her most significant parliamentary activity was the prominent role she played in the passage of the Consumer Protection Law of 1968. She also attended numerous parliamentary conferences, was president (shachō) of two publications: *Shōnen Shōjo Shimbun* and an English language gazette, and also served as chairperson of the board of directors (rijicho) of the Asian Women's Association. She was one of the very few women with truly distinguished legislative careers. Tokano Satoko died on November 7, 1971 at the age of 62.

Of the other women in the Class of '46 Matsuo Toshiko, also a socialist, was elected a total of six times, the last in 1958 as a DSP candidate. Born in 1907 she was a graduate of Nihon University. Like Tokano Satoko, she taught English - at the Yokohama YMCA Language School. She also served as principal of Nihon Joshi Eigakuin and was president of a company, Matsuo Kōsan. She travelled extensively and wrote two books: *Introduction to English Stenography* (in Japanese) and *Onna no Higagoto*, a book of random thoughts.

Yamashita Harue (b. 1901) was also elected six times, the first for the Nihon Shimpotō in 1946. She next joined the Minshutō and was elected under their banner in 1947, for the Kaishintō in 1952 and 1953, the Jiyūtō in 1955, and the LDP in 1958. She was the most successful, save one, of the conservative women elected to the lower house. From Fukushima, Yamashita graduated from Nihon Joshi Taiiku Semmon Gakkō (A physical education normal school for women) in 1922, taught for a while in Hiroshima prefecture and served as a reporter for *Mainichi Shimbun* before turning to elective politics. She was a very prominent conservative member of the Diet, often used as a showcase representative to international meetings because of her singularity as a female member of the ruling party.

The Class of 1946 also included Katō Shizuc who was elected to the House of Representatives only one other time, in 1947, as a socialist. She is well known to English reading students of Japan as Ishimoto Shizue, author of the famous book, *Facing Two Ways*, originally published in 1935. Born in 1897 in Aichi prefecture, she was nevertheless a candidate for election in Tokyo. Before the war she was one of Japan's most prominent feminists, a strong advocate of birth control and political rights for women. After graduating from Joshi Gakuin, she married Baron Ishimoto Keikichi and travelled with him to the U.S. where she met Margaret Sanger in 1920. She also brought Sanger to Japan and opened her own birth control clinic in 1934. She was arrested briefly for "dangerous thoughts" in December 1937, but was quickly released through the efforts of friends in high places. She was, however, forced to close her clinic in January 1938. She divorced her first husband and married labor leader Katō Kanjū in 1944. The latter also won election as a socialist in 1946 to create a highly unusual husband and wife team in the House.[4] In 1950 Katō Shizue was elected to the House of Councillors where she remained prominent until 1974. She did, however, fall out of favor with the left wing of the JSP following the Security Treaty crisis of 1960 when she criticized the "aimless demonstrations."

The twenty-six women who were elected for the first and only time in the initial postwar election of 1946 display remarkably similar characteristics. All but three who were socialists represented the various conservative parties. They were almost evenly divided among the three major conservative groups in 1946: Kokumintō, Jiyūtō and Shimpotō. They represented twenty-three different prefectures and their most common occupational background was as teachers. Nine of the twenty-six claimed this as their primary career. The remainder were scattered about the other occupations with, however, a surprising five coming from medicine (three physicians, one dentist, one midwife). About seventy percent of the women ever elected by conservative parties in Japan were successful only once - the election of 1946. If we eliminate from consideration the one-time-only females chosen in 1946 we are left with fifty-eight successful candidates. The party breakdown of these fifty-eight is as follows:

Party Breakdown of 58 Successful Women Candidates
(Excluding those elected only in 1946)

LDP	11	19.0%
JSP	24	41.4%
JCP	14	24.1%
DSP	5	8.6%
Komeito	3	3.4%

1947 and After

The roster of women elected to the lower house since 1947 also contains some illustrious names and interesting personalities. As of today the most famous is Doi Takako who became president of the JSP in 1986 following the party's dismal showing in the July elections. From Kobe and a graduate of Dōshisha University, she was a professor there, teaching Constitutional Law, from 1958 to 1970. She entered the political fray in the election of December 1969 at the age of forty-one and has been reelected continuously ever since. Outspoken, but regarded as flexible, her rise to the top of her party is testimony to her outstanding ability. She is considered to be an expert on foreign and defense policy and has been the subject of much attention since her assumption of the JSP presidency. In 1987 the party hastily issued a book under her name, *Seiji to Watashi*, most of which consists of interviews with and statements by other persons, including well-known foreigners. Her party made gains in the 1990 election, but her tenure as leader of Japan's number two party obviously depends on the party's electortal fortunes in the near future.

The most successful woman conservative in the House of Representatives was Nakayama Masa, who was elected eight times from Osaka (1947-1960 consecutively and 1967). She was narrowly defeated in the 1963 election, falling 141 votes short. She retired before the 1969 election, but her son, Nakayama Masaaki, replaced her on the conservative side of the aisle and he was elected every time thereafter until 1990. Nakayama Masa's father was born in the U.S. and her husband, Nakayama Fukuzō, was a conservative member of the House of Councillors.[5] She attended Ohio Wesleyan University, graduating in 1916, and enjoyed a distinguished prewar career in education before her recruitment to electoral politics. As a member of the Diet in the late 1940s she worked diligently to repatriate Japanese from overseas as chair of the Overseas Repatriation Committee. She was Parliamentary Vice-Minister for Welfare in the Fifth Yoshida Cabinet (1953-54) and has the distinction of being the first woman to rise to cabinet rank. She served for four months as Welfare Minister in the First Ikeda Cabinet in 1960.[6] She is clearly one of the most prominent women in the postwar history of the ruling party. She died in 1976.

Another socialist woman of some prominence was Fukuda Masako who was elected five consecutive times from Fukuoka from 1947 to 1955. Born in Kagoshima in 1912, Fukuda graduated from Tokyo Women's Medical College in 1934, did postgraduate work at Kyūshū University, receiving an M.D. degree in 1940. She became a physician specializing in obstetrics at several well-known hospitals, including Kyūdai. She also served in public health departments in Osaka and Tokyo and founded and headed a clinic which handled women's health problems. As an elected member of parliament she was identified with the left wing of the JSP and she became a member of the party's Central Executive Committee in which capacity she attended meetings of the Socialist International. She too was clearly a distinguished feminine personality in Japanese politics.

Kamichika Ichiko was another famous socialist Diet member who had a very colorful career. She was born in Nagasaki in 1888 and graduated from Tsuda English School (now a university) in 1913. She was a teacher and author, one of many female literary figures who belonged to the Seitōsha (Blue Stockings Society). She joined this group while a student, but dropped out of her own accord in order to graduate. Nevertheless, she was fired from her teaching position at Hirosaki Higher Girls School when her previous association with Seitōsha became known. In 1916, back in Tokyo, she stabbed and wounded her lover, the anarchist Ōsugi Sakae. She spent two years in prison, but she retained her commitment to socialism. She worked briefly as a reporter for *Mainichi Shimbun*, but her main career was in the world of letters as a writer, translator, editor and critic. From 1920 to 1937 she was married to Suzuki Atsushi. Like several other socialist women Kamichika had an education and career oriented toward English language and literature. She could appropriately be described as cosmopolitan in style and outlook. As a left wing socialist from Tokyo, she was elected five times: 1953, 1955, 1958, 1963 and 1967. In the Diet she is best remembered for leading the fight to secure passage of the anti-prostitution law in 1955. After her retirement from politics she brought suit in 1970 in an attempt to prevent the release of a film which depicted events in her life, such as the stabbing of Ōsugi. The film was entitled *Erosu to Gyakusatsu* (Eroticism and Violence). Her contention was based on the "right to privacy", but the suit was dismissed because she had written about these events anyway. The case caused a great flurry in the popular press. Her autobiography, *Kamichika Ichiko Jiden: Waga Ai Waga Tatakai* was published in 1972. Kamichika died in 1981 at the age of 93.

Yet another JSP member who was active until very recently is Kaneko Mitsu, also from Tokyo. After an unsuccessful run as an endorsed candidate in 1969, she was elected six consecutive times from 1972 to 1986. She was born in Tokyo in 1914, attended an Anglican school in Japan before going on for graduate work in the Yale University School of Public Health. She also took a degree in nursing from Toronto University. In the early postwar years she was head of the Nursing Division of the Welfare Ministry and, in 1960, she was appointed assistant professor of Nursing at Todai Medical School. Here she remained until securing her Diet seat. She also had a term as President of the Japan Nursing Association.

The most successful JCP female candidates have been Kobayashi Masako and Tanaka Michiko. Kobayashi was elected five consecutive times from Tokyo between 1969 and 1980. She claimed to have been self-educated and a day-laborer, but she later acquired certification as a teacher. She did teach elementary school for a short time.

Tanaka Michiko ran as an independent from Aichi first district and was successful in 1972, 1976, 1979, 1983 and 1986. She failed by a very slim margin in 1980 and chose not to run in 1990. Though officially listed as an independent, Tanaka Michiko supported the JCP which never ran another candidate against her. A colorful figure and stump speaker, she was born in 1922 and graduated from Nihon Joshi University, specializing in Social Work. She then served as an instructor at Mie Prefectural Normal School for Women. Shortly after the war she was hospitalized with tuberculosis and, while convalescing she met Tanaka Reizō, a Waseda University Economics professor whom she married in 1954. After her own recovery Tanaka Michiko secured a position as assistant professor of Social Welfare at Nihon Fukushi University. She is widely known for her nationwide speech tours and her tireless efforts on behalf of women's welfare. She also wrote an anonymous best-seller entitled *Mikon no Anata Ni*.

Female candidates, including successful ones, have been much more in evidence in the House of Councillors which lies outside the scope of this study. It may be mentioned in passing, however, that the House of Councillors has been more appealing to women candidates because political parties (especially the LDP) have specifically recruited women for their sex and name familiarity in the national constituency. The 252 members of the House of Councillors are elected for six year terms, half every three years. Of these, 152 are chosen in prefecture-wide elections, but the other 100 are selected nationwide. Until 1980 candidates in the national constituency ran as individuals, but beginning in 1983 a proportional representation system was introduced in which voters specify political parties. Each party prepares a list of candidates who will be declared winners depending on the number of votes for their party. Since the new proportional system came into effect, parties have often listed women as token candidates. Both before and after this new system some women elected to the House of Councillors have been "talent" candidates, including media personalities selected exclusively for their name recognition.[7]

The more successful female representatives whose careers I have encapsulated have in common the fact that they were all, save one, elected at least five times to the House of Representatives. The list, in fact, includes all women elected five times or more. They also have some other things in common. As a group they have a decidedly left-of-center anti-establishment orientation. They are well educated, foreign centered, often with English language teaching competence. They are prominent in intellectual professions, especially education. Their backgrounds, indeed, suggest what has been available in Japan to women of some means, ability and talent rather than the kind of training thought desirable for men as a background for politics. There has long been room for a small number of exceptional women of distinction in high profile positions in Japanese society. Obviously, to get as far as they did, these political women needed the support, financial and otherwise, of their families that enabled them to attend the schools they did. Truly exceptional, they also needed party endorsement and hence the qualities that enabled them to get along with the "old boys" in the political establishment. Almost all of the women represent urban constituencies where they have placed third, fourth or fifth in the multi-member district system. Because of these features women cohorts rank rather high collectively on the elite status rating scale. The overall elite rating for all eighty-four women is +6.1 The rating is boosted by high positive points in education, local government and company directorships, but brought back down somewhat by negative numbers in government service and major university attendance.

In most respects women in the Japanese Diet have been about as successful or unsuccessful as one might expect. There are enough to provide some visibility and the appearance of equal opportunity. That the number of winning candidates has tapered off, however, should be seen as an indication that electoral politics and politicians in Japan retain much of their original quality and that the "success" of the system of representative government has brought with it increasing rigidity within the membership of the LDP and other parties as well. The decline in endorsed female candidates may also be due to the fact that women in general have been encouraged to eschew partisan politics and stand above the fractious party squabbles. That most successful women at the national level have left-wing party identification is probably an indication that a woman's entrance into the world of politics is itself an expression of dissent and/or alienation. Since the LDP politically represents the "establishment", such alienated women move toward groups which offer opposition. It is clear, however, that the majority of women voters in Japan do not share this dissatisfaction at the voting booth.

In Japanese politics, as elsewhere, women seemingly must begin at or near the top. Few serve apprenticeships. Very few are hired as assistants or secretaries to male Diet members, a source of recruitment now heavily favored by the LDP. Therefore, they virtually must have "elite" backgrounds, but they also have to try harder to get endorsed and elected. A campaign, moreover, is very costly and women, like all candidates, must have sources of support in the constituency itself. Since this is accomplished by most candidates through their *kōenkai* [8] women find it particularly difficult in all but the most unconventional districts. Women in all parties have a hard time establishing and maintaining *kōenkai*. The only exception to the difficulty encountered by women is in the JCP which has actively and consciously recruited women candidates since the 1960s. Costly election campaigns for LDP candidates militate against the selection of women, but the JCP does not have that constraint. Since the JCP is not split into factions like the LDP, it is more attractive for politically minded women.

NOTES

1 See Susan J. Pharr, *Political Women in Japan* (1981), especially Chapter Two, pp. 15-41. Also, by the same author, "The Politics of Women's Rights", in Ward and Sakamoto, ed., *Democratizing Japan* (1981), pp. 221-249. Actually, of course, all generalized treatments of postwar Japanese politics make note of the enfranchisement of women.

2 There were 2,770 candidates for the 466 seats in 1946. Seventy-nine of these were women. In the April 1947 election eighty-five out of 1,590 candidates were women.

3 For women's voting rates, see Naka, *Kokkai Giin no Kōsei to Henka*, p. 174. See also Pharr, *Political Women*, p. 25. Curtis, *The Japanese Way of Politics* (pp. 204-205) provides a table showing voting rates for 1965, 1976 and 1986 broken down by sex and party preference. Women supported the LDP by five to seven percentage points less than did men, but most of this was accounted for by a five to ten percent higher support rate for independent candidates.

4 Katō Kanjū was one of a handful of moderate socialists first elected to the Diet in 1936. He was also one of the small number of persons elected before and immediately after the war, but not in 1942. Thus, he was not purged. He was Labor Minister in the coalition cabinet organized by Ashida Hitoshi in 1948. Altogether, he was elected nine times to the House of Representatives.

5 Nakayama Fukuzō, a Todai graduate and attorney, was a House of Councillors member from Osaka in the 1960s.

6 There have been five other women cabinet members: Kondō Tsuruyo, a member of the House of Councillors who was Director of the Science and Technology Agency from July 1962 to July 1963 in the second Ikeda Cabinet; Ishimoto Shigeru, also a member of the House of Councillors, who served as Director General of the Environmental Agency in the second Nakasone Cabinet from October 1984 until it was reshuffled in December 1985. In the first Kaifu Cabinet (Aug. 1989) there were two: Mayumi Moriyama,(Upper House member) as Chief Cabinet Secretary and Takahara Sumiko(a non-Diet member), Economic Planning Agency and in the third Kaifu Cabinet (Dec. 1990) Santō Akiko, an Upper House member, was named Director-General of the Science and Technology Agency. Only the position of Chief Cabinet Secretary could be considered an important one.

7   In the 1986 House of Councillors election there were fifty-two women among 237 candidates listed by parties in the proportional field, but only twenty-seven out of 253 in the prefectural races. Since, in the proportional races, one does not vote for an individual but for a party, it is safer to nominate women. In prefectural contests women sometimes run on their own, though they may also receive party endorsement. "Talent" candidates have also included men. The process began in 1962 when a TV star, Fujiwara Aki, won first place in the national constituency. In 1968, Ishihara Shintarō, a well known writer, won first place with over three million votes, almost three times the number of the second place finisher. In 1968 the top four national constituency winners were "talent" candidates. In 1974 the top spot went to Miyata Teru, a male TV personality. See Herbert Passin, *A Season of Voting* (1979), pp. 128-129; Michael Blaker, *Japan At the Polls* (1976), pp. 26-29, 57-64; and Naka, *Kokkai Giin no Kōsei to Henka*, pp. 180-185. Passin, in particular, thinks that the glamour may have worn off and the proportional system minimizes the importance of name recognition.

8   On *kōenkai*, see Curtis, *The Japanese Way of Politics*, p. 190 and Ronald J. Hrebenar, "The Changing Postwar Party System", in Hrebenar, ed., *The Japanese Party System*, p. 17 et.seq.

Chapter 10

Conclusion:
The Diet Membership in Global Perspective
■

The creation of a representative body was, in some respects, a revolutionary undertaking in the constitution of 1889. Although this constitution did not grant sovereignty to the representatives of the people, the establishmment of the Diet seemed at first glance to have been entirely the result of Japan's recent contact with the Western world. The constitution, and the parliament it provided for, was instituted from above in order to gain international respectability and treaty equality with the Western powers, but it was also a response by the *hanbatsu* oligarchy to pressure from dissenters who couched their opposition in the terms of political philosophy then current in the West. Although occasioned by these general conditions, it is well to remember George Sansom's phrase of many years ago that the Meiji constitution "was surprisingly like the constitution that would have emerged in Japan if, without reference to foreign example, the government had logically pursued the line of development that it had already taken during its conflict with opposition parties."[1]

>   With the convening of the Diet in 1890, there marched for the first time to the centre of the stage of national policy-making representatives of a 'new' class, a class which had in fact been waiting in the wings with envy and increasing ferment for some considerable time. To this class we may give the generic title of Men of Enterprise. All in all, the elections were a triumph for the middle classes, and above all for the village land-lord-entrepreneurs, who in being returned to the Diet in such numbers had come into their own.[2]

The Meiji leadership, in providing the constitution, no doubt "reaffirmed the traditional value system"[3], but "doing what came naturally" in the Japanese context was also "natural" in the context of the modern capitalist state that was emerging in Japan. If the early Diet was dominated by entrepreneurs and land-lord-capitalists who alone had the right to vote and run for elective office, this was "natural." And, it is also possible to call the Diet a "committee of the bour-geoisie" whose members, while often opposing the policies of the government oligarchy, were nevertheless vitally interested in advancing the material interests of their class. The composition of the Diet and its evolution over time clearly reflect this class bias. Both in its Imperial and National stages, the Diet was an important though not necessarily preeminent part of the "superstructure" by which the dominant class sought to augment its power. Japanese historians and others, including elected members of the JCP, have long been aware of this bour-geois character because Japan fits so well the Marxian stages of development. Shiga Yoshio was astute when he wrote that Lenin might well have been writing about immediate postwar Japan when he said (about Russia) that in the March [sic] Revolution Russia became a bourgeois democratic republic with close con-nections between the state and monopoly capitalism and a high level of competi-tion.[4]

It is axiomatic that changes in the composition of the Diet reflect changes in the structure of society and the economy of Japan. While it is unquestionable that pre-Meiji Japan had a rigidly stratified society, there is much disagreement over the class structure in modern times. That there has been progressive movement toward a fully bourgeois society is not subject to doubt. Class conflict has been muted, but there certainly has been change since the 1890s. This is apparent in this study in the sections on Occupation (Chapter Two) and Education (Chapter Three) where it is revealed that Diet members as a group stand somewhat in advance of society as a whole. For example, the percentage of Diet members who have attended universities is always about double that of the electorate. In contrast to local assemblies where career patterns of representatives closely resemble that of their constituents, the career patterns of National Diet members are consistently more "elite" than that of the general public whom they represent.[5] However, the rate of change in these career patterns and educational background does not differ significantly from the national rate. Moreover, the change is largely incremental, even in periods where great transformation is pre-sumed to have occurred. This kind of change suggests "smoothness" in the development of modern Japanese society. The cumulative effect is significant change and great differences in many features of Diet membership with much of the alteration coming in such a way as to give the impression of remaining the same. The graphs and tables in Chapters Two and Three particularly reveal the incremental and cumulative nature of the transformation.

In a recent book, *The Japanese Way of Politics*, Gerald Curtis notes in the preface that Japan has "a political system that has combined stability in terms of party power with a remarkable capacity for flexibility and change."[6] Stability in hand with flexibility is a generalization that might well be made for all of Japan in the modern era. In discussing the politics of the last thirty years, Curtis goes on to say ". . . it would be hard to imagine how this situation could have been otherwise, given the rapidity of economic and social changes during these decades."[7] These are unquestionably accurate statements and, although Curtis' context is the party politics of the last three decades, these statements about change and stability hold true for the entirety of Japan's parliamentary history. This is evident in the statistics on the composition of the representative assembly - the Imperial and National Diet - assembled in this book.

During the century covered by this study Japan moved from an "underdeveloped" or "peripheral" state barely accepted in the family of nations through several stages but always in the direction of greater wealth and power in the world community. In the process the composition of society necessarily changed, but the transformation did not come all of a sudden. Japan became more urban and less rural, the economy became relentlessly capitalistic and the culture, already secularized, became thoroughly integrated. The population, in growing increments, partook of world culture and technology until Japan became first a nation between the exploiters (First World = "core") and exploited (Third World = periphery) and then, after the Pacific War, a major "core" country herself.[8] Society became ever more urban, apparently less rural and traditional. Nevertheless, most serious observers of the Japanese social scene, even in the affluent 1980s and 1990s, see many important surviving traces of tradition. Yet, the cumulative picture is that of a society today whose physical and cultural landscape is hardly recognizable from that of its nineteenth century antecedents. The alterations, which may be regarded in sum as revolutionary, were accomplished without violent social upheaval despite several traumatic national experiences, most notably the total loss of a total war. Political transformation, including changes seen in the membership of the Diet, has come about in much the same fashion.

The most abrupt line of division in the patterns of development appears to come with the end of the war, showing up in the election of 1946. However, the Occupation era (elections of 1946, 1947 and 1949) is itself aberrant in many ways, not meshing well with the trends and patterns antecedent to the war or those in evidence from 1952 onward. What happened in many areas in 1952 and 1953 was a resumption of recruitment patterns that had been arrested by the abnormality occasioned by the war and the Occupation.[9] It is as if the Japanese body politic, symbolized by the Diet, were placed in a state of suspended animation from 1942 to 1952, during which time some alien force took over, only to be returned to its "normal course of development" in the latter year, now on an elevated plane. The elevation is the result of some rather substantial leaps in the educational background of the membership, but the upward swing follows the curve already established before the war.

The only thing peculiar about any of this is that some rather "peculiar" things happened to Japan in the 1930s and 1940s. However, even the descent into the "dark valley" of military fascism and the loss of a total war were not unique experiences. The same kinds of things happened elsewhere. What was outstanding if not unique was the equanimity with which Japan recovered to place herself back on the track from which she had been derailed. Back on the track, the nation resumed the relatively smooth, transitional pace which is reflected in the career patterns of the Diet representatives.

The changes in the character of the Diet members as well as other alterations in Japanese political culture are not dissimilar to those occurring in other advanced industrialized countries, especially in the last three decades or so. Almost everywhere in this period there has been a weakening of party identification among voters as political parties contending for control have sought ways to increase their popular appeal and either gain or remain in power.[10] Japan has been an unusual case because conservative forces have dominated the electoral scene almost continuously from the beginning. In particular, a single party has organized every cabinet since 1955. Compositional patterns of elected representatives, however, are not unique. The absence of uniqueness, however, does not mean that one should anticipate a convergence of Japanese political forms and behavior with that of Western models, including the United States. What has happened in Japan is the product of her own experience and what occurs in the future will also be so derived. "To the extent that there is a convergence in the political and economic life of the advanced industrialized democratic countries, that convergence is Japanizing the West as much as it is Americanizing Japan."[11]

Political and other developments in Japan have, of course, been very "Japanese", but being "Japanese" is not very different from being anything else. Representative institutions tend to behave in similar but not identical fashion and they tend to attract or recruit similar kinds of individuals. Some of the features of parliamentary practice that are pronounced, for example, in Britain or the U.S., are less obvious - perhaps hidden beneath the surface - in Japan. The reverse is also true. For instance, intraparty factions are more formal and obvious in Japan. Though they exist in the U.S. and Britain, they are more informal and obscure. By contrast, former military men are common in the British House of Commons, but almost unheard of in Japan, even before the loss of the Pacific War. Attorneys are legion in the American Congress, much less evident in either Japan or Britain. These are minor differences and there are many other features that are remarkably consonant - elite educational backgrounds, to mention but one.

The issue of continuity versus discontinuity was taken up in Chapter Four which also considered the importance of the end of the war as a major dividing line in Japanese history and politics. That section called attention to some of the variant interpretations of the Occupation. The role of the Occupation in promoting continuity or discontinuity has continued to arouse interest in recent scholarly literature. Sakamoto Yoshikazu has pointed out that both conservative and progressive (reformist) forces experienced discontinuity from the prewar and wartime era to the immediate postwar. This initial discontinuity affected the conservatives most seriously, but was counterbalanced in part when the "reverse course" turned against some of its own liberalizing reforms and against the Communist Party in particular. It was, argues Sakamoto, the reformists who "would be expected to have encouraged discontinuity, [but who] became the vanguard of supporters of continuity in the very reforms wrought by SCAP and the United States." Sakamoto concludes by comparing the position of the Japanese left to that of Indian nationalists vis-a-vis Britain, by noting that "the elite of the British colonies who studied in Britain and absorbed the British value system often became the vanguard of anti-British movements after returning home."[12]

The comparison seems rather strained, although one of the great ironies of the Occupation was the generation of essentially left wing reforms in Japan under the aegis of a military figure largely regarded as standing on the right wing of the American political spectrum. Socialists and Communists, who would have been viewed with great suspicion in the U.S., emerged as the chief initial beneficiaries of the American sponsored reforms. These men, however, had not absorbed the "American value system" as the Indian nationalists had perhaps absorbed the British. Because of the way the purges were conducted in Japan these leftists found themselves unexpectedly at liberty and in positions to gain prominence by championing the liberalizing early postwar reforms.

That there was some discontinuity, as Sakamoto and also Ishikawa Masumi[13] have noted, is not subject to serious doubt. It should not be overstressed, however. There is a good deal of statistical evidence suggesting that the wartime period and Occupation combined to represent a period of abnormality. Most of the prewar trends, detailed in the earlier chapters, were resumed beginning in 1952. In a way, it is as if the ten years from 1942 to 1952 simply didn't happen in Japanese electoral politics.

Purging under the Occupation began in late 1945 with the designation of war criminals. To the original list of such criminals were added in late December the names of six sitting Diet members.[14] Following the termination of hostilities the Imperial Diet, elected in 1942, met twice in emergency session in late 1945: September 4-5 and November 27-December 18. By the second of these sessions a number of persons had voluntarily resigned, so that there were fifty-seven vacancies. Most of the Diet members who had been Yokusan "recommended" candidates in 1942 had by now banded together to form the Shimpotō. Then, in January 1946 SCAP issued its most sweeping purge directive, which, among other things, banned from public office all persons who had been Yokusan recommended candidates. This rendered ineligible 381 out of 466 in the House of Representatives for the first postwar election. One week later SCAP issued another order, this time demanding that an election be held "after March 15." The government, led by Prime Minister Shidehara, was required to determine eligibility for candidacy. This it did on February 9 by including on the proscribed list not only Yokusan recommendees from 1942 but others who were associated with right wing or patriotic movements and organizations.[15]

Ishikawa and others have made much of the discontinuity, pointing out that the purges wiped out the leadership cadre in the political parties and made possible the election to the Diet of an unprecedented number of newcomers.[16] Ishikawa, moreover, emphasizes the discontinuity by stressing that only about one-fourth of the Yokusan recommended candidates and only about fifty percent of all Diet members elected in 1942 ever sat again in the National Diet. As suggested in Chapter Four, however, the continuity-discontinuity question can be given a different "spin" by noting that no less than 210 persons who were elected in the days of the Imperial Diet (that is, up to the twenty-first election in 1942) were also returned to the Diet after the war. This includes sixty-five who eschewed the 1942 election (either as unsuccessful candidates or by declining to run) but came back in 1946, 1947 or 1949[17] and eleven who stayed out of politics (at least on the surface) all through the "aberration" that is represented by the decade from 1942 to 1952: the wartime and Occupation periods combined. Steven Reed, in a recent article, has also pointed out that some of the purgees used surrogates to run in the Occupation era elections.[18]

Although the purges were initially directed against the right and ultra-nationalists, in 1949 and 1950 SCAP purged the left, singling out the Communists. This action not only promoted discontinuity in the ranks of the JCP, but compromised the promise of "democracy" which the Occupation reforms seemed to demand. Sakamoto notes that "one would only have to recall the prewar history of Japan where the repression of Communists was a prelude to repression of liberals. . . . One may also refer to the experience of many Third World nations in the contemporary world where the policy of Western countries supporting reactionary or authoritarian anti-Communist forces has not led to the blossoming of liberal-democracy, but instead to the polarization of society to the detriment of democratic values."[19]

The key to Japan's "success" as a country (i.e. its stability) is the flexibility of its political (and other) institutions. The system "works" regardless of its form.

Is it too simplistic to suggest that the internal political contradictions were worked out sometime before the "opening" of Japan, so that, despite some national tragedies and miscalculations, the nation has held together very well in modern times? The evidence for this contention is provided, in part, by the sense of continuity seen in the evolution of "democratic" political institutions in recent times, including the membership of the Diet.

But, is Japan now or has she ever been "democratic"? Does it matter? In a recent book, Ronald J. Hrebenar quotes from a lecture by Raymond Aron, delivered in April 1981:

> For the last thirty years, the same party has been in power in Japan; opposition parties, which sometimes win in local elections, do exist; newspapers which freely criticize those in power, also exist. Because of this continuity, Japan has risen to be one of the foremost nations; it is Japan which has best withstood the shocks of the oil crisis; it is Japan which has been most successful in achieving a close cooperation between the Ministry of Industry and privateenterprise; it is Japan which most successfully combines medium (even long-term) planningand the free play of the market. None of this would have been possible if, from one day to the next, the plans of the government and its priorities and values were in danger of being upset by the results of the elections. In our countries, proud of alternation in government, the changes in public opinion and in the electorate every two, four, or seven years, add to the hazards ofthe world economic climate. [20]

In this lecture Aron went on to qualify his praise for Japan and concluded that peaceful alternation, a la Britain and the U.S., was preferable to violent and, by implication, to Japan's one party rule. This, in turn, suggests that Japan is neither very "democratic" nor very stable, because of the absence of alternation. It seems to me that Aron has fallen victim to the tendency, so wisely described by Robert J. Smith, that "No analyst is ever very far removed from the biases of experience and understanding of his or her own society, which color in fundamental ways that analyst's interpretation of other systems."[21] Smith, incidentally, goes on to add that recent criticism of Japan in Western media and scholarship seeks to explain away Japan's successes, "for otherwise we should be forced to concede that a system different from our own, without becoming like us, has achieved goals we have long taken to be uniquely ours."[22]

The essence of this study is that Japan has created a system that is very solid and stable. Political systems, like other systems, covet stability. The purpose of a constitutional system, in particularly, is to perpetuate stability. No less than monarchs, the bourgeoisie, when dominant, desires constancy and regularity. A system based wholly or in part on elected representation should ideally reflect slow, gradual change rather than sudden lurches in opposite directions. This is what the Japanese political system was designed to do, both in 1889 and 1947, and it is what it has done. In this objective it is no different from other parliamentary "democracies" which are, indeed, designed to perpetuate the "rule of the bourgeoisie."

NOTES

1 George B. Sansom, *The Western World and Japan* (1950), p. 358.

2 R.H.P. Mason, *Japan's First General Election, 1890* (1969), p. 197.

3 Mason, *Japan's First General Election*, p. 204.

4 Shiga Yoshio, *Kokka Ron* (1949), p. 183.

5 Daniel B. Ramsdell, "Prefectural Assemblies in Japan: Hokkaido and Shimane, 1947-1983", *Scholarship in Review* (June 1986), pp. 14-24.

6 Curtis, *The Japanese Way of Politics*, p. vxi.

7 Curtis, *The Japanese Way of Politics*, p. 16.

8 Japan was also unquestionably an exploiter as semi-peripheral states sometimes are in the Wallersteinian model. The rhetoric of the Greater East Asian Co-Prosperity Sphere in the first half of the 1940s played on Japan's exploitative, intermediary position.

9 The 1942 election was highly abnormal, although Edward J. Drea argues that it was transitional between the two constitutional eras in modern Japan. See Drea, *The 1942 Japanese General Election*, preface. See also Reed, "The People Spoke", pp. 316-317.

10 Curtis, *The Japanese Way of Politics*, p. 190.

11 Curtis, *The Japanese Way of Politics*, p. 248.

12 Sakamoto Yoshikazu, "The International Context of the Occupation", in Ward and Sakamoto, ed., *Democratizing Japan*, pp. 67-68.

13 Ishikawa, *Sengo Seiji Kōzōshi*, pp. 1-7.

14 The six were Nakajima Chikuhei, Sakurai Hyōgorō, Ōta Masataka, Ikezaki Chūkō,, Shiōden Nobutaka, and Sasakawa Ryōichi. See Uchida Kenzō, "Japan's Postwar Conservative Parties", in Ward and Sakamoto, ed., *Democratizing Japan*, p. 317.

[15] Uchida, "Japan's Postwar Conservative Parties", pp. 323-324.

[16] Ishikawa, *Sengo Seiji Kōzōshi*, pp. 5-6. See also Curtis, *The Japanese Way of Politics*, pp. 6-7. Ishikawa does, however, point out that many of the newcomers were actually sponsored by purged old timers who provided their *jiban*.

[17] Fifty-two of this number made their comebacks in 1946, eight in 1947 and five in 1949.

[18] Reed, "The People Spoke", p. 316.

[19] Sakamoto, "The International Context of the Occupation", p. 65.

[20] Hrebenar, "The Changing Postwar Party System", p. 9.

[21] Robert J. Smith, *Japanese Society: Tradition, Self and the Social Order* (1983), p. 128.

[22] Smith, *Japanese Society*, p. 129.

Appendix A & B

Bibliography

& Index

■

Appendix A

	Total No.	A	B	C	D	Women
TABLE A-1 **IMPERIAL AND NATIONAL DIET** **Occupations Correlated with Miscellaneous Categories** **(All Members)**						
Agriculture	735	85.4	45.6	2.4	2.18	—
Business	1368	62.2	86.5	0.4	2.78	0.4
Education	402	48.0	28.4	11.9	2.77	6.2
Higher Education	93	9.7	21.5	1.1	3.20	4.3
Govt. (Central)	414	13.9	32.5	1.2	3.81	0.2
Govt. (Home Min.)	234	15.1	38.8	—	3.27	—
Total C. Govt.	648	14.4	34.5	0.8	3.64	0.2
Local Govt.	356	16.3	36.3	1.7	2.34	0.8
Journalism	424	32.5	32.3	3.1	4.09	1.4
Law	544	49.8	25.7	2.8	3.36	0.7
Labor/Soc.	120	55.0	2.5	96.7	4.58	2.5
Medicine	149	59.7	21.5	0.7	2.70	4.0
Military	55	20.0	25.5	—	2.05	—
Politics	404	41.7	4.0	1.2	4.28	3.0
Religion	20	15.0	15.0	—	2.55	—
Women's Orgs.	7	14.3	—	—	1.57	100.0
Writing	22	27.3	9.1	9.1	3.23	13.6
Blue Collar	50	20.0	—	88.0	3.52	—
White Collar	149	23.5	19.5	8.7	4.23	2.0
Soka Gakkai	10	50.0	—	—	5.50	10.0
Other/None	13	—	9.1	18.2	3.00	9.1

A = Local Assembly members
B = Company Directors
C = Union Backgrounds
D = Average number of times elected

Figures are percentages of the total number of Diet members in each occupational category.

TABLE A-2
IMPERIAL AND NATIONAL DIET
Apprenticeship, Women, Professionalism
(All Members)

	All members		Prewar		All Postwar		New Postwar	
	No.	%	No.	%	No.	%	No.	%
Company Directors	2294	41.2	1737	49.1	655	29.2	557	27.4
Local Assembly mem.	2832	50.9	2190	61.9	736	32.8	642	31.6
Union Background	299	5.4	33	0.9	287	12.8	266	13.1
Female Members	84	1.5	—		84	3.7	84	4.1
Avg. No. of times elected	3.12		2.65		4.20		3.92	

TABLE A-3
IMPERIAL AND NATIONAL DIET
NEW MEMBERS
Education

Election	1	2	3-4	5-6	7	8	9	10	11	12	13	14	15
University	15.6	16.3	9.4	20.2	32.9	31.2	25.0	36.9	50.0	47.1	52.3	52.7	59.5
Major University	12.9	13.8	7.4	14.0	28.0	24.7	20.8	29.7	45.2	42.4	46.4	47.7	54.8
TODAI	4.0	1.8	1.1	1.6	7.9	4.3	0.8	5.8	11.2	13.7	15.9	13.0	19.0
KYODAI	-	-	-	-	-	-	-	0.5	1.5	1.3	1.3	2.2	4.0
WASEDA	0.6	0.6	1.1	3.5	3.5	3.2	7.5	4.4	6.6	7.8	7.9	9.0	13.1
KEIO	6.2	7.2	3.0	5.0	5.3	7.5	2.5	4.4	10.7	5.2	6.6	5.4	5.6
MEIJI	0.9	3.0	1.1	1.6	4.8	4.3	4.2	3.4	6.6	4.6	4.0	3.6	7.5
CHUO	0.6	1.2	1.1	2.3	5.3	5.4	2.5	7.8	7.1	5.2	6.0	6.9	1.6
NIHON	-	-	-	-	-	-	2.5	1.5	0.5	3.3	2.0	4.0	2.8
HOSEI	0.6	-	-	-	0.8	-	0.8	1.9	-	1.3	2.0	3.2	0.8
TOHOKU	-	-	-	-	-	-	-	-	-	-	-	-	-
HOKUDAI	-	-	-	-	0.4	-	-	-	1.0	-	0.7	0.4	0.4
High(er) School	-	-	-	-	-	-	-	0.5	-	-	-	0.7	1.2
Middle School	-	0.6	0.8	0.8	1.3	3.2	0.8	1.5	3.6	3.9	4.0	4.0	4.0
Elementary	-	-	0.4	1.6	3.5	5.4	-	1.0	0.5	-	-	0.4	-
Private Education	46.7	50.0	47.2	45.7	40.8	38.7	35.0	29.6	18.9	17.6	14.6	8.3	4.4
Other Schools	6.5	8.4	7.9	9.3	7.5	8.6	9.2	11.7	11.2	13.1	15.9	11.6	17.1
None Listed	31.1	24.7	34.4	22.5	12.4	12.9	30.0	18.9	15.8	18.3	13.2	22.4	13.9
Total number	300	166	265	258	228	93	120	206	196	153	151	277	252
Year	**1890**	**1892**	**1894**	**1898**	**1902**	**1903**	**1904**	**1908**	**1912**	**1915**	**1917**	**1920**	**1924**

Elections three and four (1894) and five and six (1898) have been combined.
Figures are percentages of the total number of new members in each year.

Continued on next page

TABLE A-3 CONTINUED
IMPERIAL AND NATIONAL DIET
New Members - Education

Election	16	17	18	19	20	21	22	23	24	25	26	27	28
University	66.5	67.7	61.7	52.8	51.6	61.9	50.5	63.6	66.2	73.4	68.8	66.7	61.8
Major University	60.6	63.0	54.7	50.4	46.4	51.7	41.8	54.7	56.9	65.9	58.4	58.0	48.5
TODAI	24.9	22.0	22.7	15.0	15.1	18.8	11.9	14.7	23.1	37.6	33.3	28.1	14.7
KYODAI	2.9	3.9	3.1	5.5	2.2	4.5	3.9	4.4	5.6	7.3	4.2	8.8	2.9
WASEDA	12.1	15.0	10.1	12.6	11.8	11.9	10.4	9.8	6.7	5.5	6.3	8.8	5.9
KEIO	1.1	0.8	2.3	-	-	5.0	2.6	2.2	1.5	1.8	-	1.8	7.4
MEIJI	6.4	7.9	5.5	5.5	3.2	4.0	3.9	7.1	4.1	0.9	2.1	3.5	-
CHUO	4.0	6.3	4.7	5.5	2.2	3.0	3.4	4.9	6.2	5.5	2.1	3.5	10.3
NIHON	7.5	6.3	6.3	4.7	5.4	3.0	3.4	7.6	7.7	4.6	10.4	3.5	2.9
HOSEI	1.7	0.8	-	1.6	2.2	0.5	1.3	2.2	1.0	0.9	-	-	-
TOHOKU	-	-	-	-	4.3	0.5	0.7	1.8	1.0	0.9	-	-	1.5
HOKUDAI	-	-	-	-	-	0.5	0.3	-	-	0.9	-	-	2.9
High(er) School	-	-	-	-	-	-	3.1	0.9	1.5	-	2.1	-	-
Middle School	3.5	3.9	6.3	5.5	2.2	8.9	4.7	8.0	5.6	1.8	8.3	3.5	5.9
Elementary	0.6	-	-	-	-	-	0.3	0.9	0.5	-	-	-	-
Private Education	4.6	2.4	2.3	-	-	-	-	-	0.5	-	-	-	-
Other Schools	15.0	11.0	14.8	19.7	23.7	21.3	24.6	12.0	13.8	21.1	10.4	21.1	25.0
None Listed	9.8	15.0	14.8	22.0	22.6	7.9	16.6	14.7	11.8	3.7	10.4	8.8	4.4
Total number	173	127	128	127	93	202	386	225	195	109	48	57	68
Year	1928	1930	1932	1936	1937	1942	1946	1947	1949	1952	1953	1955	1958

Continued on next page

TABLE A-3 CONTINUED
IMPERIAL AND NATIONAL DIET
New Members - Education

Election	29	30	31	32	33	34	35	36	37	38	39
University	61.0	65.3	58.8	69.7	71.6	74.4	75.0	69.4	75.0	78.1	80.5
Major University	56.0	51.4	50.9	51.5	55.9	59.2	55.2	64.0	50.1	54.8	53.4
TODAI	33.9	23.6	17.6	17.2	20.0	21.6	10.5	22.2	15.5	23.4	18.0
KYODAI	1.7	2.8	8.8	2.0	1.1	4.0	5.3	-	1.2	3.1	3.0
WASEDA	8.5	9.7	8.8	14.1	10.5	13.6	10.5	5.6	6.0	7.8	11.3
KEIO	1.7	2.8	3.9	5.1	5.3	6.4	13.2	16.7	8.3	4.7	4.5
MEIJI	1.7	6.9	2.9	1.0	2.1	0.8	2.6	-	4.8	1.6	2.3
CHUO	3.4	2.8	1.0	3.0	9.5	8.0	9.2	11.1	9.5	6.3	6.8
NIHON	3.4	1.4	2.0	6.1	3.2	3.2	2.6	5.6	2.4	6.3	0.8
HOSEI	-	-	1.0	1.0	2.1	0.8	-	-	1.2	1.6	2.3
TOHOKU	1.7	1.4	2.9	1.0	2.1	0.8	1.3	-	1.2	-	3.0
HOKUDAI	-	-	2.0	1.0	-	-	-	2.8	-	-	1.5
High(er) School	1.7	-	2.9	3.0	5.3	2.4	7.9	5.6	9.5	9.4	12.0
Middle School	1.7	2.8	3.9	6.1	-	2.4	3.9	5.6	1.2	3.1	1.5
Elementary	6.8	2.8	6.9	4.0	2.1	-	1.3	-	1.2	-	-
Private Education	-	-	-	-	-	-	-	-	-	-	-
Other Schools	27.1	22.2	24.5	16.2	17.9	20.8	11.8	16.7	13.1	9.4	6.0
None Listed	1.7	6.9	2.9	1.0	3.2	0.8	-	2.8	-	-	-
Total Number	59	72	102	99	95	125	76	36	84	64	133
Year	1960	1963	1967	1969	1972	1976	1979	1980	1983	1986	1990

		TABLE A-4		
		IMPERIAL AND NATIONAL DIET		
		New Members as Percent of Total		
Election	Year	Total membership	New members	Percent
1	1890	300	300	100
2	1892	323	166	51.4
3/4	1894	629	265	42.1
5/6	1898	628	258	41.1
7	1902	376	228	60.6
8	1903	380	93	24.5
9	1904	404	120	29.7
10	1908	422	206	48.8
11	1912	413	196	47.5
12	1915	403	153	38.0
13	1917	414	151	36.5
14	1920	504	277	55.0
15	1924	513	252	49.1
16	1928	467	173	37.0
17	1930	468	127	27.1
18	1932	475	128	26.9
19	1936	481	127	26.4
20	1937	494	93	18.8
21	1942	473	202	42.7

TABLE A-4 CONTINUED
IMPERIAL AND NATIONAL DIET
New Members as Percent of Total

Election	Year	Total membership	New members	Percent
22	1946	469	386	82.3
23	1947	474	225	47.5
24	1949	468	195	41.7
25	1952	467	109	23.3
26	1953	467	48	10.3
27	1955	474	57	12.0
28	1958	471	68	14.4
29	1960	467	59	12.6
30	1963	467	72	15.4
31	1967	486	102	21.0
32	1969	491	99	20.2
33	1972	491	95	19.3
34	1976	511	125	24.5
35	1979	511	76	14.9
36	1980	511	36	7.0
37	1983	511	84	16.4
38	1986	512	64	12.5
39	1990	512	133	26.0

In many of the prewar years the total number of members listed in this table exceeds the statutory size of the House of Representatives. This is because the table includes all persons who sat in the House between one election and the next. Thus, replacements are also included.

TABLE A-5
IMPERIAL AND NATIONAL DIET
Age Distribution of New Members at the Time of Their First election

Age	Prewar No.	%	Postwar No.	%	Total No.	%
20-29			32	1.7	32	0.6
30-39	1023	29.2	309	15.2	1332	24.1
40-49	1534	43.8	868	42.7	2402	43.4
50-59	768	21.9	673	33.1	1441	26.0
60-69	170	4.9	148	7.3	318	5.7
70+	5	0.1	2	0.1	7	0.1

Average Age of All New Members

Prewar	Postwar	Total
44.76	47.34	45.70

TABLE A-6
PROFESSIONALISM
Distribution of Times Elected at Each Election

Election	1	2	3	4	5	6	7	8	9	10	11	12	13	14-15	16-17	18-19	20+
1 (1890)	321																
2 (1892)	166	156															
3 (1894)	138	75	87														
4 (1894)	129	84	61	55													
5 (1898)	162	44	34	33	25												
6 (1898)	101	104	39	29	32	23											
7 (1902)	228	36	37	20	21	15	19										
8 (1903)	93	152	36	29	20	23	12	15									
9 (1904)	120	75	100	26	25	14	19	11	14								
10 (1908)	206	58	36	53	16	17	8	10	7	11							
11 (1912)	196	90	30	26	29	6	12	7	4	5	8						
12 (1915)	153	101	54	22	14	25	5	6	8	2	1	7					
13 (1917)	151	91	64	37	16	9	17	7	3	7	3	1	7				

Continued on next page

TABLE A-6 CONTINUED
PROFESSIONALISM
Distribution of Times Elected at Each Election

Election	1	2	3	4	5	6	7	8	9	10	11	12	13	14-15	16-17	18-19	20+
14 (1920)	277	66	53	29	25	10	8	15	5	3	3	2	1	7			
15 (1924)	252	108	37	41	21	19	8	5	9	4	2	1	2	4			
16 (1928)	173	122	66	32	30	17	7	5	2	4	3	3			3		
17 (1930)	127	113	102	48	21	27	12	6	1	1	3	2	3		2		
18 (1932)	128	82	89	82	39	15	15	10	5	2	1	2	1	2	2		
19 (1936)	126	92	61	66	65	27	13	11	9	4	1	1	2	2		1	
20 (1937)	93	94	82	56	54	53	25	10	11	6	3	1	1	2	1	1	
21 (1942)	202	47	50	50	29	33	34	13	4	9		1					1
22 (1946)	385	23	17	14	12	8	1	2	4		2						1
23 (1947)	225	190	11	13	14	7	7	1	1	3		1					1
24 (1949)	195	128	113	8	11	3	3	2	1		3		1				1
25 (1952)	109	115	94	85	17	16	12	10	3	1		4					1
26 (1953)	48	118	108	89	56	14	17	9	7	1		3					1

Continued on next page

TABLE A-6 CONTINUED
PROFESSIONALISM
Distribution of Times Elected at Each Election

Election	1	2	3	4	5	6	7	8	9	10	11	12	13	14-15	16-17	18-19	20+
27 (1955)	57	64	114	73	80	47	11	12	5	7	1		1	2			
28 (1958)	68	51	54	102	63	68	36	9	8	5	5			2			
29 (1960)	59	52	51	59	89	53	51	33	5	6	4	4			1		
30 (1963)	72	42	48	46	45	77	52	46	26	4	4	4	1		1		
31 (1967)	102	59	40	48	43	31	61	38	35	19	3	3	3	1			
32 (1969)	99	89	49	31	34	32	24	51	31	30	14	2	2	3			
33 (1972)	95	75	62	52	29	27	25	24	37	25	21	11		1			
34 (1976)	125	77	70	67	40	25	14	14	16	27	14	15	6	1			
35 (1979)	76	103	71	64	61	35	22	15	13	9	18	9	10	4	1		
36 (1980)	36	78	90	63	56	60	32	21	14	14	12	11	9	14	1		
37 (1983)	84	31	70	84	51	51	45	29	20	7	7	10	6	12	3	1	
38 (1986)	64	64	38	67	72	46	49	40	23	12	9	6	4	11	6	1	
39 (1990)	133	66	46	31	49	53	35	33	26	19	7	5	3	1	4	1	

TABLE A-7
PROFESSIONALISM BY REGION AND PREFECTURE

REGION/PREF	All members Avg. times	All members Rank	Prewar members Avg. times	Prewar members Rank	All postwar Avg. times	All postwar Rank	New postwar Avg. times	New postwar Rank
HOKKAIDO	3.36	1 99	2.85	2 12	3.93	9 34	3.78	8 32
TOHOKU	3.16	3	2.71	5	4.11	6	3.90	6
AOMORI	3.04	24	2.61	25	4.24	22	3.89	25
IWATE	3.04	24	2.36	36	4.25	21	4.24	9
MIYAGI	3.93	1	3.20	4	5.34	1	5.21	1
AKITA	3.19	17	2.87	10	3.70	41	3.63	37
YAMAGATA	2.95	33	2.60	26	4.11	27	3.70	34
FUKUSHIMA	3.00	28	2.71	22	3.56	46	3.36	46
KANTO	3.29	2	2.94	1	4.14	5	3.75	9
IBARAKI	3.56	3	3.39	2	4.47	13	3.81	28
TOCHIGI	3.26	13	2.73	19	4.74	5	4.24	9
GUMMA	3.37	7	2.73	19	4.33	17	3.38	4
SAITAMA	3.12	19	2.80	14	3.65	43	3.51	42
CHIBA	3.09	21	2.80	14	3.81	38	3.47	44
TOKYO	3.46	5	3.17	5	4.33	17	3.80	30
KANAGAWA	3.07	22	2.71	21	3.80	39	3.48	43
HOKURIKU	2.91	9	2.47	8	4.14	5	3.82	7
NIIGATA	2.96	32	2.50	30	3.99	32	3.95	22
TOYAMA	2.86	37	2.53	27	3.93	34	3.18	47
ISHIKAWA	3.01	27	2.70	23	4.40	15	4.00	20
FUKUI	2.82	38	2.10	44	4.24	22	4.14	14

Continued on next page

TABLE A-7 CONTINUED
PROFESSIONALISM BY REGION AND PREFECTURE

REGION/PREF	All members Avg. times	Rank	Prewar members Avg. times	Rank	All postwar Avg. times	Rank	New postwar Avg. times	Rank
CHUBU	2.93	8	2.35	9	4.21	4	4.16	1
YAMANASHI	2.82	38	2.35	37	4.00	31	3.86	26
NAGANO	2.92	36	2.32	38	4.44	14	4.25	8
GIFU	2.62	42	2.08	46	4.29	19	3.97	21
SHIZUOKA	2.94	34	2.45	33	3.66	42	3.61	39
AICHI	3.16	18	2.50	30	4.73	6	4.56	2
KINKI	3.16	3	2.69	6	4.53	1	4.09	2
MIE	3.33	10	2.85	12	5.11	2	4.35	5
SHIGA	2.57	46	2.18	42	4.16	26	3.64	35
KYOTO	3.20	16	2.80	14	4.66	7	4.11	17
OSAKA	3.37	7	2.86	11	4.61	8	4.15	13
HYOGO	3.26	13	2.74	18	4.59	9	4.27	7
NARA	2.52	47	2.02	47	3.58	45	3.63	37
WAKAYAMA	3.33	10	3.07	7	4.27	20	3.83	27
CHUGOKU	3.10	6	2.77	4	4.26	3	3.93	3
TOTTORI	2.80	40	2.24	41	3.95	33	3.94	23
SHIMANE	2.99	30	2.53	27	4.57	10	4.30	6
OKAYAMA	3.55	4	3.32	3	4.86	4	4.03	18
HIROSHIMA	3.39	6	2.96	9	4.18	25	4.02	19
YAMAGUCHI	2.59	45	2.12	43	3.78	40	3.57	40

Continued on next page

TABLE A-7 CONTINUED
PROFESSIONALISM BY REGION AND PREFECTURE

REGION/PREF	All members Avg. times	Rank		Prewar members Avg. times	Rank		All postwar Avg. times		Rank	New postwar Avg. times		Rank
SHIKCKU	3.16		3	2.83		3	4.32	2		3.93	2	3
TOKUSHIMA	3.91	2		3.82	1		5.10		3	4.12	3	16
KAGAWA	3.28	12		3.02	8		4.04		30	3.80	30	30
EHIME	2.82	38		2.26	39		4.24		22	4.14	22	14
KOCHI	3.00	28		2.79	17		4.20		24	3.55	24	41
KYUSHU	2.99		7	2.51		7	4.08	7		3.92	7	5
FUKUOKA	2.93	35		2.41	35		3.82		37	3.76	37	33
SAGA	3.12	19		2.65	24		4.38		16	4.14	16	14
NAGASAKI	2.97	31		2.49	32		4.10		29	3.92	29	24
KUMAMOTO	3.03	26		2.44	34		4.57		10	4.39	10	3
OITA	3.25	15		3.17	5		3.53		47	3.37	47	45
MIYAZAKI	2.61	44		2.09	45		3.90		36	3.81	36	28
KAGOSHIMA	3.06	23		2.51	29		4.52		12	4.24	12	9
OKINAWA	2.71	41	10	2.26	39	10	3.64	10	44	3.64	10 44	35

GRAPH A-1

IMPERIAL AND NATIONAL DIET
OCCUPATION: AGRICULTURE

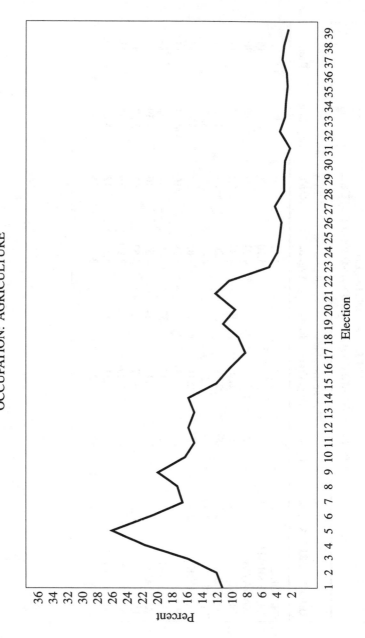

GRAPH A-2

IMPERIAL AND NATIONAL DIET
OCCUPATION: BUSINESS AND BANKING

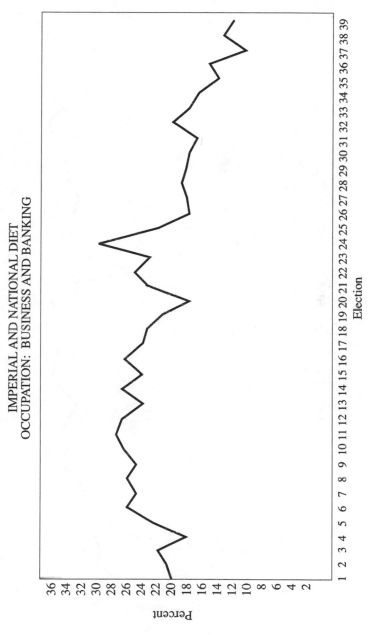

GRAPH A-3

IMPERIAL AND NATIONAL DIET
OCCUPATION: HIGHER EDUCATION

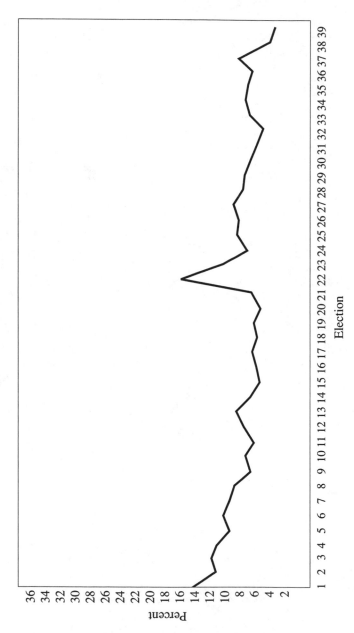

Election

Percent

GRAPH A-4

IMPERIAL AND NATIONAL DIET
OCCUPATIONS: CENTRAL GOVERNMENT

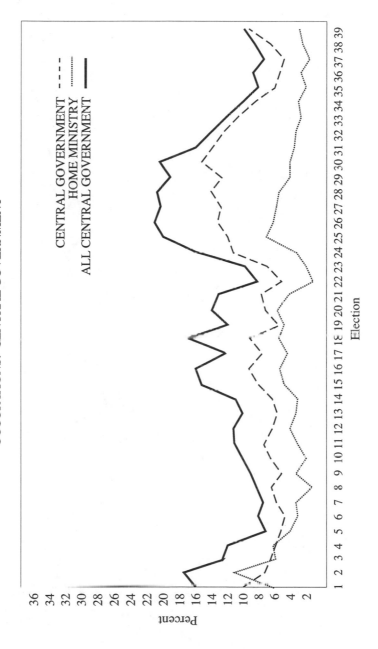

GRAPH A-5

IMPERIAL AND NATIONAL DIET
OCCUPATION: JOURNALISM AND LAW

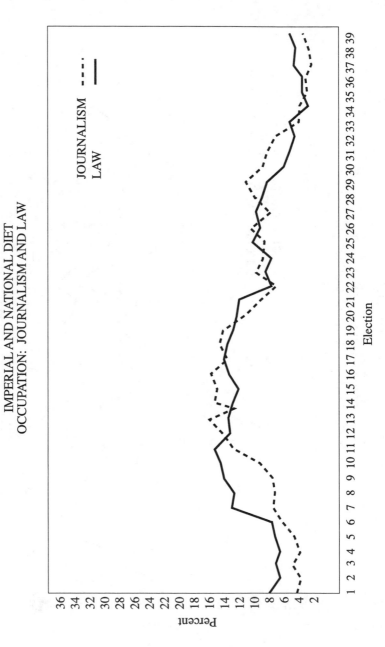

GRAPH A-6

IMPERIAL AND NATIONAL DIET
OCCUPATION: LOCAL GOVERNMENT AND POLITICS

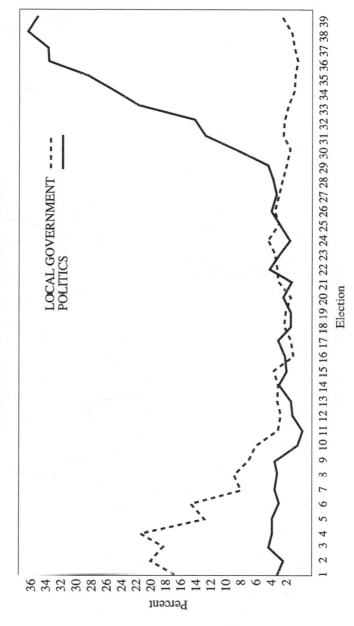

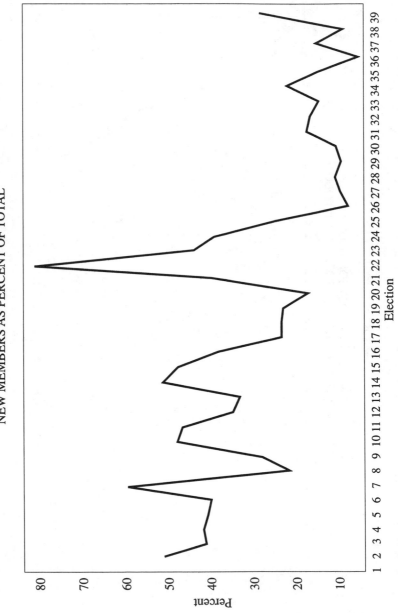

GRAPH A-7
IMPERIAL AND NATIONAL DIET
NEW MEMBERS AS PERCENT OF TOTAL

GRAPH A-8

IMPERIAL AND NATIONAL DIET
EDUCATION: MAJOR SUBJECT OF UNIVERSITY OR
PRIVATE STUDY

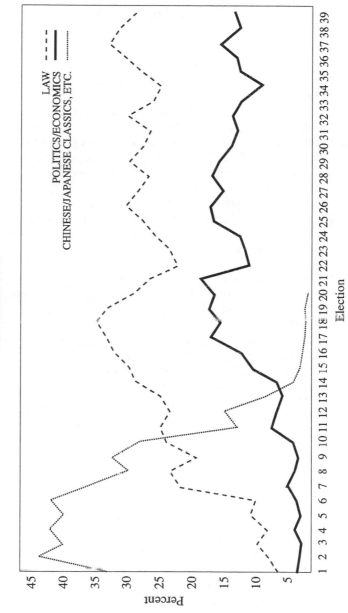

APPENDIX B

■

In the introduction were noted a number of works which have provided statistics on Japanese Diet members for portions of the time period covered here. None of the other studies is as extensive as this one, although some are rather intensive. Spot comparisons of the figures reveal slight discrepancies in most cases with a few instances where the disparities are greater. This appendix presents comparisons of the figures in this study alongside those of the others, plus explanatory comments for those who may be interested.

The other works compared are:

Haruhiko Fukui, "The Liberal Democratic Party Revisted: Continuity and Change in the Party's structure and Performance", Journal of Japanese Studies (Summer 1984).

Masumi Junnosuke, Nihon Seitō Shiron (1965-80).

Naka Kurō, Kokkai Giin no Kōsei to Henka (1980).

T.J. Pempel, "Uneasy Toward Autonomy: Parliament and Parliamentarians in Japan", in Parliaments and Parliamentarians, Ed. by Ezra N. Suleiman (1986).

Robert Scalapino and Masumi Junnosuke, Parties and Politics in Contemporary Japan (1962).

Wakata Kyōji, Gendai Nihon no Seiji Fūdo (1981).

APPENDIX B

TABLE B-1
OCCUPATIONS

This table compares Masumi's category of "Lawyers, Journalists and Teachers" with the combined figures from Journalism, Law and Education in this study.

Election	Year	This Study	Masumi (Wakata, Pempel)
1	1890	27.7%	17%
2	1892	22.5%	11%
3	1894-1	24.6%	14%
4	1894-2	22.2%	13%
5	1898-1	22.0%	14%
6	1898-2	24.6%	16%
7	1902	32.2%	25%
8	1903	29.6%	24%
9	1904	29.7%	23%
10	1908	33.8%	30%
11	1912	36.8%	29%
12	1915	37.6%	30%
13	1917	40.6%	35%
14	1920	35.0%	31%

The figures in my study are consistently higher than Masumi's. This is because I have broken down occupations more distinctly and because he lists a larger number of persons with no occupation. Masumi's figures, however, begin with 1902. In the above table the figures for 1890 through 1898 are from Wakata. Pempel appears to have copied directly from Wakata and they have all used the same source for 1902 and after.

TABLE B-2
OCCUPATIONS
BUREAUCRATS

This table compares postwar figures for "bureaucrats."

Election	Year	This study	Pempel	Fukui	Scalapino
22	1946	8.5%			
23	1947	11.0%	6.9%		
24	1949	16.1%	13.3%		
25	1952	21.2%	21.5%		
26	1953	21.8%	19.3%		
27	1955	21.5%	20.1%		
28	1958	21.5%	19.5%		18.5%
29	1960	19.9%	20.6%		
30	1963	21.7%	20.1%		
31	1967	18.5%	19.5%		
32	1969	16.5%	18.7%		
33	1972	13.6%	16.5%		
34	1976	10.4%	16.2%		
35	1979	7.8%	14.7%		
36	1980	7.9%	14.9%		
37	1983	7.1%	13.9%	10.6%	

Each work lists this category slightly differntly. In my calculations I include all "Central Government". Pempel uses "ex-Bureaucrat Diet members", Fukui identifies "High Bureaucrat", while Scalapino & Masumi used the term "ex-officials." There are sizeable differences in my figures and Pempel's, especially after 1972. Fukui's placement for 1983 at almost exactly midpoint between the two suggests that we both may be off to some degree.

TABLE B-3
OCCUPATIONS
BUREAUCRATS

This table compares Masumi's (also Wakata and Pempel) category of "Bureaucrats" with my figures for Central Government and Local Government combined.

Election	Year	This study	Masumi (Wakata, Pempel)
1	1890	33.0%	40%
2	1892	38.0%	33%
3	1894-1	31.0%	25%
4	1894-2	33.8%	27%
5	1898-1	22.3%	20%
6	1898-2	21.6%	22%
7	1902	17.5%	18%
8	1903	17.1%	16%
9	1904	15.8%	15%
10	1908	15.8%	14%
11	1912	14.3%	15%
12	1915	14.1%	12%
13	1917	13.5%	13%
14	1920	13.5%	13%

The figures in these two columns are very close beginning in 1898. Except for 1890 my figures are higher, in part perhaps because Masumi may not be including local government servants as well as Higher Civil Service appointees.

TABLE B-4
EDUCATION

Elect-ion	Year	University		Todai		Waseda	
		This Study	Naka*	This Study	Naka*	This Study	Naka*
22	1946	54.2%		12.2%		11.1%	
23	1947	64.1%	58.4%	13.5%	17.6	12.2%	9.7%
24	1949	67.3%	63.1%	17.7%	17.6%	10.0%	7.7%
25	1952	73.2%	68.5%	25.7%	25.5%	9.9%	8.4%
26	1953	72.8%	68.2%	24.6%	24.0%	10.7%	9.4%
27	1955	71.5%	68.1%	24.9%	25.1%	10.8%	8.4%
28	1958	71.1%	67.2%	23.8%	23.8%	8.7%	7.5%
29	1960	71.5%	68.7%	26.1%	26.1%	9.6%	8.1%
30	1963	72.2%	68.3%	26.8%	26.3%	10.5%	9.2%
31	1967	70.6%	68.1%	24.7%	24.5%	10.3%	9.7%
32	1969	71.7%	69.8%	25.1%	24.9%	9.2%	8.4%
33	1972	70.9%	68.8%	23.2%	23.0%	10.8%	10.2%
34	1976	73.0%	69.7%	22.7%	22.9%	11.9%	11.5%
35	1979	72.8%	70.6%	19.0%	19.6%	12.9%	12.5%
36	1980	74.4%	74.2%	21.3%	21.9%	11.9%	11.0
37	1983	75.0%	75.0%	19.8%	19.8%	11.9%	12.1%

*Naka's figures are through 1979. The figures in this table for 1980 and 1983 are from Pempel who appears to have derived his figures for the earlier years from Nakan as they are identical. The principal discrepancy here comes in overall university attendance where my figures are slightly higher. This is almost certainly because (1) I counted university attendance, not graduation and (2) I included institutions for prewar times that became universities after the war. I have listed comparative tables for other universities or other levels of educational attainment. The differences are exceedingly small.

TABLE B-5
EDUCATION
LDP MEMBERS

| Election | Year | University | | Scalapino | Todai | |
		This Study	Fukui		This Study	Fukui
27	1955	78.3%	69%		30.7%	31%
28	1958	78.8%	70%	81%	30.5%	32%
29	1960	81.2%	70%		32.3%	32%
30	1963	82.9%	73%		34.9%	35%
31	1967	84.4%	77%		34.8%	36%
32	1969	83.1%	76%		33.4%	34%
33	1972	83.0%	77%		32.2%	33%
34	1976	85.9%	81%		31.5%	32%
35	1979	84.8%	82%		28.1%	29%
36	1980	85.9%	83%		28.9%	29%
37	1983	85.9%	83%		29.0%	30%

I have higher figures percentages than Fukui for university education of LDP members. The difference is more marked at first and though the discrepancies dwindle they do not disappear. The difference is likely due to my use of university attendance rather than graduation and the inclusion on my list of schools which later became universities and are so classified. It should be noted, however, that Scalapino and Masumi come up with a higher figure for LDP members in 1958. The differences for Todai are insignificant.

TABLE B-6
NEWCOMERS AS PERCENT OF TOTAL

Election	Year	This Study	Masumi (also Wakata and Pempel)
1	1890	300	300
2	1892	166 (51.4%)	166 (55%)
3	1894-1		147 (49%)
4	1894-2	265 (42.1%)*	103 (34%)
5	1898-1		173 (58%)
6	1898-2	258 (41.1%)*	77 (26%)
7	1902	228 (60.6%)	233 (61%)
8	1903	93 (24.5%)	97 (26%)
9	1904	120 (29.7%)	109 (29%)
10	1908	206 (48.8%)	187 (49%)
11	1912	196 (47.5%)	185 (49%)
12	1915	153 (38.0%)	156 (41%)
13	1917	151 (36.5%)	136 (35%)
14	1920	277 (55.0%)	248 (53%)

*Figures are the combined totals for 1894 and 1898 respectively.

These figures are very close in most cases. I have higher totals in a few instances because I also counted replacements for persons who resigned, died, or were declared ineligible after taking their seats.

TABLE B-7
NEWCOMERS AS PERCENT OF TOTAL

Election	Year	This Study	Pempel	Naka	Scalapino
22	1946	81.7%			81.3%
23	1947	47.5%	47.6%	47.6%	47.6%
24	1949	41.7%	41.2%	41.2%	41.2%
25	1952	23.3%	23.4%	23.4%	24.9%
26	1953	10.3%	10.1%	10.1%	10.1%
27	1955	12.0%	11.8%	11.8%	11.8%
28	1958	14.4%	14.1%	14.1%	14.1%
29	1960	12.6%	12.8%	12.8%	12.8%
30	1963	15.4%	14.6%	14.6%	
31	1967	21.0%	21.0%	21.0%	
32	1969	20.2%	19.3%	19.3%	
33	1972	19.3%	18.9%	18.9%	
34	1976	24.5%	24.3%	24.3%	
35	1979	14.9%	14.5%	24.5%	
36	1980	7.0%	6.8%		
37	1983	16.4%	16.4%		

The figures are so close that comment seems superfluous. It is apparent, however, that Pempel and Naka used the same source or Pempel simply took Naka's figures. The Scalapino figures are also the same, except for 1952.

TABLE B-8
AVERAGE AGE

Election	Year	This study	Masumi (also Wakata and Pempel)
1	1890	39.95	42
2	1892	42.03	44
3	1894-1	42.04	44
4	1894-2	42.49	44
5	1898-1	42.97	45
6	1898-2	43.05	45
7	1902	44.45	46
8	1903	45.05	47
9	1904	45.21	47
10	1908	47.61	47
11	1912	47.65	49
12	1915	48.12	51
13	1917	49.31	51
14	1920	49.17	51

My figures are consistently lower, usually by about one and one-half years, than Masumi's. I am, however, confident that my figures are more accurate. I have calculated age according to date of birth at the time of the election. I have not used age as it may have been printed in the newspapers at the time. This procedure would likely add one or two years to the average age. In addition, I have included all persons seated between the time of one election and the next, thus adding to the total number to be averaged. This would likely pull down the average slightly as replacements would probably be younger, non-incumbents in most cases.

TABLE B-9
AVERAGE AGE

Election	Year	This Study	Naka (also Pempel after 1980)
23	1947	48.16	49.8
24	1949	47.83	49.6
25	1952	52.56	52.5
26	1953	51.87	51.9
27	1955	53.08	53.1
28	1958	54.14	54.0
29	1960	55.46	55.4
30	1963	56.10	56.0
31	1967	55.34	55.7
32	1969	55.06	55.0
33	1972	55.23	55.3
34	1976	54.97	54.9
35	1979	55.56	55.8
36	1980	55.12	56.1
37	1983	56.08	57.0
38	1986	56.59	57.0

These figures are extremely close, in some cases identical, from 1952 onward. My lower figures for 1947 and 1949 are probably due to the inclusion of replacements.

TABLE B-10
APPRENTICESHIP; LOCAL ASSEMBLY MEMBERS

Election	Year	This study	Masumi (also Wakata and Pempel)
1	1890	67.9%	64%
2	1892	66.9%	62%
3	1894-1	69.3%	64%
4	1894-2	69.6%	63%
5	1898-1	68.3%	62%
6	1898-2	70.4%	63%
7	1902	71.3%	60%
8	1903	70.5%	61%
9	1904	72.5%	60%
10	1908	65.2%	54%
11	1912	56.2%	44%
12	1915	55.3%	42%
13	1917	55.8%	37%
14	1920	56.3%	38%

The discrepancies here are rather great, particularly after 1902 when the number of seats increased. This may be accounted for, in part, by the inclusion of persons with service in town, city and village assemblies as well as prefectural assemblies. Finding these figures so disparate, I conducted a spot check, using 1902. I found that Masumi apparently counted membership in prefectural assemblies and, possibly, city assemblies. I discovered that, for 1902, about fifteen percent of those identified in my data had not served at the prefectural level. I, therefore, conclude that the figures put forward by Masumi and accepted by Wakata and Pempel are incorrect as stated and, in fact, misleading. For the period from 1902 to 1920 Masumi does identify his figures as prefectural assembly membership. In another section, however, he lists both prefectural and city assembly members who later entered the Imperial Diet. Thus, it is Wakata and Pempel who have misused Masumi.

TABLE B-11
APPRENTICESHIP: BUSINESS BACKGROUND

This table compares my category "Company Directors" with the category "Business Entrepreneurs" used by Masumi, Wakata and Pempel.

Election	Year	This Study	Masumi (also Wakata and Pempel)
1	1890	34.0%	33%
2	1892	37.8%	37%
3	1894-1	37.0%	38%
4	1894-2	34.0%	38%
5	1898-1	41.3%	45%
6	1898-	42.7%	44%
7	1902	46.3%	41%
8	1903	46.8%	47%
9	1904	47.8%	47%
10	1908	54.3%	56%
11	1912	61.0%	59%
12	1915	60.3%	57%
13	1917	55.3%	56%
14	1920	59.1%	57%

The figures are very close. We are counting the same things.

Bibliography

■

Abe, Hakaru. "Education of the Legal Profession in Japan", in A.T. von Mehren, ed., *Law in Japan* (1963), pp. 153-187.

Akita, George. "The Meiji Constitution in Practice: the First Diet", *Journal of Asian Studies* (Nov. 1962), pp. 31-46.

Aoki Yasuya. "Kokkai Giin no Keireki", *Hyōron - Shakai Kagaku* (17: 1980).

Aoyama Takenori. *Gikai Kōsei no Mondai to Kentō* (1977).

Asakawa Hiromi. "Seikai - Sesshu Eriito no Kōzai", *Jiyū* (5: 1977).

Baerwald, Hans. *Japan's Parliament: an Introduction* (1974).

Baerwald, Hans. "Parliament and Parliamentarians in Japan", *Pacific Affairs* (Fall 1964), pp. 271-282.

Baerwald, Hans. *Party Politics in Japan* (1986).

Baerwald, Hans. *The Purge of Japanese Leaders Under the Occupation* (1959).

Benjamin, Roger and Kan Ori. *Tradition and Change in Postindustrial Japan: the Role of Political Parties* (1981).

Berger, Gordon Mark. *Parties Out of Power in Japan, 1931-1941* (1977).

Berton, Peter. "The Japan Communist Party: the 'Lovable' Party", in Ronald J. Hrebenar, ed., *The Japanese Party System* (1986), pp. 116-141.

Blacker, Carmen. *The Japanese Enlightenment* (1964).

Blaker, Michael K., ed., *Japan at the Polls: the House of Councillors Election of 1974* (1976).

Bogdanour, Vernon and David Butler, ed. *Parties, Democracy and Elections: Electoral Systems and Their Political Consequences* (1983).

Bowen, Roger. *Rebellion and Democracy in Meiji Japan. A Study of Commoners in the Popular Rights Movement* (1980).

Braudel, Fernand. *The Perspective of the World.* Vol. 3 of *Civilization and Capitalism 15th-18th Centuries* (English translation, 1984).

Brett, Cecil C. "The Komeito and Local Japanese Politics", *Asian Survey* (Apr. 1979), pp. 366-378.

Campbell, John C. *Parties, Candidates and Voters in Japan: Six Quantitative Studies* (1981).

Clark, Rodney. *The Japanese Company* (1979).

Clayton, Stephen. "More Lawyers Than Meet the Eye", *PHP* (Nov. 1984), p. 8.

Cleaver, Charles G. *Japanese and Americans: Cultural Parallels and Paradoxes* (1976).

Clubok, Alfred B. "Political Party Membership and Subleadership in Rural Japan. A Case Study of Okayama Prefecture", in Bernard Silberman and Harry Harootunian, ed., *Modern Japanese Leadership* (1967), pp. 385-409.

Cole, Allan B., George O. Totten and Cecil Uyehara. *Socialist Parties in Postwar Japan* (1966).

Curtis, Gerald. "Big Business and Political Influence", in Ezra F. Vogel, ed. *Modern Japanese Organization and Decision Making* (1975), pp. 33-70.

Curtis, Gerald. *Election Campaigning: Japanese Style* (1971).

Curtis, Gerald. *The Japanese Way of Politics* (1988).

Doi, Takako. *Seiji to Watashi* (1987).

Drea, Edward J. *The 1942 Japanese General Election: Political Mobilization in Wartime Japan* (1979).

Duke, Benjamin C. *Japan's Militant Teachers: a History of the Left-Wing Teachers' Movement* (1972).

Duus, Peter. *Party Rivalry and Political Change in Taisho Japan* (1968).

Enomoto, Shukei. "Shoki Shūgiin Giin Senkyō-ku no Sakkaku", *Shiryū* (3: 1987), pp. 69-73.

Flanagan, Scott C. and Bradley Richardson. *Japanese Electoral Behavior: Social Cleavages, Social Networks and Partnership* (1977).

Foster, J.J. "Ghost-hunting: Local Party Organization in Japan", *Asian Survey* (Sept. 1982), pp. 843-857.

Fujita, Taki. "Women and Politics in Japan", *Annals of the American Academy of Social and Political Science* (Jan. 1968), pp. 92-95.

Fukuda, Kan'ichi. *Fujin Sansei Kankei Shiryō Shū* (1986).

Fukui, Haruhiko. "The Liberal Democratic Party Revisited: Continuity and Change in the Party's Structure and Performance, *Journal of Japanese Studies* (Summer 1984), pp. 385-435.

Fukui, Haruhiko. *Party in Power. The Japanese Liberal Democrats and Policy Making* (1969).

Gendai Seiji Kikō Kenkyūkai, ed. *Gendai Seijika no Sōgan: Shūgiin Zengiin Roku* (1977).

Haley, John O. "The Myth of the Reluctant Litigant", *Journal of Japanese Studies* (Summer 1978), pp. 359-390.

Hall, John W. and Richard Beardsley, ed. *Twelve Doors to Japan* (1965).

Hammond, Susan Webb. "From Staff Aide to Election: the Recruitment of U.S. Representatives", in Harold C. Clarke and Moshe Czudnowski, ed., *Political Elites in Anglo-American Democracies: Changes in Stable Regimes* (1987), pp. 209-230.

Haruta, Kunio. *Nihon Kokkai Jishi* (1987).

Hattori, Takaaki. "The Legal Profession in Japan: Its Historical Development and Present State", in A.T. von Mehren, ed. *Law in Japan* (1963), pp. 111-152.

Havens, Thomas R. *Valley of Darkness. The Japanese People and World War Two* (1978).

Hayama, Akira. "The Decline of Class Politics? Japanese Party Politics in Comparative Perspectives", *Asian Profile* (Apr. 1988), pp. 113-126.

Hayashida, Kametarō. *Nihon Seitō Shi*, 2 vol. (1927).

Hōgaku Seminā Zōkan. *Gendai Gikai Seiji* (1977).

Hoshi, Hajime. *Senkyō Daigaku* (1924).

Hrebenar, Ronald J. "The Changing Postwar Party System", in Ronald J.

Hrebenar, ed., *The Japanese Party System* (1986), pp. 3-31.

Hrebenar, Ronald J., ed. *The Japanese Party System. From One-Party Rule to Coalition Government* (1986).

Hrebenar, Ronald J. "The Komeito: Party of 'Buddhist' Democracy", in Ronald J. Hrebenar, ed., *The Japanese Party System* (1986), pp. 147-180.

Hrebenar, Ronald J. "The Money Base of Japanese Politics", in Ronald J. Hrebenar, ed., *The Japanese Party System* (1986), pp. 55-79.

Ienaga, Saburō. *Ueki Emori Kenkyū* (1960).

Ishida, Takeshi. "The Development of Interest Groups and the Pattern of Political Modernization in Japan", in Robert E. Ward, ed., *Political Development in Modern Japan* (1968), pp. 293-336.

Ishida, Takeshi. "Interest Groups Under a Semi-Permanent Party: the Case of Japan", *Annals of the American Academy of Political and Social Science* (1974), pp. 1-10.

Ishikawa, Masumi. *Dēta Sengo Seijishi* (1984).

Ishikawa, Masumi. *Nihon Seiji no Tōshizu* (1985).

Ishikawa, Masumi. *Sengo Seiji Kōzōshi* (1978).

Itō, Yukio. "Seitō Seiji to Teichaku", in Sakano Kōji and Miyaji Masato, ed. *Nihon Kindaishi ni Okeru Tenkanki no Kenkyū* (1985).

Izumi, Shoichi. "Diet Members", in Francis R. Valeo and Charles E. Morrison, ed. *The Japanese Diet and the U.S. Congress* (1983), pp. 61-77.

Japan. Kokkai. Shūgiin. Shūsan Hōseikyoku. *Gikai Seido Shichijūnen Shi*. 12 Vol. (1960-1962).

Japan. Kokkai. Shūgiin. *Shūgiin Giin Ryakureki* (1940).

Japan. Kokkai. Shūgiin. *Shūgiin Giin Tōreki Roku* (1957).

Johnson, Chalmers. *An Instance of Treason. Ozaki Hotsumi and the Sorge Spy Ring* (1964).

Kahn, Herman. *The Emerging Japanese Superstate. Challenge and Response* (1970).

Keene, Donald. *Dawn to the West. Japanese Literature in the Modern Era. Fiction* (1984).

Kim, Young C. "Political Recruitment: the Case of Japanese Prefectural Assemblymen", *American Political Science Review* (Dec. 1967), pp. 1036-1052.

Kubota, Akira. *Higher Civil Servants in Post-war Japan. Their Social Origins, Educational Backgrounds, and Career Patterns* (1969).

Kyogoku, Jun'ichi. *The Political Dynamics of Japan* (1987).

Lipset, Seymour M. and Stein Rokkan, ed. *Party Systems and Voter Alignments: Cross National Perspectives* (1967).

McCormack, Gavan and Yoshio Sugimoto. *Democracy in Contemporary Japan* (1986).

Maeda, Hideaki. *Kokkai Giin no Chii to Kensen* (1978).

Mason, R.H.P. *Japan's First General Election, 1890* (1969).

Masumi, Junnosuke. *Nihon Seitō Shiron*, 77 vol. (1965-1980).

Masumi, Junnosuke. *Postwar Politics in Japan, 1945-1955* (1985).

Matthews, Donald R. *U.S. Senators and Their World* (1960).

Mellors, Colin. *The British M.P.: A Socio-Economic Study of the House of Commons* (1978).

Mishler, W. and A. Hildreth. "Legislatures and Political Stability: an Exploratory Analysis", *Journal of Politics* (Feb. 1984), pp. 25-59.

Mori, Kishio. *Kokkai Giin no Himitsu* (1982).

Najita, Tetsuo. *Hara Kei in the Politics of Compromise, 1905-1915* (1967).

Naka, Kurō, et.al., ed. *Kokkai Giin ni Okeru Keireki Patān no Renzoku to Henka* (1982).

Naka, Kurō, ed. *Kokkai Giin no Kōsei to Henka* (1980).

Nihon Kokusei Chōsakai, ed. *Shūgiin Meiroku* (1977).

Ori, Kan. "The Diet in the Japanese Political System", in Francis R. Valeo and Charles E. Morrison, ed. *The Japanese Diet and the U.S. Congress* (1983), pp. 11-23.

Ōtsu, Jun'ichirō. *Dai Nihon Kensei Shi*, 10 vol. (1927-1928).

Ōuchi, Tsutomu. *Fuashizumu e no Michi* (1967).

Ouchi, William. *Theory Z: How American Business Can Meet the Japanese Challenge* (1981).

Ōyama, Ikuo. *Gendai Nihon no Seiji Katei* (1925).

Packard, George R. III. *Protest in Tokyo: The Security Treaty Crisis of 1960* (1966).

Passin, Herbert. *A Season of Voting* (1979).

Pempel, T.J. *Policy and Politics in Japan: Creative Conservatism* (1982).

Pempel, T.J. "Uneasy Toward Autonomy: Parliament and Parliamentarians in Japan", in Ezra N. Suleiman, ed. *Parliaments and Parliamentarians* (1986), pp. 106-153.

Pharr, Susan J. *Political Women in Japan. The Search for a Place in Political Life* (1981).

Pharr, Susan J. "The Politics of Women's Rights", in Robert E. Ward and Sakamoto Yoshikazu, ed. *Democratizing Japan* (1987), pp. 221-249.

Pittau, Joseph. *Political Thought in Early Meiji Japan 1868-1889* (1967).

Ramsdell, Daniel B. "Prefectural Assemblies in Japan: Hokkaido and Shimane, 1947-1983", *Scholarship in Review* (June 1986), pp. 14-24.

Ramseyer, J. Mark. "Reluctant Litigant Revisited: Rationality and Disputes in Japan", *Journal of Japanese Studies* (Winter 1988), pp. 111-123.

Reed, Steven R. "The People Spoke: the Influence of Elections on Japanese Politics, 1949-1955", *Journal of Japanese Studies* (Summer 1988), pp. 309-339.

Richardson, Bradley and Scott C. Flanagan. *Politics in Japan* (1984).

Robins-Mowry, Dorothy. *The Hidden Sun. Women of Modern Japan* (1983).

Sansom, George B. *The Western World and Japan* (1950).

Scalapino, Robert A. *Democracy and the Party Movement in Prewar Japan. The Failure of the First Attempt* (1953).

Scalapino, Robert A. "Elections and Political Modernization in Prewar Japan", in Robert E. Ward, ed. *Political Development in Modern Japan* (1968), pp. 249-291.

Scalapino, Robert A. and Masumi Junnosuke. *Parties and Politics in Contemporary Japan* (1962).

Shiga, Yoshio. *Kokkaron* (1949).

Shillony, Ben-Ami. *Politics and Culture in Wartime Japan* (1981).

Shiōden, Nobutaka. *Kyōsan Shugi Shakai Shugi Undō no Jissai* (1941).

Shiōden, Nobutaka. *Shiōden Nobutaka Kaikoroku* (1964).

Smith, Robert J. *Japanese Society. Tradition, Self and the Social Order* (1983).

Spaulding, Robert M., Jr. "The Bureaucracy as a Political Force", in James Morley, ed. *Dilemmas of Growth in Prewar Japan* (1971).

Steslicke, W.E. *Doctors in Politics: the Political Life of the Japan Medical Association* (1973).

Stockwin, J.A.A. "The Japan Socialist Party: a Politics of Permanent Opposition", in Ronald J. Hrebenar, ed. *The Japanese Party System* (1986), pp. 83-115.

Storry, Richard. *A History of Modern Japan* (1972).

Suleiman, Ezra N., ed. *Parliaments and Parliamentarians in Democratic Politics* (1986).

Tagawa, Daikichirō. *Kokka to Shūkyō* (1938).

Takabatake, Michitoshi. *Gendai Nihon no Seitō to Senkyō* (1980).

Takane, Masaaki. *The Political Elite in Japan* (1981).

Takase, Den. *Ichi Daigishi no Negoto* (1957).

Taylor, H. *Qualifications of Politicians* (1967).

Thayer, Nathaniel. *How the Conservatives Rule Japan* (1969).

Tomita, Nobuo, et.al. "The Liberal Democratic Party: the Ruling Party of Japan", in Ronald J.Hrebenar, ed. *The Japanese Party System* (1986), pp. 235-285.

Tomita, Nobuo, et.al. "Prerequisites to Ministerial Careers in Japan, 1885-1980", *International Political Science Review* (No. 2, 1981), pp. 235-255.

Tsuji, Kan'ichi. *Giin Shukusha* (1950).

Tsuji, Kan'ichi. *Seijika to Iu Mono* (1955).

Tsuneishi, Warren M. *Japanese Political Style. An Introduction to the Government and Politics of Modern Japan* (1966).

Tsurumi, Yusuke. "The Liberal Movement in Japan", in Sir Valentin Chirol, Yusuke Tsurumi, SirJames Arthur Salter, ed. *The Reawakening of the Orient and Other Addresses* (1925),pp. 67-89.

Tsurutani, Taketsugu. *Political Change in Japan: Response to Postindustrial Challenge* (1977).

Uchida, Kenzo. "Japan's Postwar Conservative Party", in Robert E. Ward and Sakamoto Yoshikazu, ed. *Democratizing Japan* (1986), pp. 306-338.

Uchida, Nobuya. *Fusetsu Gojunen* (1951).

Ueki, Emori. *Ueki Emori Nikki* (1955).

Wakata, Kyōji. *Gendai Nihon no Seiji to Fūdo* (1981).

Wakata, Kyoji. *Japanese Diet Members: Social Background, General Values and Role Perception* (1977).

Wallerstein, Immanuel. *The Modern World System.* Vol. 1: *Capitalist Agriculture and the Origins of the European World-Economy in the Sixteenth Century* (1974). Vol. 2: *Mercantilism and the Consolidation of the European World-Economy 1600-1750* (1980).

Wallerstein, Immanuel. *The Politics of the World Economy* (1984).

Ward, Robert E. and Sakamoto Yoshikazu, ed. *Democratizing Japan. The Allied Occupation* (1987).

Ward, Robert E., ed. *Political Development in Modern Japan* (1968).

Watanuki, Joji. *Politics in Postwar Japanese Society* (1977).

Wray, Harry and Hilary Conroy, ed. *Japan Examined: Perspectives on Modern Japanese History* (1983).

Yamato, Hiroshi. "Political Parties and the Diet", in Francis R. Valeo and Charles E. Morrison, ed. *The Japanese Diet and the U.S. Congress* (1983), pp. 25-38.

Yoshino, M.Y. *Japan's Managerial System* (1968).

Youn, Jung-suk. "Candidates and Party Images: Recruitment to the Japanese House ofRepresentatives, 1958-1972", in John C. Campbell, ed. *Parties, Candidates and Voters in Japan* (1981), pp. 101-115.

Yuzu, Masao, ed. *Kokusei Senkyō to Seitō Seiji* (1977).

Index
■